D0778287

PRAY TO WIN!
Alfred Armand Montapert

You hold in your hands one of those rare books that will benefit you every day of your lifetime. *PRAY TO WIN!* is more than a prayer book. It is a blueprint that shows you God's Plan for your Success!

Rarely will you find so much practical real-life wisdom between two covers . . . as clear, refreshing and beneficial as a dipper of cool spring water on a hot summer day.

Learn what true prayer is . . . why all prayer is answered . . . how to develop your Spiritual Dimension . . . and how you can use the Higher Power of God to find your FULL POTENTIAL and the secret of lasting JOY!

Money is material prosperity, JOY is Spiritual Prosperity. The combination of the two is the ULTIMATE. This joyful book shows you how to bring that unbeatable combination into your life.

Prayer's real purpose is to put God at the center of our lives. Learn to really pray and your cares will drop off like autumn leaves.

PRAY TO WIN! is a dynamic book which explains in simple words how to make an eminently successful life . . . GOD'S WAY. We need prayer to raise us up to the level where all God's mercies and blessings flow in abundance.

Here are TRUTHS you have been seeking all your life . . . TRUTHS that will help you make hundreds of right decisions every day.

Prayer is POWER. You cannot live greatly without it. Read how eminently successful businessmen tell the secrets of the Spiritual Development which was the foundation for their ABUNDANT LIFE!

"Through prayer I find God and God finds me." With the Power of God in our hearts, we realize how God's love enhances our existence. This Love transforms our spiritual life into a paradise.

This book is about ESSENTIAL KNOWLEDGE . . . Indispensable Truth we must know. When it comes time to die, will you wake up and realize that You have not lived? LEARN TO PRAY AND GROW HAPPY!

BOOKS OF VALUE
2458 Chislehurst Drive
Los Angeles, California 90027

DEDICATION
TO
ALDOPH PHILLIP GOUTHEY, B.D., D.D.

This book is dedicated to my pastor and teacher and friend for over twenty five years. This dear man helped me more than any other man during my long lifetime. Although he has been gone over twenty years you will find him in all these pages. His lectures and prayers were classics and you will find the cream of his best work between the covers of this book. He truly was a man of God. He loved the mountains and he himself was as rugged as a mountain, but his heart was as tender as the heart of a child. What a privilege and a blessing to know a Godly man like Dr. A. P. Gouthey. You will only meet a few great people during your lifetime, be careful how you treat them.

Printed in the United States of America by

BOOKS of VALUE
2458 CHISLEHURST DR., LOS ANGELES, CA 90027

SOWING THE SEEDS OF WISDOM · INSPIRATION · LOVE · HAPPINESS

PRAY TO WIN!

A BLUEPRINT FOR SUCCESS

By

ALFRED ARMAND MONTAPERT

Discover the secrets of successful living, and
release Life's Greatest Potential. Prayer
is a natural instinct of mankind. More things are
wrought by prayer than this world dreams of.
The benefits and blessings are all spelled out in
PRAY TO WIN! for your personal use.
Don't overlook your real wealth, your natural
treasures. The NEW HAPPY SPIRITUAL LIFE
that you will experience through PRAYER is a key
to unlock the doors to a RICH, JOYOUS LIFE!

BOOKS OF VALUE • LOS ANGELES

IDEA
Who supplies another
with a constructive thought
has enriched them forever.

—Alfred Armand Montapert

Library of Congress Cataloging in Publication Data
Montapert, Alfred Armand.
    Pray To Win!
    Prayers, Spiritual Development, Well Being,
    Successful Living, Prosperity

Copyright © 1986 by Alfred Armand Montapert

ALL RIGHTS RESERVED, NO PART OF THIS BOOK MAY BE REPRODUCED IN ANY
FORM OR BY ANY MEANS, WITHOUT PERMISSION IN WRITING FROM THE PUBLISH-
ER. LIBRARY OF CONGRESS CATALOG CARD NO. 85-73037

Printed in the United States of America by
BOOKS OF VALUE   ISBN# 0-9603174-4-9

BOOKS BY THE SAME AUTHOR:

DISTILLED WISDOM
Thoughts That Successful Men Live By

THE SUPREME PHILOSOPHY OF MAN
The Laws of Life

PERSONAL PLANNING MANUAL
A Roadmap For Your Life

THE WAY TO HAPPINESS
Formulas To A Better and Happier Life

AROUND THE WORLD ON THE QE2
Your Lifetime Dreams Realized

INSPIRATION & MOTIVATION
Ideas For Successful Living

WORDS OF WISDOM TO LIVE BY
An Encyclopedia of Wisdom in Condensed Form

ADDITIONAL COPIES MAY BE ORDERED FROM:

BOOKS OF VALUE
2458 Chislehurst Drive
Los Angeles CA 90027

THE GREATEST RESPONSIBILITY
ENTRUSTED TO MAN
IS THAT OF
DISCOVERING AND DEVELOPING HIMSELF

Man's total development is the meaning and purpose of life. It is the continual remaking of yourself so that at last you know how to live. To be what you are, and to become what you are capable of becoming. To serve God and humanity. This is the true life and . . . life forever.

CENTRAL ARKANSAS LIBRARY SYSTEM
JACKSONVILLE BRANCH
JACKSONVILLE, ARKANSAS

PREFACE

For the last thirty years I have spent full time to STUDY how to LIVE . . . BE . . . and HAVE . . . the BEST. The foundation for my success is found in the Bible. MONEY IS MATERIAL PROSPERITY . . . JOY IS SPIRITUAL PROSPERITY. This is the unbeatable balanced combination for Successful Living we all seek.

Words are a rickety vehicle to convey one's emotions and the writer's sorrow is that he FEELS MORE than he can ever put into words. But, cut some words and they will bleed for they are vascular and alive. Many of the experiences in this book are better felt than told. This is my eighth book; in each one I have done my best to help mankind. My greatest passion is to make some contribution to God and mankind for the multitude of blessings I have received.

When I discover something of great worth, I feel a strong desire to share it with others, in the hope that my discovery will enrich their lives as it has mine. Such is the case with *"PRAY TO WIN!"*. You will find no "preaching" here, I am a learner. You may accept or reject the information, the vital decision rests with you.

The Law of God as revealed in the Bible, gives me the greatest benefits and satisfaction. Christianity is the "WAY OF LIFE" that I choose to live. IN THE BIBLE I FIND THE SIMPLEST STATEMENT ON CONDITIONS, THAT MAKE FOR THE BEST EXISTENCE THAT THE WORLD HAS EVER HAD, HAS NOW, OR EVER WILL HAVE.

The WORD of God finds its counterpart in the Nature of MAN, in Natural Law, and in Common Sense. It fully meets the needs of man, anticipates and provides for mankind' s highest SPIRITUAL, MENTAL and PHYSICAL good.

Man reaches God through prayer. Prayer is a natural instinct, a relationship, an attitude. Prayer is the door to our Spiritual development which is our true fortune. The NEW HAPPY SPIRITUAL LIFE that you will experience through prayer is a key to unlock the doors to a RICH, JOYOUS LIFE!

PREFACE, *CONTINUED*

THE MOST IMPORTANT THING TO LEARN IN LIFE IS HOW TO LIVE! Life is good when you WIN! Be a WINNER! It's your own fault when you lose. This work explains in simple layman's language how to PRAY TO WIN! Everybody loves a WINNER! The reason you will win is that when you PRAY you will have the Higher Power helping you do better than you know how.

People tear their shirts off trying to find and attend seminars that teach them SUCCESSFUL LIVING. The Basis for Successful Living is found in the BIBLE, but people do not take time to study and practice GOD'S WORD. This work will give you the essence of the Bible and lends itself to developing a COMPLETE WHOLE PERSON capable of handling anything that may come your way.

When we come to LIFE we come to GOD, and the finite may not investigate the Infinite. BUT, we SEE the results of a Supreme and Eternal Power that governs the Universe and man.

Today man is ignorant of his wonderful INNER BODY and SOUL, HIS INNER UNIVERSE. He does not truly "KNOW HIMSELF." In his quest to solve his problems man overlooks his own NATURE. The primary purpose of this *PRAY TO WIN!* book, is to develop the INNER MAN, MORAL GROWTH, and GOODNESS ... Practical lessons in SUCCESSFUL LIVING ... and to increase the VALUE and JOY of human life, and decrease the amount of suffering.

Basically, your inner qualities are your real wealth, not what you have in the bank, not on your financial statement. These INNER QUALITIES REPRESENT YOUR INTANGIBLE WEALTH. They are what YOU ARE. The success we seek is the product of all these qualities, PLUS our equitable share of the material. This is the real foundation for BALANCED SUCCESSFUL living and a truly successful life. When you combine GOLD and GOODNESS you have the Ultimate. MONEY IS MATERIAL PROSPERITY ... JOY IS SPIRITUAL PROSPERITY!

THE MOST ABSOLUTELY POTENT THING ON EARTH, IS A MAN SO GOD-MASTERED AS TO MAKE POSSIBLE THE RELEASE OF HIS ENTIRE FULL POTENTIAL. THIS IS OUR GOAL. Life is a series of turning points, they never end, and they make life interesting and exciting. May you profit greatly from this book, and may you find helpful information that will bring you the desires of your heart.

Alfred Armand Montapert
Los Angeles, California

TABLE OF CONTENTS

TABLE OF CONTENTS

LIFE'S GREATEST GOAL
IS
TO BUILD A MAN OR WOMAN

Far more important than what a man achieves is WHAT HE IS. TO BUILD A MAN IS THE GREATEST PROJECT ON EARTH FOR EACH OF US. Men of genius are not nearly as important to civilization as men of God. WHAT MEN ARE, IS WHAT MAKES THEM SUPERIOR OR INFERIOR. It frequently happens that great intellectual ability is a curse because it is not accompanied by great integrity. We have far too many who aspire to place and power but whose inspiration is not equal to their aspiration. After those who build buildings, bridges, jets and space ships are forgotten, we shall still remember and honor those who make it their first business TO BUILD A MAN OR WOMAN.

THE FIRST STEP . . . TO SUCCESSFUL LIVING

"Seek ye first the Kingdom of God and His righteousness;
and all these things shall be added unto you."
This constitutes the entire ministry of Jesus Christ.

— *Matthew 6:33*

LOVE AND KINDNESS

All things are TRANSIENT on this earth, be it power, glory, wealth, and even entire civilizations.

All we can do is to put our full LOVE and KINDNESS into our lives, professions, and families. Making a work of art of the precious years that are granted to us. This is my prayer for you the reader!

You have in your hands one of those rare books
that will benefit you throughout your lifetime.

A SPIRITUAL FOUNDATION FOR YOUR LIFE.

THE SECOND STEP . . . TO SUCCESSFUL LIVING

Use THE HIGHER POWER OF GOD which is available to you. It is communication with the Father by PRAYER so your needs may be met. Prayer is a NATURAL INSTINCT of man, and more things are wrought by Prayer than this world dreams of. Have you learned the techniques of effective Prayer?

God wants you to
LIVE . . . BE . . . AND HAVE . . . THE BEST.

THE THIRD STEP . . . TO SUCCESSFUL LIVING

DEVELOP YOUR SPIRITUAL DIMENSIONS, THE WHOLE PERSON. Everyone has three Divine Dimensions . . . Physical . . . Mental . . . Spiritual. Why operate on two cylinders when you have three? This book will help you develop your SPIRITUAL DIMENSIONS. The QUALITY of your life, your VALUES, the foundation of your life, all depend on solid beliefs. ENJOY A PARTNERSHIP WITH THE HIGHER POWER. Then you will reach the highest and best quality of life known to mankind. This is the secret of Successful Living.

Read on . . . BE SOMEBODY

Study to shew thyself approved unto God,
a workman that needeth not to be ashamed,
rightly dividing the word of truth.
— 2 Timothy 2:15

The beginning of WISDOM is to know that there are things you don't know. You can live and die successfully without knowing plenty. HOWEVER, there is ESSENTIAL KNOWLEDGE, meaning indispensable truth, you MUST know. I will do my best to spell it out for you.

PRAY AND LIVE SO ENTHUSIASTICALLY YOU CANNOT FAIL!

Prayer is a natural instinct of mankind. A prayerful individual unites with the Higher Power, then lives with confidence and joy. Real inner-wealth radiates in the FACE and LIFE. The main object of PRAYER is not to get a person into Heaven, but to get Heaven INTO a person. LIFE'S GREATEST LESSON!

THERE IS ALWAYS AN ANSWER TO PRAYER . . .
When you have learned how to PRAY!

People who neglect prayer are starving a natural instinct. PRAYER is the missing element between our present mediocre life and the GOOD peaceful abundant life promised by our Lord. Today we are developing only the intellect at the cost of the moral senses, the sense of beauty, goodness, integrity, character, and above all, the sense of the Holy. We are raising educated devils, which spells disaster to the individual and all mankind.

HUMAN DEVELOPMENT

Life's greatest achievement is the continual
remaking of yourself . . . so that,
at last you know how to really live!

THE CHALLENGE OF LIFE for each of us is to BECOME the BEST person we are capable of becoming. In GOODNESS, in LOVE, in KINDNESS, in CHARACTER, in HELPING EACH OTHER, in the GENEROUS QUALITIES, including the indwelling presence of God, and all the permanent qualities of the SPIRITUAL SOUL, that we can enjoy throughout the eternal years.

FOOD FOR THE SOUL

WE NEED FOOD FOR THE SOUL

The emptiness of the human soul is the greatest evangelistic opportunity in both East and West. The central neurosis of the world is the SOUL'S emptiness. Men cut themselves off from the root of their being . . . GOD . . . so life becomes dull and meaningless. It is the same problem everywhere.

— *Dr. E. Stanley Jones*

WE NEED OUTSIDE HELP

Both science and the scriptures conclude that man,
unaided by light outside of himself,
is incapable by some mysterious law in his nature,
of finding his way through the complicated maze called life
to the high levels of secure, compensating destiny.

For what shall it profit a man,
if he shall gain the whole world,
and lose his OWN soul?

— *Mark 8:36*

Think that over, my friend, for if you truly understand and practice this, you have the best advice on SUCCESSFUL LIVING ever given to mankind.

HOW TO REACH YOUR
FULL POTENTIAL

In order to lay a good solid foundation I am making the introduction section several pages long. If you are going to build a hut you do not need much of a foundation, BUT if you are going to build a GOOD LIFE you must have a strong foundation. You must have Solid Beliefs to build your life upon. Actually, we are laying the solid foundation supports, block by block, that are needed in order to reach our FULL POTENTIAL. So, have a little patience as we walk through the introduction section hand in hand to the first chapter.

RESPONSIBILITY

Learn the rules of Life . . . Obey the rules of life. They are spelled out for you in this book. Each individual must take over the responsibility of his own life. How can I make the days ahead most productive and meaningful? If each individual developed his own personal resources, we would produce the Golden Age for the whole world.

However, it may be necessary for us to pass through a series of crises before we shall wake up to the fact that we live in a world of Divine Law and Order. The heroes of the world will be those who live in accordance with the WORD OF GOD and feel the JOY and INDWELLING PRESENCE of GOD. JOY is a union with the unchanging God, and prayer is the cement of that union. Learn to really pray and your cares will drop off like Autumn leaves.

The capacity to enjoy life is inborn in all living beings, but JOY, like LIFE, does not sustain itself. It must be cultivated. The noxious weeds of worry and strife, rush and rumpus, must be constantly rooted out. Each of us must be the gardener who labors together with God, if the finest things of life are to come to full flower and fruit.

LEARN

If we are willing to take hours on end to learn to play a piano or operate a computer, or fly an airplane, it is sheer nonsense for us to imagine that we can learn the high art of getting guidance through communion with the Lord without being willing to set aside time for it. It is no accident that the Bible speaks of prayer as a form of waiting on God.

— Paul S. Rees

THEN ACT

MAN HAS TWO CREATORS . . . his GOD . . . and HIMSELF:

The FIRST Creator, GOD, furnishes the raw material and other gifts;

The SECOND Creator, is what WE make of ourselves. Each individual builds his own monument . . . or digs his own pit. Your life will be no better than the plans you make and the action you take. YOU are the architect and builder of your own life, fortune, destiny. The Spiritual factor can tremendously increase your potential for SUCCESS-FUL LIVING. Be mindful of the things of GOD . . . know you are not doing things by yourself. You will find that when you add the power of prayer, you will do better than you know how. Miracles will often happen. Keep in an attitude of prayer and the spiritual power will help you. With God as your partner, how can you lose?

"I can do all things through Christ which strengtheneth me."

— Philippians 4:13

IT TAKES MORE THAN POSITIVE THINKING

It takes the power of a positive FAITH in God . . . which gives you the positive outlook. MIGHTY FAITH makes the heart full of the POWER OF GOD. The most powerful force in the world is the positive attitude in the mind and heart of a believer who has the indwelling presence of God.

The only limit to the POWER OF GOD
lies within YOU!

If you have the capacity to fully understand . . . and truly obey these last seven lines you are well on your way to SUCCESSFUL LIVING!

WHAT PRAYER IS

PRAYER is an ATTITUDE and a RELATIONSHIP . . . powered by DESIRE.

Prayer is an ATTITUDE much more than it is anything else. An attitude of "My Father knoweth that I have need of all these things." Prayer is then an attitude of mind, an emotion of the heart, a companionship of my spirit with the Great Spirit.

PRAYER IS UNION WITH THE SUPREME POWER BY WHICH WE LIVE. God is my source . . . my source of birth, life, breath, comfort, strength, health, peace of mind, joy, love, faith and hope.

RELATIONSHIP: God abides within my soul . . . "The Kingdom of God is within." He is my best friend, a real personality which we call the Holy Spirit. Prayer is the tie between the individual and the Great Spirit. It is the human soul searching for this RELATIONSHIP.

DESIRE: Prayer is the soul's sincere DESIRE uttered or unexpressed. This desire can be great or small. Prayer connects you to the Higher Power. Men cannot live greatly without it. YOUR FAITH IS YOUR FORTUNE.

PRAYER is the key to Successful Living. Through prayer, I find God and God finds me. THE WHOLE ESSENCE OF PRAYER DEPENDS UPON OUR FAITH. IT IS THE BELIEF THAT OUR HEART EXERCISES, THAT BRINGS RESULTS.

Behold, I stand at the door and knock:
if any man hear my voice and open the door,
I will come in to him,
and will sup with him,
and he with me.

— Revelation 3: 20

DEFINITION OF PRAYER

One can define prayer many ways . . . as an uplifting of the soul to GOD. As an act of love and adoration toward HIM from whence comes the wonder which is LIFE. In fact, prayer represents the effort of man to communicate with an invisible being, creator of ALL that exists, supreme wisdom, strength and beauty, father and saviour of each one of us. Far from consisting in a simple recitation of formulas, true prayer represents a mystic state when the consciousness is absorbed by God. This condition is NOT of an intellectual nature.

Prayer demands no book knowledge or degrees, neither does the sense of love or of beauty. The simple and uneducated are conscious of God as naturally as the warmth of the sun, or the perfume smell of a flower. But this God, so approachable by those who know how to Love . . . is hidden from those who know only how to understand. Thought and words are at fault when it is a matter of describing this condition.

Prayer finds its highest expression in a soaring of love out of the heart or spirit of the true believer . . . not through the obscure night or fog of the intellect.

PRAYER HISTORY

In nearly all ages people have prayed to the higher power. The ancient city of Jerusalem was principally a religious institution. The Romans erected temples everywhere. Our ancestors of the middle ages covered with cathedrals and gothic chapels the soil of christendom. In our own time, above each village rises a belfry. In the course of our history, prayer has been a need as elemental as that of working, of building, of conquering or of loving. In truth, the sense of the holy appears to be an impulse from the very depths of our NATURE, a fundamental activity.

In one form or another, as far back as it is possible to trace human history, man's deepest concern has ever been to reach things beyond the ken of his intellect. The savage at his crude altar, the Aborigine sacrificing to his gods of wood and stone, the fire worshipper turning his face to the rising sun, and modern man with his multiple religions, creeds, doctrines, dogmas and philosophies all testify to the fact that man can no more escape the call of the Eternal than he can escape the fact of his own being.

PRAYER BRINGS STRENGTH AND JOY

Prayer to God has been the mainspring of my life. Whatever my influence or success in this world may have been, or is today, I can sincerely and reverently say that it has all been the result of faith and prayer. Both the physical and spiritual functions of prayer are needed to guide us confidently through a maze of doubt and fear, and present us daily before mankind radiant and full of courage. Prayer has helped me when all other aids and agencies proved futile and without hope. Our entire being is stimulated and inspired by prayer. This is because we are each endowed with a spiritual dimension.

Without prayer, no man has spiritual strength. I can reflect on ordeals that only the great power of God could have brought me through. It is unfortunate that so many people are not aware of this great power of God, which is available to all if they will only call upon Him for it.

PRAYER IS POWER. When the will and mind of man are in harmony with the creative spirit that undergirds the universe, man has new resources for effective living. In these miraculous ways prayer constantly changes the quality and the course of our lives.

Even though America from the beginning of its settlement has been motivated by religious faith, it is doubtful whether our people ever have had greater need for Divine help and guidance than they do today.

If my people, which are called by my name, shall humble them-selves, and pray, and seek my face, and turn from their wicked ways; then will I hear from heaven, and will forgive their sin, and heal their land.

— II Chronicles 7:14

Dostoyevsky said, "Be not forgetful of prayer. Every time you pray, if your prayer is sincere, there will be new feelings and new meanings in it, which will give you fresh courage and you will understand that prayer is an education." I believe that learning to pray is an important process in the growth of a Christian's life. In personal tribulation, in the hour of temptation, in the struggle against injustice, in every human crisis, the source of Power is available for us through prayer.

THE INNER HAPPINESS. To be able to say and mean, "I put everything into your hands, Lord. Thy will be done," is the only hope of happiness in this life.

ESSENTIAL KNOWLEDGE

We have been told that the realm of knowledge is so vast that to touch more than the fringe of it during a lifetime of study is quite impossible. In one sense, that is true. In another sense, it is quite untrue. If, by knowledge, one means all that pertains to life, the universe and to the earth on which we live, then, of course a lifetime is not long enough to investigate such unthinkable realms. If, by knowledge, one means essential information concerning such facts as have to do with fulfilling the prime objective of the Creator, then a lifetime, be it short or long, provides more than sufficient time to acquire such essential knowledge.

Christianity opens to us a whole realm of essential knowledge, and it is a means of acquiring essential knowledge. Why do I use that word essential? Because after all, much that we call knowledge is not, in the last analysis, essential knowledge. Essential knowledge then, is the knowledge that gives point and meaning to life itself. Essential knowledge is "indispensable truth that I must know."

The Bible is God's revelation to man. It meets all the tests, provides all the needed truth and points to the highest life known. This revelation is at once the vindication of a God who is infinite in wisdom and mercy, and who has made full provision for man whose limited knowledge demands such a revelation.

The Bible deals with eternal values and is a source of help with the mundane things we have to deal with every day. We need the Bible to guide us in our everyday living. The Bible is the Word of God and is the best guide to life. It gives us confidence, hope, peace of mind, inspiration in our everyday living. That is one of the many reasons I say, "to know God is to be adjusted to daily living. To know is . . . to experience God . . . to fellowship with God . . . to enjoy God . . . to appreciate God. NO MAN WILL LIVE THE WAY HE IS DESIGNED TO LIVE WITHOUT HAVING GOD IN HIS HEART, AND NOTHING WILL SATISFY A MAN THAT IS LASTING AND PERMANENT EXCEPT HAVING GOD IN HIS HEART."

But how to "know God?" . . . The only way to "know God" is to experience Him, to fellowship, to appreciate, to enjoy Him. Physical birth is for a physical world, but there is a realm above the physical. To enter that realm *"ye must be born again from above . . . by the Spirit,"* into the Spiritual World. Such a birth is essential knowledge.

PRAYER . . . MANKIND'S GREATEST POWER

Prayer is a natural instinct of mankind. A prayerful individual unites with the Higher Power, then lives with confidence and joy. Real inner wealth radiates in the FACE and LIFE.

Here are the truths that each of us has been seeking all our lives. *PRAY TO WIN!* is breath-taking in its magnitude. It is like going into a treasure house and opening the different doors. One room is full of diamonds. The next room is full of rubies. The next room full of pearls.

GOD IS OUR SOURCE . . . our source of birth, life, breath, comfort, blessings, strength, health, peace of mind, joy, love, faith and hope.

NO ONE IS REALLY LIVING UNTIL THEY HAVE LEARNED TO SHARE THEIR RESPONSIBILITY OF LIFE WITH GOD.

The object of Prayer is to experience God.

Alexis Carrel, the noted scientist said, "It is by prayer that man reaches God and that God enters into him. Man needs God as he needs water and oxygen."

Prayer is an ATTITUDE. The ATTITUDE of putting YOUR trust in God. Prayer is an attitude much more than it is anything else. An attitude of "My Father knoweth that I have need of all these things." And here is the importance of and the necessity for prayer.

The objective of this book is to have you richly live with God as your partner and to die rich, with a life of service to God and Mankind. This study of prayer, a spiritual phenomenon, is the observation and experience gathered and derived from the course of a long career among the most diverse people. Is it not important that we should know all the activities of which we are capable? Life demands we conduct ourselves in the way prescribed by the most profound and the most subtle needs of our nature.

PRAYER POWER

Man is basically a spiritual being . . . his equipment for living far surpasses any visible resources available in his environment. His spirit calls out for a greater destiny. It demands a greater satisfaction than is ever possible within the confines of the visible universe. This longing is spiritual. And God has provided man with the resources he needs in the spiritual realm to satisfy the longings of his heart and to fulfill his destiny to a far greater extent than we would dream.

The key to this power is the USE of it. And it is available to every individual. When we round out our life to include a well developed spiritual awareness we become a powerful, resolute individual who is capable of meeting life's problems, capable of reaching our highest desires for our own lives and contributing to the higher attainment of others. We are capable of deep abiding love, devotion to our family, loyalty to our jobs, courage in times of danger, strength in times of temptation, power in times of trial.

This world was made for man. Man is God's agent here on earth. There is a supreme power outside of man and a power within every man. It is up to each of us to recognize this power and use it if we would live the way we are designed to live.

Tolstoy admonished, "To Know God is to live." The first purpose of Prayer is to Know God. PRAYER IS THE MEANS BY WHICH WE OBTAIN GOD'S POWER.

Our Lord said, *"The things which are impossible with men, are possible with God,"* in Luke 18:27. The beginning of power is opening our minds and hearts to God and being receptive to His presence, His Spirit, His Voice and His will.

I don't understand the mystery of prayer any more than I understand the mystery of electricity and I am an Electrical Engineer. But I do know that man builds a generator that develops out of the magnetic field that marvelous power electricity. God made electricity and I believe the God who made a power to light our homes did not forget to make a power to light up our lives. God made Prayer Power to help His children along the way of life.

SOURCE OF POWER

The Power of Prayer. God is an inexhaustible source of power. In my life I can remember events some of them so serious, that only the almighty power of God could bring me through. It is unfortunate that so many people are not aware of this great power of God, which is available to all if they will only call upon Him for it.

The greatest need of the world today is prayer and the practicing of God's way of life. When we analyze the problems of the world today we see that they are caused by thinking of self first. God's way of life is for people to think of the welfare of others, be helpful and so live from day to day. Prayer will develop this attitude of mind on the part of an individual. It is the only way people can live harmoniously with each other and at the same time get the greatest contentment from life, by showing Love and Kindness.

The mistake of men is, and ever has been, to think of the physical man as the real man and the physical world as the real world. The real man, the scriptures insist, is the spiritual man, and the real world is the spiritual. The real man does not, because he can not, live on stocks and bonds, houses and lands, mortgages and commodities. By every scientific test he is made for God and spiritual things. With God he must have fellowship or be in this and every other world, a bewildered, unhappy, discontented creature. It is not WHERE we are or WHAT we have that makes us happy or unhappy. No generation ever had so much; no generation has so little. We must find God or lose everything.

The greatest legacy my parents ever gave me was taking me to Sunday School and Church and bringing me up to know God. His infinite love, mercy and power, and conversations with Him through prayer, have meant more to me than anything in my life.

For what reason does the sense of the holy play such an important role in the fulfillment of LIFE? It is not Science that nourishes the inner life of man ... it is the FAITH of the soul. Prayer is the tie between the individual and the Great Spirit. It is the human soul searching for this relationship. Men cannot live greatly without it.

PRAYER POWER

THE GREATEST THING THE GREATEST MAN EVER DID WAS TO PRAY! We do not need prayer to influence God on our behalf. We need prayer to RAISE US UP TO THE LEVEL where all God's mercies flow in abundance. On this level, prayer becomes the ATTITUDE indicated by Jesus Christ when he said, *"Only believe and thou shall see the glory of God."*

PRAYER FORTIFIES AND STRENGTHENS. From my own experience I can say that prayer is a spiritual armor that fortifies and strengthens one in times of discouragement, trouble or sorrow. Man must continually rededicate himself to God. Both silent and vocal prayer fortify one's faith and strengthen one to meet emergencies of life with courage and without fear. A famous scientist has said, "The most powerful form of energy one can create is prayer. Prayer, like radium, is a luminous and self-generating force of energy."

Our Lord, emphasizing the same truth, says, *"If ye keep my commandments, ye shall abide in my love."* The word "if" means "On the condition that; a supposition or condition." In other words, "if" means equal possibilities in both directions. Whether we stay in correspondence, or get out of correspondence, depends entirely on the "if" of cooperation. If the rose bush stays in the ground, it will abide and bloom . . . and it will abide and bloom as long, and only as long, as it stays in the ground.

THE HIGHEST POWER

Things go better when we are in harmony with –

The Divine Power that governs the Universe . . .
The Supreme Power that governs Nature . . .
The Unseen Power that heals Mankind . . .
The Almighty Power that gives abundant –

LIFE . . . LOVE . . . JOY

In GOD'S POWER we live, move, and have our being.

SUPREME POWER

All about us we are constantly reminded of a great power that has set up inexorable laws by which we must abide for our safety, health and well-being. Although we take it all for granted we do have the assurance that the sun will rise each morning and set each evening, and we are able to calculate in advance, for years to come, the exact movement of each.

We can depend upon the tides and the seasons. The day, the month, the year, and even the tenth part of the minute used by the industrial engineer, or the fractional part of a second used by the physicist are all the result of man's confidence in the absolute orderliness of the Creator.

We are a part of a great unchanging system of orderliness and of a universe controlled by a Supreme Power we call God, and it behooves us to practice the orderliness which is Godliness. Even the most cynical must admit that conformity to the laws of God in the universe have their own rewards.

The power which has established and maintains this orderliness in the universe is available to us to guide and empower our lives if we will draw upon it. God is not merely a Creator of a universe who has set the world spinning and left it to go its merry way. His infinite care is demonstrated in the cause and effect, action and reaction pattern built into the universe. Everything is made to perpetuate itself. There is available to every living thing the resources within its environment that it needs to sustain its life.

Modern man demands to know the how of all he accepts. There is no scientist who can explain the mystery of physical birth, the mystery of the electron, the bewildering phenomenon of germination, or the baffling riddle of a lily's growth. Who can explain with reason and logic why a caterpillar goes into his cocoon and later comes out a beautiful butterfly?

Every creature known to science, except man, is perfectly built for adjustment to the present physical environment of our world. It would not tax the genius of a scientist at all to definitely establish the fact that a fish is built for water. His gills, fins and entire make-up prove conclusively that water is his environment. Just so, the wings and general make-up of a bird argues that it was built for air. By exactly the same method of study, man reveals himself to have been created by God, for fellowship with God.

PRAYERS TEACH US
HOW TO LIVE

The subject of prayer is so wonderful, so marvelous. This book will revolutionize your attitude about prayer. People think they have to beat themselves with thongs and whip up their attitude in order to get them into the right mental place.

Just open up the blinds and let the sunshine in. The sun is always there. You don't have to beg the sun to shine. All you have to do is get in the right mental attitude and open up your mind and heart and the sun will come in. This little book could change this whole nation if people took the right attitude and relationship to prayer.

PRAY TO WIN! will reveal:
    Prayer the GREATEST ASSET of every person.
    Prayer the GREATEST POWER given mankind.

"The effectual fervent prayer of a righteous man availeth much."

This is the day of information explosion. And the basic question everyone should ask . . . is, the age old question . . . Where did I come from? Why am I here? How can I discover myself and live a rich full life that I was designed to live, and how can I best serve my fellowman? And, if possible do some work that would live after I die. I HAVE FOUND OUR REAL FULFILLMENT IS MY ONENESS WITH GOD. This is the only thing that will ever satisfy man's spiritual nature, and this spiritual nature is in fact the foundation for my other dimensions which are my physical being, and my mental being.

"When we depend upon organizations, we get what organizations can do . . . When we depend upon education, we get what education can do . . . When we depend upon man, we get what man can do . . . But when we depend upon prayer, we get what God can do."

— *E. M. Bounds*

By PRAYER, belief, faith, hope and service we achieve the Ultimate Victory . . . ONENESS WITH GOD. Prayers can't be answered unless they are prayed. Daily prayers dissolve your cares.

HOW TO PRAY

How must one pray? What are the formulas or techniques? We have learned the techniques of prayer from Christian apostles from St. Paul up to the crowd of anonymous apostles who for twenty centuries have initiated the peoples of the west to the religious life. Christianity has brought God within the reach of Man. It has given HIM a countenance. It has made HIM our Father, our Brother, our Saviour. TO REACH GOD THERE IS NO LONGER NEED OF A COMPLEX CEREMONIAL OR OF BLOODY SACRIFICES. Prayer has become easy and its technique simple . . .

To pray it is only necessary to make the effort of reaching out towards God. This effort must be effective and not intellectual. There is no need to be eloquent in order to be heard. For example, a meditation on the greatness of God is not a prayer, unless it is at the same time an expression of Love and of FAITH. Whether short or long, whether vocal or only mental, prayer should be like the conversation of a child with its father. One prays as one loves, with one's WHOLE BEING.

HABIT

Man is a bundle of habits. When prayer becomes a habit it operates on the Character. ALL CONDUCT IS INSPIRED BY PRAYER. Thus understood PRAYER becomes a "Way of Life". It is necessary therefore to pray frequently. "Think of God more often than you breathe," said Epictetus. To pray on rising and then to behave the rest of the day like a pagan is absurd. Very brief thoughts or mental invocations can hold a person in the presence of God.

A MORAL BUILDER

We should have prayer in the public schools. In 1952 the Charlatans kicked God out of the U.S. Public Schools. NOW they wonder why the young people are giving us HELL. In practice, the moral and religious activities are bound together. The moral sense vanishes soon after the sense of the holy. MAN HAS NOT SUCCEEDED IN BUILDING, as Socrates desired, A MORAL SYSTEM INDEPENDENT OF ALL CHRISTIAN DOCTRINE. Societies in which the need for prayer has disappeared are generally not far from degeneracy. That is why all civilized peoples . . . unbelievers as well as believers, must be concerned with this grave problem of the development of every basic activity of which the human being is capable.

IGNORANCE OF THE HOLY

WHAT ARE THE CAUSES OF OUR IGNORANCE? First, our false prosperity makes people think they do not need God. Second, we have legislated prayer out of the schools. The highly educated usually are egotistic, proud Pharisees incapable of faith and love. When times are good the sense of the holy is on the way to disappearance . . . However, when times get tough and people skip a few meals they start praying to God, as there is no place else to go.

The habit of prayer, though exceptional among the whole population, is relatively frequent among the groups that have remained faithful to the ancestral religion. It is within these groups that it is still possible today to study its beneficial influence.

Prayer is always followed by a result, if made under proper conditions. Nevertheless, prayer is looked upon by modern men as a useless habit, a vain superstition, a remnant of an uncivilized existence. In truth, many people are completely ignorant of its effects. But in an emergency that involves life or death, everyone will pray!

God is sorry about much of our blindness, and cries often that we are to be pitied who content ourselves with so little. God said he has infinite treasures to bestow. Blind as we are, we hinder God and stop the flow of His graces. But when He finds a soul penetrated with a lively faith, He pours into it His graces and favors plentifully.

Yes, we often stop this torrent by the little value we set upon it. Let us make way for grace; let us redeem the lost time, for perhaps we have but little left. Death follows us close, our souls are at stake. For unless we know God, we are not truly living.

These are turbulent days. They are days of uncertainty and of difficult decision. MAN HAS WALKED AWAY FROM GOD. He is doing his own thing and is playing fast and loose. He has abandoned God for the schemes and devices of his own making. Unless man and his children return to God, man will destroy himself the same as the Roman Empire only with a more diabolical end.

THE INNER MAN
THE BRIDGE TO GOD

THE SPIRITUAL DIMENSION OF MAN: Every intelligent person knows that man has three dimensions: BODY — MIND — SPIRIT. Our outside world of space, stars, sun, moon, galaxies is wonderful. A marvel of creation, a complex universe of Law and Order. But, do you realize you have just as wonderful a world inside of you . . . as there is outside of you?

There is much talk nowadays about self-realization and self-fulfillment, but this will never be reached if the personality is left incomplete through neglect of the inner life.

When a man becomes aware that the significant part of his being is the invisible and immortal part, then the world is seen to be what Keats called "a vale of soul-making," and everything becomes worth-while because it has an august end in view. Life is then significant.

We are born with no ready-made self or soul provided. A babe in a shawl is a little bundle of possibilities, including the materials for a self of infinite worth. And the first incentive towards leading the inner life is the desire to reach the end for which we were created. St. Augustine cries, "My life shall be a real life, being wholly full of Thee." And Coventry Patmore repeats the same truth in his famous saying, "God is the only Reality, and we are real only so far as we are in His order, and He is in us."

The biggest thing that any human being can do is to make of himself a cleansed channel through which the power of the spiritual world may flow.

Sooner or later every person must learn that only the love of God can satisfy the inherent desires of the Heart. One can have both hands full of worldly goods and be empty and miserable inside. Man's real wealth is inside where everlasting Joy flows like fountains of living water. The Joy of the Lord is your real wealth, your personal gold mine. My life is full of years and this is my testimony.

MAN LIVES IN TWO WORLDS

One is the material or PHYSICAL WORLD.
One is the SPIRITUAL WORLD.

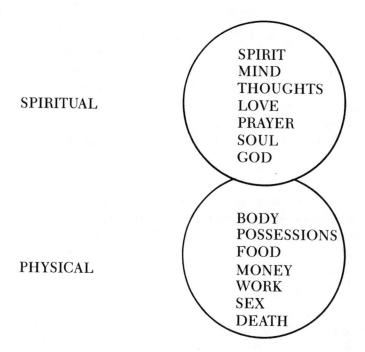

SPIRITUAL

SPIRIT
MIND
THOUGHTS
LOVE
PRAYER
SOUL
GOD

PHYSICAL

BODY
POSSESSIONS
FOOD
MONEY
WORK
SEX
DEATH

The mistake of men is, and ever has been, to think of the physical man as the real man and the physical world as the real world. The real man, the Scriptures insist, is the spiritual man, and the real world is the spiritual.

TRY TO SEE THE UNSEEN

It took me many years to realize that there are two realms . . . the Physical and the Spiritual. The things of the Spiritual are UNSEEN. Very soon I learned to see the UNSEEN. Then I had the right approach to the Spiritual Realm, and many answers came to me. These were the things that were in the Spiritual Realm and were eternal. For we walk by FAITH and not by sight. *"For the things which are seen are temporal; but the things which are not seen are eternal."*

— *II Corinthians 4:18*

PRAYER THE MAINSPRING OF LIFE

FAITH. The simple word "faith" sums up what I am convinced makes the difference between attaining or not attaining the greatest values of life.

It takes strength of character to use Faith in God. Yet the more it is used, the more it keeps forever building greater strength of character. It gives beliefs you can hold fast to when everything else may seem to be crumbling. It is my conviction that faith is stronger than disbelief; faith can overcome fear and hopelessness in you; just as the whole history of mankind has been lighted up by the faiths that have triumphed over the forces of darkness. The Lord admonished . . . *"According to your FAITH be it unto you."*

He is a fool who tries to live without prayer. Just as he is a fool who tries to live without eating and breathing. And for the same reason. Only in the case of prayer the reason or reasons for it are much more vital and far-reaching than are the reasons for eating and breathing. Breathing and eating are only the repair work which we do on the house in which we live.

The soul . . . the YOU of you . . . is much more important than the house in which you live. You will outlast the house. The word LIFE has very limited meaning as it is applied to anything physical. Only the you of you is eternal. And you can only live eternally as you cultivate correspondence with your spiritual environment.

God is spiritual environment. He is only contacted by prayer. He who tries to substitute something for prayer is trying to find a way to live without breathing. Without prayer you will lose your soul and when you do you will have lost the vital spiritual faculties which differentiate you from animals. Your life will be meaningless and useless, a glorious misfit.

The Creator gave us a set of instructions built into our very nature. Right and wrong are not merely words and phrases. They are in the nature of things, and if you transgress the Laws laid down, imposed by the nature of things, you will pay the penalty.

CHAPTER ONE

THE IMPORTANCE OF PRAYER

Any study of prayer must properly begin with the importance of prayer. Study is never in order until the importance of a subject is established. The importance of prayer is indicated by two things: the type of mind that it has always intrigued, and the emphasis placed upon it by Christ.

I know of no really great man in history who has not been a man of prayer. *"Fools,"* says the Bible,*"make a mock at sin."* Just as surely it might be added, only fools neglect to use the greatest source of human strength available to man: PRAYER.

Not even God can save a fool from his folly —
that is, from the result of his folly.
From the Law of Action and Reaction there is NO escape.

The human side of life is as inseparably joined to prayer as it is to breathing. It was on the human side that Christ was bound by the law of prayer. He could and did live for long periods without food, but He could not live without prayer. Granted that here appears perhaps the greatest mystery of His dual life, but the fact that He could not live without prayer outweighs the mystery. The deeply thoughtful person is not greatly troubled by mystery. It confronts him everywhere.

Even the simplest things are as mysterious as they are simple. Simple men soon learn to take mystery for granted. They are more interested in facts than they are in mystery. The WHY of things intrigues their investigations more than the HOW of things. HOW prayer sustains life is a mystery entirely beyond the ken of finite mind.

WHY it is necessary to sustain life through prayer is entirely within the reach of investigation. By experimentation . . . and there is no other scientific approach to any problem . . . any man, even the simplest of men, can establish both the fact and the necessity of and for prayer.

HOW a switch conducts either light, heat, or power at the will of the person who operates the switch is a mystery as profound as electricity itself. The FACT that it does all three is within reach of a child. WHY the switch makes or breaks the connection between the light bulb, the heating apparatus, or the mechanism that furnishes power is also within reach of the simplest mind.

The mystery of the switch, then, is not nearly as important as the USE of the switch. The fact and the results are the two important things. Granted that somewhere there is a master-mind who knows more about electricity, the switch, and the various mechanisms for the use of electricity than the average user, the fact still remains that one does not need to know all about either electricity, the switch, or the mechanism in order to use and enjoy the benefits of light, heat, and power.

As with electricity so with prayer. There is a Master-mind back of the mystery of prayer Who has given all necessary directions for its use. All we need to know is that certain results are obtained by following directions. The directions are simple.

Again, as with electricity so with prayer. On every switch there are two simple words: Off and On. Simply operate the switch in either direction and results are obtained. If it is light we want, simply throw the switch to ON and light we get . . . providing, of course, everything is in order. The same is true of heat and power. And those three words . . . LIGHT, HEAT and POWER indicate the first phase of our scientific study of prayer. All three have to do with the major premise of this study; namely, the importance of prayer.

LIGHT is defined as, "the condition of illumination necessary for vision." The word "vision" in this definition is related in its first meaning to physical sight. But the word vision as used in the Bible goes much deeper than physical sight. That is indicated by Our Lord. The words, *"Eyes to see,"* as used by Him, evidently mean power of spiritual discernment.

Accurate vision is one of the most essential physical faculties. Impaired vision is one of the greatest of all physical handicaps. Both observations are true of the spiritual realm. No more tragic words could be written or spoken of any person than the words, *"having eyes to see but they see not."* No more graphic words were ever spoken concerning blindness than the words of Our Lord descriptive of the religious life of His day: He said, *"The blind lead the blind, and all alike fall into the ditch."*

The words, "The ditch," at once conjure mental pictures of mud and slime and filth – a breeding place for pests and a dumping place for rubbish. It was this sort of a RELIGIOUS DITCH to which Our Lord referred. And it seems that the spiritual blindness that lands one in such a ditch is hopelessly incurable. *"Let them alone"* was Christ's injunction. *"They be blind leaders of the blind. And if the blind lead the blind, both shall fall into the ditch."* Matthew 15:10-20 is the whole tragic story of spiritual blindness told in a few sentences.

The evolution of religious blindness is always the same: Blindness, religion, the ditch. It is the law of the spiritual world. The words, "shall fall into the ditch" indicate cause and effect. The CAUSE is religious blindness that mistakes external things for spiritual values. The EFFECT is the ditch. Once the law has worked itself out, says Christ, there is nothing that can be done for the religionist. The proof of that is that Christ never made a single convert from among the Pharisees. *"Let them alone,"* He enjoined His disciples. Wonder why I do not have sense enough to obey Him?

And remember, the moment you begin to put the emphasis upon external things, you become a Pharisee . . . and Pharisees are the only class Christ ever did pronounce hopeless. I advise you to read and reread Matthew 15:10-20 until you have developed "eyes to see."

The point of this whole discussion is, spiritual vision is entirely dependent upon the proper use of prayer. In due course we shall come to the proper and the improper use of prayer. At the moment the point of emphasis is, No prayer, no light . . . no light, no spiritual discernment . . . no spiritual discernment and you become the easy prey of every religion and religionist that infests the tangled jungles of morbid confusion . . . until at last you "fall into the ditch" to rot in the mud and slime of religiosity, hopelessly forsaken by even God Himself, and the place where you fall will be marked only by a slab with the words, "Let him alone," scrawled upon it.

HEAT is a word capable of wide application. We usually think of it as simply the opposite of cold. While that is one meaning of heat, it is by no means all its meaning.

In physics the scientist knows heat as, "a form of energy possessed by bodies, made manifest by their temperature, change of state," etc. In practical application science knows a half dozen uses for heat. There is the heat of combustion, the heat of formation, the heat of fusion, the heat of evaporation, heat of solution. Then there is latent heat and specific heat. These terms in their specific, scientific application may be unfamiliar to the average layman, but their practical use is not unfamiliar to him. They are a part of his daily life. Combustion, formation, fusion, evaporation, and solution are all essential to his daily existence.

Again, as with the physical so with the spiritual. The heat of combustion is necessary to burn out the chaff of both sin and non-essential trash. God likens Himself to *a consuming fire.* He promises to act in our lives like *a refiner of silver.*

It is prayer that kindles and furnishes fuel for these refining fires. It is prayer that fuses us into oneness with the high purpose of God. It is prayer that keeps the constant temperature of devotion upon our heart life.

Heat has been referred to as the one indispensable thing essential to spiritual well-being. Mere religion is the result of no spiritual warmth. And mere religion is the one thing that God hates. A religionist is the frigid, barren waste that is as useless to God as the ice cap at the magnetic pole. As Jesus said about religionists in Matthew 6:5, *"And when thou prayest, thou shalt NOT be as the hypocrites are: for they love to pray standing in the synagogues and in the corners of the streets, that they may be seen of men. Verily I say unto you, they have their reward."*

POWER, like heat, is a word of wide variety of meaning and application. But of all the various and varied applications of the word God has singled out one more essential than all others to spiritual life and the progress of His Kingdom upon the earth. In fact, He has made the progress of His Kingdom contingent upon the exercise of this particular form of power.

We frequently mistake religious pow-wow for spiritual power. There may be a great deal of pow-wow without power. On my grandfather's farm there was a pump that would squeak and scream and rattle and shake without producing a drop of water . . . as David would say, "Selah!" *"From your inward parts,"* said Christ, *"there shall flow water."* What water? Acts 1:8 is the answer, *"Ye shall receive power"* . . . to *"be witnesses unto me"*. THAT is the essential power referred to a moment ago.

Christ is the essential need of the world. It is said of one Philip that he "preached Christ." That kind of preaching is so unfamiliar to even the very religious now-a-days that they cannot take it. We have been so busy with our creeds and doctrines and pet -isms that witnessing Christ is pretty nearly a lost art. That loss is traceable directly to a loss of prayer life. Prayer and prayer alone keeps Christ real and gives power to make Him real to others.

DO YOU KNOW ANY POWER THAT CAN HELP ME?

Here is the importance of prayer . . . all through the Bible the exhortation is: "To trust God . . . Have Faith in God . . . Wait on God." No one is a true Christian until he has learned to share the responsibility of life with God. If Prayer to God is my greatest power, it is up to me to use it. Prayer is important, for I must pray and ask, in order to receive. Prayer is releasing God's Power, and we need all the help we can muster. THEN we have man's powers PLUS God's Powers.

When people are in trouble, what do they care about doctrines and dogmas? What do they care about the recital of creeds? When they are in trouble, they will ask you anxiously, "DO YOU KNOW ANY POWER THAT CAN HELP ME?" What is your answer? Do I have an answer? Do you have an answer? The time fast approaches when men will seek refuge and alas they shall find none unless they have learned to put their trust in the living God.

You ask, "What is the matter with my life, I don't seem to be getting ahead?" I can answer you. And I can answer you without knowing a thing in the world about it. You need to get some positive force in action. The positive force to get into action is . . . not a mere mental statement of certain facts . . . but you need to get a positive force at the seat and source of your being that will so clean the streams of life out that they will literally be full with power. Power of a positive faith. You don't believe that will work? I challenge you to try it!

"All things are possible to him that believeth," God has said. Times without number God did say to men and women, *"according to your faith."* ACCORDING . . . both to the extent and quality of it . . . *"according to your faith be it unto you."* In the record of His earthly ministry there is no problem, no disease, no question that confronts us as individuals which faith did not master. It could do the same for us now. What the world wants to know is DO YOU HAVE ANY FAITH IN GOD? *"By faith,"* it says, *"their weaknesses turned to strength."*

May such a vision of our ability in God send us out to become the essential dynamic force in our community, and in our nation, and in our world. May this word of truth so rivet itself in our minds that it will awaken us in the night, it will disturb our cheap content, and make us eternally dissatisfied until we join forces with God in such a dynamic way that everybody we touch will feel the power in our lives.

CHAPTER TWO

PRAYER IS AN ATTITUDE AND A RELATIONSHIP

My first title for this study of prayer was "THE SCIENCE OF PRAYER." However, the word science, as applied to the subject of prayer may sound cold and critical. My object is to kindle new and hotter fires of prayer in all our hearts. This will lend itself to a joyful and richer life. The word science means "knowledge obtained and shown to be correct by accurate observation and thinking." That is not the full meaning of the word science by any manner or means, but it does indicate both the method and the objective that I shall use and that I have in mind.

Science is concerned with the HOW of things only as far as experimentation is necessary in order to obtain and observe certain specific results and classify the knowledge gained. That being true, I shall concern myself with rules and regulations only as far as rules and regulations have to do with accurate knowledge concerning prayer. In fact, most of us have already read so many books on "how to pray" that, by following all these rules and regulations, we have pretty nearly lost prayer . . . true prayer . . . itself.

Even though I may bore you with repetition, I shall remind you again that the disciples did not ask to be taught HOW to pray. By observing the prayer life of Christ, they saw and were impressed with the importance of prayer and their concern was to be taught that phase of prayer. *"Teach us to pray"* was their request in Luke 11:1.

Once the importance of prayer is established in the thinking of any individual and he begins to use prayer as the most important fact and factor in his life, he will learn by experience all he needs to know about "how to pray." That is the truth I tried to emphasize in the last chapter, drawing an analogy with the most common thing in modern life . . . electricity.

I tried to show that in order to enjoy the benefits of electricity about all one needs to know is the location and the use of a switch. Light, heat, and power can be obtained by the simple application of that knowledge. Advance knowledge of electricity is a little more complicated. So it is with prayer. We shall come to the graduate and post-graduate work in due time.

In the meantime, the important thing is to pray. The results are sure, even though you are not too expert in the use of the switch. You may even fumble the switch a bit in the dark, but the results are sure. Whether you use your right hand or your left hand on the switch makes no difference . . . much to the horror, I suppose, of the strictly orthodox right-handed switch throwers. Many a fumbling south-paw switch thrower has obtained amazing results!

In answer to the oft repeated, "I do not know how to pray," one can only use the common slang word of the street, "bunk!" You know how to ask for what you want, do you not? Well, said Jesus Christ, *"Ask, and ye shall receive."* You know how to look for what you want, do you not? Well, Jesus Christ said, *"Seek and ye shall find."* You know how to knock on a door where you want admittance, do you not? Well, Jesus Christ said, *"Knock and it shall be opened unto you."* It is as simple as that . . . ask . . . seek . . . knock. No elaborate directions are given. Prayer only becomes complicated when we complicate it.

Most "sermons" I have heard on prayer finally discourage rather than encourage prayer. They make the whole subject so forbidding by rules, regulations, and restrictions that one is impressed with the difficulties more than with the importance of and the necessity for prayer. True, there are some restrictions in the realm of prayer, but they are as simple as prayer itself. We shall give attention to some of these restrictions in due course. At the moment, they need give us no concern . . . need give us no concern because they are for the most part removed by prayer itself.

What I am concerned about, at the moment, is that we shall pray. The point that I am trying to make, above all others . . . and fear that I shall not make . . . is, by not praying we rob ourselves of the vital, essential things of life itself. And what are the vital and essential things of life? We know clearly enough what they are not. Christ has told us that. Life, He said, is more than meat, more than drink, more than raiment. He did not say that these things have no part nor place in life. They do.

But there is something more than these things that makes meat, drink, and raiment meaningless unless it is present. That something more is . . . Well, it is that something more. It is something that frees life of the hindrances to its full development and makes it the normal, natural thing that God intended it to be. The passage from which I am gleaning this information is the very familiar one in Matthew 6:26-34.

In order to show how far . . . how very far . . . man has removed himself from natural, normal living, Christ uses the birds and the lilies to illustrate. Birds, He said, do not spend all their time "sowing and reaping and gathering." They live. Lilies, He said, do not spend all their time "toiling and spinning." They just live and grow. But human beings can live no such carefree life . . . do I hear someone protest? The word can't is not the word. WON'T is the word.

God's orginal thought was that man should live just as carefree as the birds and lilies. That still is His thought. What else could Christ mean in verse 30? *"If God so clothe the grass of the field . . . shall He not much more clothe you?"* He took the entire responsibility for life at the beginning.

In this passage, He is trying to take that responsibility again. We have built up the vastly complicated business of toiling, spinning, sowing, reaping, gathering, and hoarding. The net result is worry with all its attendant evils. That is what Christ is trying to cure.

Worry is the most vicious and deadly thing in human experience. There is no evil that is not traceable directly to it. There is no good that ever comes of it. There is only one cure for it . . . prayer.

The point usually overlooked in the study of the passage under consideration is, it is only a part of a discussion of prayer that begins in Matthew 6, verse 5. The whole object is to free life of its complications by turning the responsibility for life back to God, where it belongs. That is the something more to which I referred a moment ago.

And may I say . . . and I have purposely reserved what I am about to say to the last because I want us to always remember this important fact . . . NO ONE IS A TRUE CHRISTIAN UNTIL HE HAS LEARNED TO LEAVE THE RESPONSIBILITY FOR LIFE WITH GOD. And there is the importance of, and the necessity for, prayer . . . not the vastly complicated business of prayer as outlined in the average "sermon" and book on prayer, but the simple, natural committing of life to God by faith taught by Jesus Christ. Prayer is an attitude much more than it is anything else. An attitude of *"my Father knoweth that,"* I *"have need of all these things."*

Try that simple method of living and note the results. A thousand "problems" will melt away like snowbanks under a June sun, things you now "fear" will be erased from your thoughts like haunting pictures from a blackboard. "Worries" and "burdens" will drop from your life like icicles from the eaves when the sun strikes them. Clouds of "depression" will drift from your sky like thunderheads driven by a wind. Try it, I say, and for the first time in your life you will know what Christ meant when He said, *"Let not your heart be troubled."* Trouble cannot abide if *"ye believe in God."* Belief shifts the responsibility for life to God, where it belongs.

> *"Humble yourselves therefore under the*
> *mighty hand of God, that He may exalt*
> *you in due time: casting all your cares*
> *upon Him: for He careth for you."*
>
> — *Peter 5: 6-7*

"AS A MAN THINKETH IN HIS HEART SO IS HE."

LIFE'S FIRST LESSON . . . YOUR ATTITUDE

Have a happy, loving attitude. A positive attitude is mature health. This is the best state of psychological and spiritual health that can be obtained on this earth. HAPPINESS depends not upon things around me, but on my ATTITUDE. EVERYTHING in my life will depend on my ATTITUDE. The quality of your life depends upon your ATTITUDE. It is not how much you do, or what you do, it is HOW you do it, how you react to things that is important. Your attitude rules the "HOW". You can make it difficult OR you can make it a breeze.

RELATIONSHIP

People should discuss the presence of God in their lives with other people more. God is my Father, my partner, my life . . . His word is food to my soul, my cup runneth over. My God and I walk through the fields together, we walk through the days together, we are good friends.

BEING HAPPY

A marvelous thought came to me one day that is priceless, and I use it daily. I realized that I had the tremendous power to choose . . . so why not be happy? It's just as easy to choose to be happy as to be unhappy.

I have available to me the love and help of the HIGHEST POWER (GOD), who maintains the functions of the entire Universe. So I make myself available to this Power and this Unseen Force helps me with my writing. Helps me in everything I do. Helps me to be happy. This Supreme Power is the best thing I have going for me in my life.

Whenever a man analyzes his life, he finds that all of his happiness comes from doing good and loving others; and that all of his unhappiness comes from selfishness and hate.

THE GOLDEN RULE

"Whatsoever ye would that men should do to you,
do ye even so to them."

— Matthew 7:12

THE TWENTY-THIRD PSALM

Every night for over twenty years, my wife and her mother prayed out loud the Twenty-Third Psalm together. This is a marvellous way to close every day . . . an attitude and a relationship with God the Father. When a person goes to sleep with beautiful comforting thoughts, they sleep sound and with great peace. This enhances health, well-being and serenity.

THE LORD IS MY SHEPHERD I SHALL NOT WANT: HE MAKETH ME TO LIE DOWN IN GREEN PASTURES: HE LEADETH ME BESIDE THE STILL WATERS. HE RESTORETH MY SOUL: HE LEADETH ME IN THE PATHS OF RIGHTEOUS-NESS FOR HIS NAME'S SAKE. YEA, THOUGH I WALK THROUGH THE VALLEY OF THE SHADOW OF DEATH, I WILL FEAR NO EVIL: FOR THOU ART WITH ME; THY ROD AND THY STAFF THEY COMFORT ME. THOU PREPAREST A TABLE BEFORE ME IN THE PRESENCE OF MINE ENEMIES; THOU ANOINTEST MY HEAD WITH OIL; MY CUP RUNNETH OVER. SURELY GOODNESS AND MERCY SHALL FOLLOW ME ALL THE DAYS OF MY LIFE: AND I WILL DWELL IN THE HOUSE OF THE LORD FOREVER!

There is perhaps, in all literature, no picture of a satisfying, replete, or happy present so graphically and poetically sketched as the word picture given by David in the Twenty-Third Psalm. It is a portrait of life as it can be lived when you have given yourself into God's hands in the way we have suggested.

The mountains in the distance lean, light-washed and cloud-crowned, against an early morning sky. Fingers of light, two hours ago, lifted the curtain of night from a sleeping world, and the morning star melted into the dawn. A thousand dewdrops, cradled on leaf and grassblade, caught the first rays of the sun and wreathed their transparent faces in flashing smiles.

The birds, in one great burst of song, made martial music for the marching feet of day, and the brook that flowed through the pasture set rippling fingers to the keyboard of its mighty organ and played open diapason, while columns of light came rank on rank. Hillside and valley flamed with blossoms of a dozen hues, and the willows along the stream shook out their green hair in the first breath of breeze.

A flock of sheep has spread itself over the pasture like the rolling tide of a mighty ocean of silver, and the clouds have spread their sails for the voyage of the day.

THE TWENTY-THIRD PSALM
CONTINUED

Lambs stray from their mothers and come galloping from their explorations, like tiny puffballs of white and black blown in by the wind. Their scampering feet flush a thousand grasshoppers that rise in a variegated rush on wings of green and yellow, brown and gray gauze. Contented bleats roll in a soft chorus from wooly throats, while the shepherd reclines dreamily against a sun-warmed stump, listening to a song sparrow's merry lay as it sits atop a cherry bush, and to the poignant call of the meadowlark that has chosen for his rostrum the topmost rock of a huge stonepile.

The sun climbs higher and higher, and heat, like a spreading blanket, covers pasture and flock. One after another the sheep drop in the high sweet clover and dreamily chew the cud.

And there, my friend, you have a pen-picture of God's replete present. A satisfying replete present is necessary for two very important reasons: First, the heart of each one of us can know contentment in no other way. Second, we can be permanently useful in no other way. Our heart union with God liberates us from the pangs of heart hunger, and brings us to the banqueting hall of a plentiful present. The "heart" of living a full, rich, satisfying life depends upon our oneness with God.

BENEFITS

I am in a preferred position. Why? Because I have been enjoying the enormous benefits of Prayer for many years. If I did not share my secrets of Successful Living with you I would be dishonest. I've found the answer . . . I LEARNED TO PRAY.

The correspondence with the Divine Power is my greatest asset, my greatest joy, my strength and the food necessary for my soul.

It works, because it is a natural law that fulfills my Spiritual Nature. I have oneness with the Divine Power of God. It is a form of LOVE that you can only experience, impossible to define. Even the songs of a bird cannot be defined, only experienced. Imagine having this solid feeling of well-being and joy in your body every day! WHAT A FANTASTIC WAY TO LIVE!

I remember reading about being full of the Joy of the Lord. This is peace of mind, plus strength, plus confidence, plus Love, etc. This is a greater Power than any words can tell . . . a satisfied soul, the Summum Bonum, the Love of Almighty God.

You can't buy it. It is priceless, but it is free to those who honestly seek spiritual fellowship and friendship with the nature of God. There is a vast supply of these Blessings. Only you can experience them and enjoy them. Like eating a meal, no one can eat for you, it's a personal effort. Once you have eaten at God's banquet table, you will never more eat out of the world's garbage pails.

If the heart of you is in fellowship with God you will be fifty percent happier, fifty percent more prosperous. It is a paying business to walk in fellowship with God. You have thought of prayer maybe as something indulged in by weak minded folk. When you intelligently pray you are using one of the great scientific forces in this world which makes for a clear intellect for you, a wholesome healthy body, and a normal wholesome walk on the level that you were created to walk.

The man who prays intelligently will be more courageous, more contented, more industrious, more productive. If your prayer does not lift you to that realm, then your prayer is simply mockery. If prayer is real, it will do every bit of that for you. Some businessmen could afford to invest in this sort of thing. No wonder Roger W. Babson, the greatest business statistician, said that "The greatest undeveloped natural resource is the souls of men." He was right, if prayer makes men more healthy, more courageous, more industrious, it does exactly what it is supposed to do.

> The world has yet to see what GOD can do
> WITH and FOR and THROUGH and IN
> a person who is fully and wholly consecrated to HIM.
> — *Dwight L. Moody*

CHAPTER THREE

THE TEMPERATE ZONE OF PRAYER

In studying or reviewing the various aspects of prayer, one must use a great deal of what I am pleased to call accommodated language. Any great spiritual truth must finally be discerned or sensed rather than expressed in exact and critical language. I am about to use a word with reference to prayer which indicates rather than expresses a truth that I think is in order at this stage of our study. The word is "zone". The word zone means, "to divide into areas."

By and large, as with our world, the realm of prayer can be divided into three zones: the torrid, the temperate, and the frigid. None of these words exactly expresses or describes, but they do indicate something to which our attention should be called, I think, before we proceed to other aspects of our study. Reversing the order of statement, let's think of the frigid zone of prayer for a moment.

One meaning of the word frigid is "stiff, formal, dull." That is the meaning of the word that I have particularly in mind. This zone of prayer is bounded by the idea that all prayer is limited to a regular order of things and cannot under any circumstances be expected to go beyond that natural order. In other words, supernaturalism, other than what is observed in Nature, is not to be expected.

One does not need to think very long or very deeply on this view of prayer to be convinced that, if it is accepted, prayer ceases to be the effective spiritual power that the Bible reveals it to be. On the contrary, it becomes a mere mechanical routine devoid of hope or inspiration.

It is no more a challenge to faith than planting beans or dahlia bulbs . . . and IF PRAYER IS ANYTHING, IT IS A CHALLENGE TO FAITH. It must be, or both prayer and faith will soon become words belonging exclusively to a rationalistic philosophy of God, life, and Nature itself. Either prayer reaches into a realm beyond mere natural phenomenon, or the word itself is entirely misleading.

Prayer is defined as, "the act of entreating earnestly." Well, why "entreat earnestly" if all life is bounded by, and confined to, a natural order of things that not even God can change, regulate, or influence? Breath, time, and energy used upon such an exercise could be put to much better and saner use . . . for instance, blowing dust off geranium leaves or blowing up paper sacks in order to burst them and hear the noise. But prayer, as we shall see after awhile, does go beyond a mere natural order of things and change, regulate and influence.

Opposite this rationalistic frigid zone of prayer is the torrid zone. Here, formalism is exchanged for fanaticism. The idea that God is neither amenable to any law nor controlled by any circumstance is the prevailing idea in this realm. The slogan is, "God can do anything." In other words, God can and does answer prayer purely from the standpoint of His ability to do so. This view of prayer is as dangerous to intelligent faith as the cold formalism of the frigid zone.

In the one case, faith is frozen to death; in the other case, faith is burned to death. In this realm, fanatics expect beans without planting and dahlias without ever having heard that dahlias grow from bulbs. Such petitioners never know exactly where or how to find God, and if they do by accident find Him, they have no idea in what mood they will find Him.

If their unintelligent prayers are not answered, they slanderously charge "God's will" with the full responsibility for their stupid misconceptions and insane "beating of the air." The only reason they can ever find for failure is, they did not pray long enough nor loud enough.

Fury is mistaken for fervor; vehemence, for assurance of victory; and gymnastics, for abounding grace. Such praying is fire out of control; a locomotive under a full head of steam, but off the tracks churning the dirt into clouds of dust; abounding energy tearing itself to pieces like a windmill in a hurricane without a speed governor.

Contrary to both the torrid and the frigid zones of prayer, and yet taking the good out of both of these realms, is the temperate zone of prayer. This zone is exactly what the word temperate indicates . . . "free from extremes." This is the zone of intelligence. Petitioners in this zone do not expect God to break away from all law to answer unintelligent or erratic prayer, nor do they expect to find God so bound by law that He cannot control law for their help in an emergency.

"And Moses stretched out his hand over the sea; and the Lord caused the sea to go back by a strong east wind all that night, and made the sea dry land, and the waters were divided. And the children of Israel went into the midst of the sea upon the dry ground; and the waters were a wall unto them on their right hand, and on their left."
— *Exodus 14: 21-22*

They move between these two extremes. Law to them is an elastic medium for the interchange of love and service between God and man . . . that He can, will, and does suspend natural laws that influence natural causes for the highest good of those who intelligently seek and find His will.

The truth that must be kept constantly in mind is that God does not need to change either His position or His intentions to answer prayer. The whole scheme of redemption is so perfect that it includes every possible physical and spiritual good. Ralph Waldo Emerson writes, "A little consideration of what takes place around us every day would show us that a higher law than that of OUR WILL regulates events."

We do not need prayer to influence God on our behalf. WE NEED PRAYER TO RAISE US UP TO THE LEVEL WHERE ALL GOD'S MERCIES AND BLESSINGS FLOW IN ABUNDANCE. On this level, prayer becomes the attitude indicated by Jesus Christ when He said, *"Only believe and thou shalt see the glory of God."*

"The Kingdom of God is at hand" was and is the message that Christ brought to men. Mark you, "at hand". The Kingdom is not something that God must be persuaded by long and loud praying to give. It is *"His good pleasure to give you the Kingdom,"* said Christ. The banquet table is loaded with every good. *"Come; for all things are now ready"* is the invitation issued to all. "Come" is the only condition laid down.

True, there are certain statements made by Our Lord which safeguard such passages against the unworthy. These passages shall have our attention in due time. It is enough at the moment to know that prayer is not the vastly complicated exercise that it is usually represented to be. It is mostly a grateful acceptance of abundant provision.

The best proof of our love for God and our devotion to Him is our intelligent acceptance of His abundant provisions. Neglect of these provisions is the surest evidence of unbelief. Praise is the highest form of prayer and gratitude is the most intelligent response to graciousness.

"What shall I render unto Him for all His benefits?" questioned David. He answered his own question: *"I will take the cup of salvation."* The word is take, not talk. Many a person has talked his prayer to death and has committed spiritual suicide by begging for what is already "at hand. " When invited by a host to "help yourself," why spend an hour begging for what has been graciously and generously placed at your disposal. The mark of a good guest is to accept as graciously as graciousness has provided. Too many of us have been mighty rude guests in "the house of the Lord."

"They ate their meat with gladness" has a spiritual as well as a physical application. If you doubt it, TRY CULTIVATING GRATITUDE AND WATCH YOUR LIFE GROW IN GRACE. Try saying, "Thank you," and watch your life flood with every benefit. God is the gracious Host; He is looking for gracious guests. To cultivate such graciousness is to live in the intelligent temperate zone of prayer.

I am reminded of the words of the song . . .

"Turn your eyes upon Jesus,
look up into his wonderful face,
and the things of this world
will grow strangely dim
In the light of His wonders and grace."

THE HIGHEST POWER

Things go better when we are in harmony with
The Divine Power that governs the Universe . . .
The Supreme Power that governs Nature . . .
The Unseen Power that heals Mankind . . .
The Almighty Power that gives abundant
LIFE . . . LOVE . . . JOY
In GOD'S POWER we live, move, and have our being.
— *The Laws of Life*

BECOME SOMEBODY

The question to be asked at the end of any educational step is not what has the person learned . . . BUT what has the person BECOME? To become the WHOLE PERSON you are capable of becoming is the ULTIMATE IN LIFE. This is the theme of this book . . . TO HELP YOU BECOME ALL THAT YOU WERE MEANT TO BE.

PRAYER IS A NATURAL INSTINCT OF MANKIND

PRAYER IS MANKIND TALKING PERSON TO PERSON TO HIS CREATOR

"What things soever ye desire, when ye pray, believe that ye receive them, and ye shall have them . . . whatsoever ye shall ask of the Father in my name, he may give it you."

— *Mark 11:24*
John 15:16

Prayer, mysterious as it may sound to our ears, and beyond, infinitely beyond, out of immediate comprehension, prayer makes it possible for God to do what He cannot otherwise do. In other words pray, thus you make it possible for my Father to do what He has in mind to do for you, but cannot otherwise do unless you do live thus closely and intimately with Him.

Through prayer God does what it is often impossible for us to do. Pray for our daily bread. We could fill this book with personal testimonies how God gives food, clothes, money, jobs, cars, healing and other blessings in answer to prayer.

Pray big prayers to an ALMIGHTY GOD. God invites and commands to ask BIG THINGS. *"Ye have not, because ye ask not."* James 4:2. The Bible certainly promised miracles in answer to prayer and faith. The miracles of the Bible are given as examples for us.

If ye shall ask any thing in my name, I will do it.

— *John 14: 14*

If ye abide in me, and my words abide in you,
ye shall ask what ye will, and it shall be done unto you.

— *John 15: 7*

Some praying makes one feel so good, it is heavenly, even though we are living in a world of suffering, greed, and struggle. The Almighty miracle working God still answers prayers as he did in the Bible times and for our fathers. Here one can learn how to pray in the will of God, grow in FAITH, really get the blessings from God and live the joyful, successful life of daily answered prayer. This is Life . . . to Know God. Why be satisfied with crumbs of life, when you could sit at the Lord's banquet table? He is just a prayer away.

CHAPTER FOUR

WHAT IS PRAYER?

The verses in Matthew, Chapter Six, raise a question which I think should occupy our thought at this point in our study of prayer. When I state the question, I shall doubtless seem to some to be going backward instead of forward. The fact is, in order to go forward at all, it is necessary at some point in this series of studies to raise the question that I have in mind. To have raised the question sooner would have been, it seems to me, to have raised it too soon. To raise it much later would be to raise it too late. The question is . . . What is prayer?

There are many definitions of prayer. But the trouble is, none of them quite defines prayer. The reason probably is, IT IS ALMOST IMPOSSIBLE TO CAGE A PURELY SPIRITUAL FUNCTION IN A DEFINITION. Spiritual functions, like emotions, do not lend themselves to definitions. They sweep beyond the boundary of words and penetrate to depths beyond the reach of intellectual investigation.

A few chapters back, I referred to prayer as an attitude. An attitude, so the psychologists tell us, is an "instinctive mental reaction." An instinctive reaction is a combination of functions which takes its rise from sources so deeply hidden that it is quite impossible to locate the fountain. The fountain is something built into the indefinable life of us that functions spontaneously . . . like the sense of direction inherently built into the wild goose or a homing pigeon. As far as any scientist knows, a goose or homing pigeon does not reason. Both birds "Instinctively react."

A goose flies by a chart upon which
the National Geographical Society could never improve.
— *Oliver Wendell Holmes*

So the normal heart of man reacts. And I use the word normal advisedly. The normal man is the man who has experienced spiritual adjustment to God. All others are either subnormal or abnormal. Normal creatures are creatures whose natures are not perverted by maladjustments. Man out of fellowship with God is a perverted creature. In fellowship with God, he instinctively reacts to all proper spiritual adjustments.

That is the reason why Christ pronounced very few don'ts and do's. Don'ts and do's, to a real Christian, are about as necessary as educating a wild goose or a homing pigeon in the art of directional flying.

What is true of the Christian's conduct is true of his prayer life. "PRAYER," says the poet, "IS THE CHRISTIAN'S VITAL BREATH." He instinctively breathes and he instinctively prays. A radio installed in an airplane, and properly tuned in, tells you instantly when you are on or off the "beam". The heart of you, properly tuned in on God, tells you when you are on or off the beam.

What is known as an "automatic pilot" can now also be installed in an airplane. This instrument, when properly adjusted, instantly makes all necessary corrections and keeps the airplane in the proper altitude and on course . . . and flies the ship infinitely better than any pilot can fly it.

So with the heart of us. If, properly adjusted to God, will do a better job of keeping the Christian on course than volumes of religious don'ts and do's can possibly do. The only way you can mess up an "automatic pilot" on an airplane is to try to help it out. The way to mess up your life and spoil your prayer life is to try to help it out . . . or allow someone else to help it out . . . with endless directions and instructions. Just one thing is necessary . . . a proper relationship. And "relationship" is the word to which I would call attention at this point.

GOD
is at the center of man.

— *Eckhart*

The trouble is, we have come to think of prayer as an act only. While prayer is an act, it is much more an attitude and a relationship. The word relationship indicates inter-dependence. The true relationship between God and man is not independent on either side. Man has no source of supply apart from God and God finds what He most craves and needs in fellowship with man.

On man's side, prayer is as inseparable from spiritual life as breathing is inseparable from physical life. On God's side, prayer makes access to man possible. About the only "rule" I know of that is necessary for prayer is the rule of keeping our essential relationship with God in adjustment.

Once again, the illustration I used a moment ago is apropos at this point. To install radio equipment in an airplane is not sufficient. The equipment must be kept in "tune in" condition. A dead set is as bad or worse than no set. In fine, clear weather a pilot has comparatively little use for his radio. When he flies into what is known as "soup", he needs all of his equipment . . . and needs it badly. And when he flies into the soup, it is a bad time to make repairs if he has allowed his equipment to get out of adjustment during clear weather.

He must keep his relationship with the source of his help constantly. Many a pilot has crashed because he was not particular to keep this relationship. His radio is the eyes and ears of his ship. If his eyes and ears are in adjustment, he gets either on or off course signals and is able to fly his course as accurately as though he were flying contact. Through his "head phones" he hears the signals. No one else hears them unless he is wearing the phones that pick up the signals. The pilot not only finds his course, but the operator in the radio tower finds him. Both are able to keep in touch.

The analogy I am using does not carry all the way through, nor does it say all there is to say about prayer, but it does say what I am anxious to get said at this point in our study. True prayer is the prayer that finds God and the prayer that makes it possible for Him to find us.

True prayer enters into the life of God and makes it possible for Him to enter into our lives. God Himself becomes the "answer to our prayer." And that is exactly what I want this chapter to leave with us. So many of us are mere petty beggars. We pray only when we want or need something. God is a mere convenience. What He can DO for us is more than what He IS to us. WHAT HE IS TO US IS THE TRUE MEANING OF PRAYER.

How long do you enjoy a relationship when you have reason to believe the only reason it is continued is what can be gotten out of you or from you? Well, how far beyond that has your prayer life gone? When things go wrong, or you need something, you come running. Your prayer life has become a one-sided thing with you always on the receiving end.

One day my wife came to my study. She tiptoed in and sat down. I finally looked up and asked, "What do you want, dear?" "Oh, nothing" she said, "I just wanted to be where you are." That is what God craves . . . and that is prayer at its best and on its highest level.

"Your heavenly Father knoweth what things ye have need of." The question is . . . Do you know what things your heavenly Father has need of? His need is your greatest need . . . a relationship for the sake of that relationship. There is profit in such a relationship but the profit is only a by-product. The relationship is the thing . . . and the thing is that relationship.

> "Behold, I stand at the door, and knock:
> if any man hear my voice, and open the
> door, I will come in to him, and will
> sup with him, and he with me."
>
> — *Revelation 3:20*

GOD

The Sun with all its planets moving around it
can ripen the smallest bunch of grapes
as if it had nothing else to do.
Why then should I doubt HIS power?

— *Galileo*

THE BIBLE ... GOD'S WORD TO MAN

"This little volume," said the venerable Schliermacher, holding up a Greek New Testament before a group of English students, "contains more valuable information for mankind than all the other writings of antiquity put together."

The Bible is the foundation of all literature worth preserving. It is the central sun of the entire constellation of the world's best thought. From it all, human genius borrows its light. To it, human progress owes its greatest debt. It is the fountainhead of life and it reveals the best way to live and the only comfortable way to die.

Without the Bible, there is neither sense nor meaning to life. Have what we may, and get what we can, we shall have nothing and get only frustration unless we have and find Him. Modern life is only another name for muddled existence.

Again, the Bible stands alone when it comes to its power to transform character and life. Its strange white light searches the conscience and condemns the guilty. It smites like a hammer, burns like fire, cuts like a sword, and finally, leads the penitent gently to the Cross and there sheds its "beams around" him and whispers tenderest comfort into his broken heart.

Individuals have been transformed from criminals, thugs, gangsters and other worthless characters into worthy, strong and noble leaders. The hopeless, forlorn, sorrowing and defeated have found courage and comfort and confidence that they could have drawn from no other source.

Hold it tightly to your heart, for soon your little day will be done, and when the shadows lie deep across the west, it will hold your trembling hand and guide your unsteady feet through the sunset path into the presence of Him who breathed inspiration into the heart and mind of those who penned its sacred pages. Never, under any circumstances, allow yourself to be without it. Hide it in your heart, that you may not sin against God, and by so doing, fail to achieve your own highest good.

MAN'S FINEST HOUR!

The QUALITY of a person's LIFE . . .
is the RESULT of CONVICTIONS to high IDEALS,
DISCIPLINE of WORK and of PROBLEMS,
HIGH STANDARDS and CHARACTER,
FAITH in GOD and LOVE with COMPASSION.
COURAGE to fight LIFE'S BATTLES . . .
even with some defeats.
When he has done his BEST, worked his HEART out
for NOBLE CAUSES, and lies battered and exhausted
on the field of battle . . .
THEN he is VICTORIOUS.
THIS IS MAN'S FINEST HOUR!
FOR TO BUILD A MAN . . . IS LIFE'S
GREATEST PROJECT . . . FOR EACH OF US!
— *Alfred A. Montapert*

CHAPTER FIVE

WAIT ON THE LORD

For the next two chapters I propose a series of short essays built around a single word which, perhaps, more than any other one word, reveals the true science of prayer . . . if I may use the word science in its broad meaning of applied knowledge. The word to which I refer is . . . WAIT. The particular passage with which I shall begin this series of essays is Psalm 27:14 . . . *"Wait, on the LORD: be of good courage, and he shall strengthen thine heart: wait, I say, on the Lord."*

The repetition in this passage is for double emphasis. Repetition generally is not considered good form. God is more interested in enforcing important truth than He is in good form. Bad form is preferable to lack of understanding or misunderstanding. If bad form makes essential truth more effective, then by all means let us have bad form.

That is evidently David's mood. Under the urge of the Holy Spirit, he repeats, *"Wait, I say, on the Lord."* I know the mood well. To see important truth slip past half-hearted, half-awake, mind-wandering listeners is the most disconcerting experience ever experienced by the man with a message. Hence, in his anxiety to enforce what he knows to be essential truth, he frequently resorts to bad form in the interest of overcoming mental and spiritual lethargy.

I am the light of the world:
he that followeth me shall not walk in darkness,
but shall have the light of life.

— John 8:12

To the person who is serious and who thinks . . . a rare combination indeed . . . the exhortation, *"Wait on the Lord"*, would be sufficient. Into all the ramifications of God's all-sufficiency and man's complete dependency, his mind would immediately go. But since such listeners are so rare, David repeats, *"Wait, I say, on the Lord."*

The word wait in our English language has but a single meaning for the average person . . . to linger or tarry. In the Hebrew language it has a diversified meaning depending on what thought the writer or speaker wishes to convey. We shall have occasion to look at several of these words with their delicate shading of meaning as these studies unfold.

The particular word used in this passage is the Hebrew word knaw-vaw . . . to bind together, especially by twisting. The thought is that to make prayer effective one must cultivate the habit of keeping one's life all bound, tangled, twisted into the life and purpose of God. Here again we come to the attitude and relationship to which I have already called attention, which is, in and of itself, true prayer . . . an attitude of expectant waiting and the relationship to God which obligates Him to reveal Himself.

WE GET WHAT WE EXPECT. THERE IS A LAW OF LIFE THAT BRINGS TO US WHAT WE EXPECT. Whether we get good, bad, or nothing, depends entirely on what relationship we bear to God. To bear the relationship of sons and daughters and to cultivate that relationship assures us of good and only good. *"All things work together for good"* to those who sustain a proper relationship to God by living in His revealed purpose.

That is an easy passage to quote; it is a difficult one to apply. Much that seems to be bad is bound to come to a Christian in a world like this. Many things seem to be bad because our vision is both selfish and short-sighted.

MY PRAYER

May God give me . . .
TEARS ENOUGH to keep me tender.
HURTS ENOUGH to keep me in sympathetic touch with those
who are in trouble.
FAILURES ENOUGH to make me ever aware of my dependence
upon God.
SUCCESSES ENOUGH to assure me that I labor together with
HIM.
And a spiritual experience that will enable me to always keep first
things in first place, so that when I come into the Kingdom of God
I shall feel at home.

We lose someone or something by death or circumstances and immediately we judge the loss by the rule of the present. We grieve and rave and indulge in self-pity until we completely break the relationship essential to the working out of God's purpose in our life. There is where waiting comes in. Instead of waiting to see what God's purpose is, we go running frantically in every direction seeking human explanations, comfort, and sympathy. God has no opportunity to reveal or explain.

We hug our sorrow, disappointments, and losses to our hearts like Jacob when he thought . . . mark you, thought . . . he had lost Joseph. *"He refused to be comforted,"* says the story in Genesis 37:35. He only saw the seeming present loss. Had he "waited on the Lord," the whole story would have in the course of time unfolded.

It did unfold, but Jacob had already belittled himself by whining and grieving. He made himself miserable, and everyone around him miserable for several years because he spent his time nursing his loss and grief instead of "waiting on the Lord." He *"refused to be comforted,"* the story says, *"and he said, For I will go down into the grave unto my son mourning."*

The fact is, what seemed to be loss was pure gain. Joseph was not dead. He was fulfilling the purpose of God in Egypt. Jacob spent his time whining and bawling. To put it mildly, that was a mighty unbecoming way for a Christian to behave! To put it bluntly, Jacob's whine and his tears were evidence of unbelief!

In his self-pity he completely forgot God's word to him . . . Genesis 31:3 . . . *"I will be with thee."* With that promise it was his business to go steadily on believing that God was with him and that all things were in the purpose of God. Abraham had such faith and vision. When called upon to offer his son Isaac, he simply said, "Very well. I do not understand, but whether I understand or not is no business of mine. This is God's business and behind it all is His promise." That is "waiting on the Lord." And mark you, the passage says, *"Wait on the Lord."*

We get into difficulty and we wait on everybody except the Lord. The passage in Jeremiah 17:5 that reads, *"Cursed be the man that trusteth in man,"* has broader application than some have imagined. When we run to people with our sorrows and problems, we rob ourselves of one of the most important ministries of the Holy Spirit; namely, to "guide" us "into all truth."

The futility of human council should be obvious to spiritual people. Human fellowship is one thing; making little gods or goddesses of people is quite another thing. In your deepest sorrows and problems no human being can truly help you. They may give you a sop by encouraging your self-pity, but they can give you no permanent help. Your sorrow or problem is a purely personal sorrow or problem. Only God knows all there is to know about it.

Every sorrow and problem has a past and a future. It may be unwittingly you are responsible for the loss you suffer. You grew fast (like a barnacle to the hull of a ship) to someone or something, and the "loss" was to save you from even a greater loss in the Kingdom of God.

And all too frequently, instead of "waiting on the Lord" to find out His reason for doing a given thing, we proceed to grow fast to someone or something else and by so doing prepare ourselves for another loss. Or Jacob-like we "refuse to be comforted" and by so doing exaggerate our misery until it becomes an obsession. WE BECOME ONE OF THOSE WHO ARE NEVER QUITE HAPPY UNLESS WE HAVE AT LEAST A LITTLE MISERY.

Even our best friends in time become tired of listening to a tale of woe. Protracted sorrow is evidence of several things:

(a) Unbelief... No matter how loudly you protest you cannot believe that *"All things work together for good to those who love the Lord"* and spend your time grieving over a loss. There is no such thing as misfortune for a Christian. "All things" are in the purpose of God. That is fortune, not mis-fortune. We miss the fortune by labeling it mis-fortune.

(b) PROTRACTED SORROW REVEALS A LACK OF VISION. The end of a matter is what really matters. Vision sweeps beyond the present. It trusts until the reason for things is disclosed. "I wait with joy the coming years," says John Burroughs. Mark you with joy, not jaw. "Rejoice in the Lord, always" is the formula. To do other than that is to question the integrity of the Lord.

(c) To fail to "WAIT ON THE LORD" for a full disclosure of the meaning of events is to lose the real meaning of prayer. PRAYER IS NOT WORDS: IT IS AN ATTITUDE AND A RELATIONSHIP. I shall keep repeating that until it becomes the paramount truth of this whole book. Wait is the word that cultivates both the attitude and the relationship.

> *"But they that wait upon the Lord*
> *shall renew their strength;*
> *they shall mount up with wings as eagles;*
> *they shall run, and not be weary;*
> *and they shall walk, and not faint."*
>
> — *Isaiah 40: 31*

We have lost something very valuable
in the last 100 years ...
What do you think it is?
It is the art of praying and helping one another.

BENEFICIAL INACTIVITY

To be unhurried, free from burning ambitions and little jealousies, is more than merely a wholesome state of mind, it is positively a blessed state of mind.

Most of us are more in need of a deeper sense of contentment with life as it is, than we are of a deeper understanding of life.

We have been so much with the business of living that we have forgotten how to live.

We have heard so many sermons on life that life itself has become as hazy as the average philosophy about it.

What most of us need is some time free from anxiety . . .

Time to watch a pair of birds carrying flies and worms to a nest full of young.

Time to watch a squirrel frisk from branch to branch and from log to log with apparently nothing on his mind except to frisk.

Time to watch a hawk make lazy circles on wide-stretched wings as though practicing some graceful maneuver.

Time to sprawl on the grass or a bed of dry leaves in a patch of sunlight and watch the clouds sail away on mysterious voyages to far places across endless seas of blue sky.

Time to just think and dream of nothing until both heart and mind become so still that God can speak to us of things that really matter.

CHAPTER SIX

TRUE PRAYER

The word "wait" occupied our attention in the last chapter. The same word shall engage our thought in this chapter. The word wait, as used by David in the 27th Psalm, we found to be revealing of both the attitude and the relationship to which I have repeatedly referred and which must exist and be maintained before any prayer life can be established and developed . . . or better still, before even prayer itself can come into being.

Now, I shall use another passage in which the word wait occurs, but which introduces another aspect of prayer. Because of its lack of flexibility, the English language fails miserably betimes to reveal some delicate shading of meaning that the inspired writers had in mind. Indeed, our comparatively crude English language sometimes completely obscures the thought that the inspired writers wished to convey.

An example in point is Psalm 62:5. The Hebrew word, translated "wait", hardly carries the meaning of wait at all, as we understand and use the word. It means to "stand still and keep silent." There is the same attitude of expectancy that we find in the Hebrew word used by David in Psalm 27, but in addition there is introduced what I shall call, for the want of a better expression, the inactive or passive phase of prayer.

Is it not indispensable that we should know all the activities of which we are capable? Success is our heritage IF we pray and obey the word of God. NO ONE SHOULD IGNORE PRAYER, THE MOST PROFOUND AND THE MOST SUBTLE NEED OF OUR NATURE. THE SPIRITUAL SHOWS ITSELF JUST AS INDISPENSABLE TO THE SUCCESS OF LIFE AS THE INTELLECTUAL AND THE MATERIAL.

THE SENSE OF THE HOLY MANIFESTS ITSELF CHIEFLY BY PRAYER. Prayer, like the sense of the holy, is, from all the evidence, a spiritual phenomenon. It is by systematic observation of the man who prays that we shall learn in what consists the phenomenon of prayer, the technique of its production, and its effects.

Prayer seems to be essentially a tension of the spirit toward the immaterial substratum of the world. One can define it equally as AN UPLIFTING OF THE SOUL TO GOD. As an act of love and adoration toward Him from Whom comes the wonder, which is life. In fact, prayer represents the effort of man to communicate with an invisible being, creator of all that exists, supreme wisdom, strength and beauty, father and savior of each one of us.

True prayer represents a mystic state when the consciousness is absorbed in God. The state is not of an intellectual nature. Also, it remains as inaccessible, as incomprehensible to the philosophers and to the learned. As Alexis Carrel says, "This spiritual world differs profoundly from the physical from which, none the less, it is inseparable. God can only be encountered outside the dimensions of space and time; beyond the intellect, in that indefinable realm, which according to Ruysbrock the Admirable, can only be penetrated by love and longing." Just as with the sense of beauty and love, it demands no book knowledge. The simple are conscious of God as naturally as of the warmth of the sun, or the perfume of a flower.

There is no need to be eloquent in order to be heard. In judging the value of prayer by its results, our most humble words of supplication and praise seem as acceptable to the Master.

One prays also by action. The accomplishment of duty is equivalent to prayer. The best way of communing with God is without doubt fully to accomplish His will. *"Our Father . . . Thy Kingdom come, thy will be done on earth as it is in Heaven."* And doing God's will manifestly consists in obeying the laws of life, as they are inscribed in our tissues, our blood and our spirit.

> *Fear God and keep His commandments:*
> *for this is the whole duty of man.*
> — *Ecclesiastes 12:13*

Prayers, which rise like a great cloud from the surface of the earth, differ from each other as much as the personalities of those who pray. A blind man, seated by the wayside, shouted his supplications more and more loudly in spite of those who wanted to silence him. *"Thy faith hath made thee whole,"* said Jesus, who was passing that way.

At its loftiest, prayer ceases to be a petition. Man lays bare to the Master of all things that he loves Him, that he thanks Him for His gifts, that he is ready to accomplish His will, whatever it is. Prayer becomes contemplation.

Where and when to pray? One can pray anywhere. In the road, in a car, in a railway carriage, in the office, in the school, in the factory. But one prays better in the fields, the mountains and the woods, or in the solitude of one's own room.

There are also the liturgical prayers offered in church. But whatever the place of prayer, God only speaks to the man who has established calm within himself.

Inward calm depends at the same time on our organic and mental state and on the milieu into which we are plunged. To pray on rising and then to behave the rest of the day like a pagan is absurd. Very brief thoughts or mental invocations can hold a man in the presence of God. All conduct is then inspired by prayer. Prayer becomes a way of life. And, prayer is always followed by a result, if made under proper conditions. "No man has ever prayed without learning something," wrote Ralph Waldo Emerson.

Prayer acts on the spirit and on the body in a way which seems to depend on its quality, its intensity and its frequency. It is easy to perceive the frequency of prayer, and to a certain extent its intensity. Its quality remains unknown, for we have not the means of measuring others' faith and their capacity for love. Yet, the way in which he who prays lives, can enlighten us on the quality of the invocations he puts up to God. One who attains divine love becomes serene and satisfied within himself.

MY DAILY PRAYER

Dear Lord, may the WORDS of my MOUTH, and the MEDITA-
TIONS of my HEART, be acceptable in thy sight.

Go with me LORD, this day wherever I go, and be my GUIDE,
my STRENGTH, and my JOY.

FILL me this day with THY INDWELLING PRESENCE, and
keep me in THY WILL and THY WAY.

TEACH ME LORD, so that I will do the IMPORTANT THINGS
FIRST, each day. Help me to organize and plan my work so that I
may accomplish as much as possible in the shortest possible time.

Keep me busy doing the things that are constructive, and help me
to achieve my FULL POTENTIAL.

HELP ME, O LORD, to keep my nose out of other people's
business.

Cultivate in me a sense of humor that will make the lives of others
more pleasant. May my thoughts be good, happy, constructive,
creative, pleasant and positive.

DELIVER ME from every tendency to have a criticizing and
complaining nature.

KEEP ME from speaking evil of anyone.

Let MODERATION be my watchword.

And finally, O LORD, give me THY NATURE, fill me with
DEEDS instead of WORDS. EXPAND MY FAITH that I may
meet life's problems with CONFIDENCE and VICTORY. Help me
to walk with THEE, and to BELIEVE and LIVE by THY PROM-
ISES. Make me a USEFUL, PURPOSEFUL, and FRUITFUL
servant of thine, so that when my little day is done the Master
Teacher will say . . . "WELL DONE."

CHAPTER SEVEN

TRUE PRAYER IS BRIEF...
SIMPLE... PRIVATE

Jesus Christ was the personification of simplicity. Simplicity has been defined as "an exact balance between too little and too much." Jesus Christ was neither too much of man nor too little of God. In Him the human rose to its most sublime heights and the Divine so clothed itself with the human as to show God to best advantage. He walked among men, God manifested in the flesh and yet He walked among men a man in the truest sense. By being the perfect balance of Deity and humanity, He revealed what was in the mind of God when He said, *"Let us make man in our own image and in our likeness."*

His humanity never compromised His Diety nor did His Diety detract from His humanity. It is impossible to compromise true greatness. Pure gold is pure gold whether it is wrapped in velvet or buried in a trash pile.

Its true value is stamped upon it and that value is recognizable by all who have eyes to see and ears to hear. Only brassy folk mistake the ring of pure gold for the dead clank of counterfeit. A pure gold coin need never announce itself as pure gold. Only pretense need walk on borrowed stilts.

I have a conviction that had there been room "in the inn" for His birth, Jesus Christ would have preferred to be born as He was. The common people were His people because they were common. They were not put to the necessity of either pretense or assumed dignity.

They *"heard Him gladly"* because they recognized in Him one of their own. His language was the language of the fields and the forest. His manner was the manner of the work-a-day man. His theology was as simple as the life of the birds and the flowers. His sympathies were and are, so He said, as broad as a father's concern for a son who took his fling in a far country, and His provisions are as comprehensive as the provisions made by the father upon his son's return from the far country.

Whatever subject He discussed, He clothed it in language of one-syllable words, and there was no linguistic circumlocution to reach a given point. He was direct to the point of bluntness. A spade was never fitted with a velvet handle and called by another name.

He was as ancient as God, but He was as modern as man's need of and for God. He did not need to be stilted because He was and is God. He did not need to assume dignity because He was the embodiment of dignity. Only hypocrisy need pretend and only insincerity need mouth pious phrases. Long-winded debate is for those whose theology will not stand alone, and long-winded public prayers are for those who seek no higher reward than the applause of those who are too shallow to detect fraud when they see and hear it.

Christ worshipped as He talked . . . with the simplicity of a child and with the abandon of complete naturalness. Worship, He taught, is a thing of the heart and the heart speaks a language that is characterized by fewness of words. Words, He said, may betimes even cause the sweet incense of worship to stink.

His prayer life was confined almost exclusively to the seclusion of mountain fastnesses and His public appearances were never heralded by newspaper publicity and trumpet blasts. Most of His journeys were made on foot so He could contact common men at their work-a-day tasks. He did depart from that rule once. On that occasion He rode upon the back of an ass.

He condemed those who sought high seats in the synagogue and He labeled long prayers in public hypocrisy. PRAYER, HE SAID, IS A THING FOR THE EARS OF GOD ALONE. It is the communion of love and therefore is not for public use. His law is to be read in public, so He said, and men are to talk about it *"by the way."* It may be discussed while waiting for the fish to bite, while sowing seed in the field and while pushing a plane in a carpenter's shop; but prayer is for the closet.

There behind closed doors one may be simple, direct, brief, and natural. There is no audience to impress and no stage setting to glamourize what cannot be glamourized without complete loss. Christ did not discourage public assembly. Indeed, He encouraged it, but He did discourage public prayer both directly and inferentially. THE DIRECTIONS ARE SIMPLE . . . *"When thou prayest, enter into thy closet, and when thou hast shut thy door, pray to thy Father which is in secret; and thy Father which seeth in secret shall reward thee openly."* True prayer will lend itself to no other environment. Nor will true prayer lend itself to many words.

DEVOTION IS THE KEY-NOTE OF TRUE PRAYER AND DEVOTION IS A SONG WITHOUT WORDS SUNG BY THE HEART FOR THE EARS OF A BELOVED ALONE. Even love becomes pretense when given too much publicity. But three words are needed to express all the fullness of love . . . "I love you." Devotion is not a thing of words. Love makes few demands and still fewer requests. Demands and requests are superfluous. Love is ever in search of ways and means to demonstrate itself. Therefore, said Christ, *"Your Father knoweth what things ye have need of, before ye ask him."*

With this background we are now ready to study the prayer that Christ instructed us to pray:

Our Father, which art in heaven, Hallowed be thy name. Thy Kingdom come, Thy Will be done in earth, as it is in heaven. Give us this day our daily bread. And forgive us our debts, as we forgive our debtors. And lead us not into temptation, but deliver us from evil: For Thine is the Kingdom, and the Power, and the Glory, for ever. Amen.

— *Matthew 6:9-13*

Note several things:

1. Simplicity is its badge of sincerity. A show of scholarship and eloquence are as foreign to true prayer as a horse's hoof is foreign to a housefly.

2. There are but two requests in the whole prayer . . . and, strictly speaking, they are not requests. They are reminders of dependence upon God and interdependence among men. They have to do with bread and faults. Bread only God can supply. Faults are taken care of by the rule of personal adjustments.

3. The whole prayer is direct and down-to-earth. In the prayer, God reveals Himself as the one behind the scenes giving direction to all personal and world affairs. Nothing escapes His notice and nothing comes to pass without His will. The prayer is given and worded for the purpose of revealing that one fact. And prayer, true prayer, is for the purpose of keeping us reminded of that one fact.

Now, note the wording in the Fenton translation:

"Our Father in the Heavens your Name is being Hallowed" . . . That is what David meant when he said, *"The Heavens declare the glory of God and the earth showeth His handiwork."* Only fools can miss the truth that God is working out His purpose in and with and through His creation. That is what we are being reminded to keep uppermost in our thoughts.

"Your Kingdom is being restored" . . . That is to remind us that redemption is active and positive in its final results.

"Your will is being done both in the Heavens and in the Earth."

"Give us today tomorrow's bread" . . . That is to remind us that tomorrow is in God's thinking as well as today.

"Forgive us our faults as we forgive those offending us". That is to remind us that we set the rule and standard of and for our own judgment.

"You will not lead us into temptation but rather deliver us from evil." And right there the prayer ends. Ends because it has covered everything.

THE LORD'S PRAYER

You can bring more love into your life, conquer stress, fear, loneliness, disappointment, anger and hatred by daily using a simple tool . . . "The Lord's Prayer", it can work a miracle in your life.

— *Dr. John Huffman*

THE WAY

Show me the way —
 Not to fortune or fame,
Not how to win laurels
 Or praise for my name —
But show me the way
 To spread the Great Story
That *"Thine is the Kingdom
and Power and Glory."*

— *Helen Steiner Rice*

FOUNDATION FOR LIFE

Life must begin at some point of contact with the Infinite God, whose language is the language of life, and whose fellowship is the meaning of life. LIFE BEGINS AT THE POINT WHERE CONTACT IS MADE WITH FULL ENVIRONMENT. THIS IS THE FOUNDATION FOR ALL SUCCESSFUL LIVING, AND IT IS DEMONSTRATED IN THE LIVES OF ALL INTELLIGENT MEN EVERYWHERE.

— *The Supreme Philosophy of Man*

ACCORDING TO YOUR FAITH

The supreme work which any of us can do and accomplish is to have FAITH IN GOD. There is perhaps no word, so much and so often, on the lips of Jesus Christ either directly, or inferentially, as the single five letter word . . . FAITH. It amazes me when I re-read the passages once again which in the ministry of Christ deal with this question of faith. For instance, it is said of Him in Matthew 13:58, "*And he did not many mighty works there because of their unbelief,*" in a certain town. It is the town where He was born. Why was God limited? Why is God limited now? Because of THEIR LACK OF FAITH.

FAITH IS A POSITIVE DYNAMIC FORCE THAT PUTS MEANING AND POWER INTO THIS BUSINESS OF LIVING. Jesus said, "*All things are possible to him*" . . . who what? What did he say? What is the Bible definition? Here is my definition of faith that I have quoted. FAITH IS A POSITIVE DYNAMIC THAT GIVES FORCE AND MEANING AND POWER TO THE BUSINESS OF LIVING.

Some of the most successful men, whose names appear in the hall of fame and in the records of history, are men who began this business of positive thinking in terms of faith in God. The Bible is very careful to warn us that these men were men of "like passion" with those of us who are in this present. They were not without their faults and their weaknesses but they were men of faith, and that is the reason why they are listed in God's hall of fame.

When last I was in London I spent a little time in Westminster Abbey looking at the names of the great who have tramped down through the records of history, who made their names famous, who immortalized their memory. While looking at their busts, sitting there on marble pillows, reading the record of their deeds chiseled into the marble, I said to myself, "That's great to have an honored place in the halls of Westminster Abbey. That's great." But it is infinitely greater to have a place in God's hall of fame. The reason why Moses, Noah, Abraham and Gideon, Sampson, David and Paul have their place in God's hall of fame is they were men of faith.

CHAPTER EIGHT

WHAT IS TRULY EFFECTIVE PRAYER?

In effective . . . prayer . . . we focus our thinking,
and fully accept the answer
to our prayer.

— *Ernest Holmes*

These studies have now brought us to the place where it is time to consider how to make prayer effective . . . or perhaps a better way of putting it is, what is truly effective prayer?

The reason or reasons for prayer we have already considered. There is, however, one aspect of prayer which belongs properly to the realm of reason or reasons, which has not had as much attention as its importance warrants, namely: the attitude of a Christian towards life itself.

One's attitude towards life may at first flush seem to some to have no relationship whatever to prayer. I assure you, however, that it is neither remotely nor indirectly related to the whole subject of prayer.

For instance . . . it is impossible to question any circumstance of life (once it is fully committed to God) without fostering unbelief. I do not need to argue that unbelief is as deadly to true prayer as a killing frost is deadly to fruit and flowers. What many of us have not seen, however, is that questioning is a form of unbelief . . . many times the most subtle and deadliest kind of unbelief.

TRUST

All that I have seen teaches me to trust
the Creator for what I have not seen.

— *Ralph Waldo Emerson*

Need I reiterate what I have so frequently written, namely THAT ONCE A LIFE IS FULLY COMMITTED TO GOD, THINGS NO LONGER HAPPEN IN THAT LIFE, THEY COME TO PASS IN THE PURPOSE OF GOD. It is never very difficult to believe that concerning good things, but it is usually a different case entirely concerning untoward things.

Good things we take as a matter of course. Our sorrows, loss of someone or something, breaking of ties and relationships and whatever else may be listed under the general heading of difficult circumstances, most of us view with intense grief. So matter-of-fact are we concerning our good things that we frequently forget to even express gratitude, but we seldom forget to whine when so-called bad things come our way. If expressed gratitude is a mark of good breeding and fine spiritual quality, whining is a mark of bad breeding and spiritually it is a mark of downright unbelief.

For a Christian to question any circumstance of life is to question the wisdom, mercy and faithfulness of God. His word is that He will make *"all things"* work together for good to those who love Him. Faith declares that that must be so whether it can see or not. Unbelief whimpers in the dark and questions, why did God do thus and so?

I am aware that the question "why" may express mere puzzlement, but when it is accompanied by protracted grief and complaining, it is downright unbelief. It becomes what the Apostle Paul, in Philippians 4:6, calls "fretting" . . . and fretting, says the dictionary, is a mood of "peevish complaining." And complaining takes many forms. It even masquerades as a spiritual quality. Unwilling to admit its true quality, it justifies itself on the grounds of supersensitiveness which can only be accounted for by a superior spiritual relationship.

It has a right to whine, it contends, because it suffers so much more deeply than just ordinary mortals. That is a form of egoism as well as unbelief. Not anything will so quickly and so completely ruin a true prayer life as fretting, repining and complaining. *"Carest thou not that we perish?"* whined the disciples when the storm was on and total loss seemed imminent. *"O thou of little faith"* was Christ's stern rebuke to their peevishness that tried to masquerade as trust. A silent, restful, confident attitude would have demonstrated trust. Their peevish, whimpering whine in the dark demonstrated unbelief.

What I am trying to emphasize is clearly revealed IN THE LIFE OF JOB AND IN THE LIFE OF THE APOSTLE PAUL... BOTH KNEW THE DEEP SECRET OF QUIETLY ACCEPTING EVERY CIRCUMSTANCE OF LIFE AS A PART OF GOD'S PURPOSE. TO THEM JOY AND SORROW, LOSS AND GAIN, HARD AND EASY TIMES WERE OF EQUAL VALUE IN THE SCHEME OF THINGS THAT BRINGS A CHRISTIAN TO THE "FULLNESS OF THE STATURE OF MEN IN CHRIST JESUS." IN OTHER WORDS, THEIR PRAYER LIFE HAD REACHED THE HIGHEST LEVEL ATTAINABLE, NAMELY: "IN ALL CIRCUMSTANCES" THEY "PRAYED THE PRAYER OF THANKSGIVING." In still other words, they discovered what every person must discover who covets a true prayer life, namely: that expressed gratitude is the highest and most effective form of prayer.

There are three statements in the Book of Job that sum up and place final value on his life. First, the statement that reveals Job's attitude when loss and sorrow came: *"The Lord giveth, and the Lord hath taken away,"* he said. Then came the revelation of his prayer life: *"Blessed be the name of the Lord."* And that ended it. He makes no further reference to the circumstance that occasioned the prayer. Second, it is said, *"In all this Job sinned not with his lips"* . . . and this has direct reference to whining and complaining, as you will see by the context. Third, *"the Lord gave Job twice as much as he had before"* . . . *"The Lord blessed the latter end of Job more than his beginning."* There in a nutshell is the whole secret of having and getting.

Gratitude attracts grace and thankfulness begets tantamount benefits. WHIMPERING AND FRETTING CUTS OFF THE FLOW OF GOD'S BLESSINGS AS SURELY AS TURNING THE FAUCET CUTS OFF THE FLOW OF WATER. "The prayer of thanksgiving" is as compelling as irresistible force exerted upon utter weakness.

> *"Do not fret . . . but in all circumstances*
> *pray the prayer of thanksgiving . . . "*
>
> — *Philippians 4:6*

Said the Apostle Paul, "*I have learned, in whatsoever state I am, therewith to be content.*" Such a state of composed faith does not come easily or naturally. SCHOOLING IN THE UNIVERSITY OF BOTH JOY AND SORROW IS THE SECRET OF GRADUATING CUM LAUDE IN THE FINE ART OF PRAYER. No life can be all good and joy and peace in a rough and troubled world like this.

Did you ever see a beautiful flower growing in the midst of a briarpatch? So grows joy in a world like this. And as with the flower growing in the briar patch, so with life. The flower must protect itself against the briars . . . protect itself by quietly blooming while the briars bristle all around. That is the stark reality of life as it must be lived.

He does not know a true prayer life who cannot say with the Apostle Paul, "*I know both how to be abased, and I know how to abound . . . I am instructed both to be full and to be empty . . . to abound and to suffer need . . . and in all circumstances I do not fret . . . but pray the prayer of thanksgiving*" . . . The simple science of all this is, no one knows how to abound gracefully who has not been abased and no one can know the deep secret of confidence who has not been worked through adverse circumstances.

David could only say, "*Thou art with me*" after having walked through "*the valley of the shadow of death.*" There in the shadows he learned that God has purpose in all He does. That inspired confidence. And confidence took all the whine out of him. Amid untoward circumstances, he learned to "*pray the prayer of thanksgiving.*"

And having learned that lesson, he achieved the highest and most effective form of prayer. In closing this chapter may I repeat, who learns gratitude has learned how to use the most compelling force in the universe.

A PRAYER OF GRATITUDE

During your lifetime there are people who have
crossed your path who have helped you immensely.
Thank God for these people, for they are as
angels sent from Heaven. Give thanks for these
dear ones from the depths of your heart, for
their love and efforts have enhanced your life
and made your journey happier and given you
encouragement and satisfaction.

THE JOY OF LIFE

The true joy of life is being used for a PURPOSE that is only mine to fulfill. A PURPOSE which I recognize and BELIEVE to be a mighty one.

The joy of life is to give my best and be truly used in doing some good. My greatest passion is to be a creative force of Nature. I must do my noblest and walk hand in hand with God into the future . . . into the forever.

This is my duty for the Gift of Life.

APPRECIATION

The deepest principle in human nature is the craving to be appreciated. IF YOU HAVE BUT A WORD OF CHEER, SPEAK IT WHILE THE ONE IS ALIVE TO HEAR!

Angels come to visit us,
and we only know them when they are gone.

EVERY PERSON BUILDS
HIS OWN INNER WORLD

As we grow during the course of our lifetime, we acquire worth-while values that become what we are as individuals . . . what we stand for, our character, personality, goodness, integrity, completeness, etc. There are no two people alike, we are all unique individuals. Truthfully, we all should be in the Smithsonian museum.

There is one truth which we cannot appreciate too early or too well; namely this, that in the last analysis, every man lives in a world of his own making. The world in which we live is made up of the thoughts of our mind and the soul qualities. The environment YOU fashion out of YOUR thoughts . . . YOUR beliefs . . . YOUR ideals . . . YOUR philosophy . . . is the only climate YOU will ever live in. And as these qualities are very much within our control, it holds true that, in a very real sense, every man himself builds the world in which he lives.

So, whether the inner world in which he lives is one of difficulties, fears, doubt, gloom and despair, or of cheerfulness, sweetness and light, is the result of every person's own making. Whether we see the bright side of things or the dark, the hopeful or the ugly, the cheerful or the gloomy, is a matter, not of logic, but of habit of thought, habit of point of view, habit of interpretation; and the difference? – the difference between content and discontent, between happiness and misery, and, not infrequently, between prosperity and adversity, between success and failure.

It is commonly thought that happiness is a matter of worldly good fortune, but close observation indicates that outward circumstances have little to do with contentedness and peace of mind. We find, in this world, some men unhappy and miserable who apparently have everything that their heart can desire, while, close by, individuals who have nothing are the very embodiment of sunshine and happiness.

YOUR RESPONSIBILITY

Difficulties, problems, and challenges,
are the name given to the things,
which it is our business to overcome.

CHAPTER NINE

INTENSE DESIRE IS THE POWER
FOR TRUE PRAYER

Last chapter we raised the question, what is effective prayer? I did not raise the question, what makes prayer effective, because true prayer is always effective. It does not need to be made effective any more than electricity needs to be made effective. ALL ELECTRICITY NEEDS IS A MEDIUM. ALL PRAYER NEEDS IS A MEDIUM. Our problem is with ourselves, not primarily with the force with which we are dealing.

Prayer is as ever present as electricity. All it needs is a conductor. It invades and pervades every part of our living atmosphere. It is as omnipresent as God himself. It does not have the opportunity to manifest and demonstrate itself because most of us are high resistance. Christ could not do *"many mighty works"* in Nazareth because of the unbelief of his listeners. Just so, prayer is limited by human bad connections.

Understanding on our part is the prime requisite to the use of prayer. Once that understanding is attained, prayer is as easy to use as electricity . . . and with the same degree of certainty as to results. I do not say that our understanding is capable of encompassing all the mystery of prayer. It is not . . . any more than our understanding is capable of comprehending all the mystery of electricity. But, comprehension of the mystery is not necessary to its use. All we need to know is that *"all things are possible"* to him who makes himself a conductor for the limitless energy that God puts at our command.

Our problem, I repeat, is with ourselves, not primarily with prayer itself. How to open and keep open the circuit that conducts the limitless energy of prayer is the only question with which we need concern ourselves. There are numerous passages of scripture which reveal the secret. They only await our careful study.

Like any other "book of instructions" they are useless when ignored, misunderstood or bungled. God's problem is to get His "Book of Instructions", The Bible, read plainly. Most of us come to it with our minds so cluttered that the Book becomes a mere convenience. We are not in search of facts; we are in search of evidence . . . real or distorted . . . to prove that we are right.

Whether we are right or wrong is not, it seems, a matter of great concern with most of us. We want to prove ourselves right even though we are wrong. Therefore, I say, the "Book of Instructions" is ignored, misunderstood or bungled. Mark 11:24 is an illustration in point . . . *"Therefore I say unto you, What things soever ye desire, when ye pray, believe that ye receive them, and ye shall have them."* The important word in the passage is ignored in favor of less important words in order to prove what the passage is not primarily emphasizing. "Believe" is the word that most preachers and readers emphasize. I do not underestimate faith, but I am trying to point out that this and numerous other passages show that FAITH, LIKE PRAYER ITSELF, CAN OPERATE ONLY WHERE CONDITIONS ARE CONDUCIVE TO ITS OPERATION. "DESIRE" is the word in this passage that needs double underscoring . . . and strange to say, I have never heard a preacher or an expositor dwell upon it.

Faith in its place is just as important as desire, but the point is, desire is the power; faith makes it possible for the power to operate. That statement may seem to raise an impossible question like, for instance, which is first, the hen or the egg? No hen, no egg. No egg, no hen . . . so both must be first! And that, of course, is impossible. So, we start all over . . . and come out at the same place.

In the case of desire and faith, however, no such problem presents itself. DESIRE, as I have said, is the power. FAITH is the medium that conducts the power. The medium is of no value if there is no power. Hence, in this case, the power is of first importance.

Strictly speaking, it cannot be said of either desire or faith it is superlatively great. Each in its place, as I have said, is equally great. But it can be said that one or the other is first in importance. Desire, in this case, is first in importance because it is the power that produces.

> Thou hast given him his heart's desire,
> and hast not withholden the request of his lips.
> Selah.
>
> — *Psalm 21:2*

And now for a closer look at the word desire:

The word itself is of Latin derivation and means to crave earnestly. Strong as this definition is, it does not quite indicate the full meaning of the word desire used by Our Lord. He uses a word which in addition to the meaning just indicated carries the deeper meaning of requirement. The earnest craving then of our English word must spring from actual requirement.

Necessity is the requisite that compels the action of faith and guarantees an affirmative answer. Note how this ties into the passage I have quoted so frequently throughout this series of studies: *"Your Father knoweth what things ye have need of"*. "Have need of" are the words on which an affirmative answer hangs. All things being equal, so-called failure of prayer is traceable to this one source. Usually we hear even preachers say lack of faith is the reason why prayer is not answered. But the point is, faith only becomes active where there is necessity. WHERE NECESSITY IS, FAITH SPRINGS SPONTANE-OUSLY.

SO-CALLED FAITH THAT MUST BE WHIPPED UP OR WORKED UP IS NOT FAITH AT ALL. It is but a psychological reaction that is absolutely death dealing to true faith. In this realm not only fanatics are born but skeptics as well. More than once I have watched a group of people work themselves into a frenzy of emotional-ism and mistake mere physical reactions for the "evidence" that their prayer (?) would be answered. I knew it would not. They later found it was not. At the moment, of course, I was listed as an unbeliever.

Later I have seen these victims of emotional psychosis completely repudiate prayer and become confirmed scoffers. And I have never seen one of them who developed a stable spiritual life. Here is the deep reason why Christ urged all who would truly pray to develop their prayer life "in secret".

None of these untoward things can possibly happen to the person who quietly closets himself with God. There in the closet necessity speaks quietly in the ear of the Father and faith compels an answer. *"He knoweth what things ye have need of."* The answer is on its way before we pray. Necessity has invaded the realm of supply before words can be uttered.

If I were asked to state in a word the greatest hindrance to true prayer, I would answer . . . words. It is Christ himself who tells us that words defeat the true purpose of prayer. The heart speaks the wordless language of desire. From that source alone comes true prayer . . . for all true prayer is desire. And all true desire is born of necessity. Where necessity is there is the Father with supply. *"Before you ask,"* He says, *"I will hear."* He listens only to your heart. If words voice true desire they are true prayer. If they do not they are little short of blasphemy. Believe that and you are well on your way to a true prayer life. Reject it and you will never truly pray.

THE AMAZING POWER OF PRAYER

When man's Divine Conviction goes straight out
from his spirit . . .
and carries its effective communication straight into
the heart of the Great Spirit of God . . .
EXPECT a MIRACLE from the INFINITE POWER
from which all things proceed.
For only HEARTS SPEAK TO HEARTS
and it is the language of the heart that God hears.

GOD'S POWER WITHIN

In order to get the results desired there is a proper way to pray, according to the Bible. Jesus Christ is our intercessor, our divine intervener between us and the Father. In the Bible, Jesus did not say to pray to Him. He said to pray to the Father in His name . . . *"And in that day ye shall ask me nothing. Verily, verily, I say unto you, Whatsoever ye shall ask the Father in my name, he will give it you. Hitherto have ye asked nothing in my name: ask, and ye shall receive, that your joy may be full."*

— John 16:23,24

When it comes to praying we must go by the rules which say we must ask the Father through the Lord Jesus. There is great joy in knowing that God our Father will answer our prayers. This is a more direct way and will give better results.

"Therefore if any man be in Christ, he is a new creature. Old things are passed away; behold, all things are become new."

— II Corinthians 5:17

Realize God's power you have within when you have the "NEW NATURE" . . . *"For this cause I bow my knees unto the Father of our Lord Jesus Christ, of whom the whole family in heaven and earth is named, that he would grant you, according to the riches of his glory, to be strengthened with might by his Spirit in the inner man; That Christ may dwell in your hearts by faith; that ye, being rooted and grounded in love, may be able to comprehend with all saints what is the breadth, and length, and depth, and height; And to know the love of Christ, which passeth knowledge, that ye might be filled with all the fulness of God. Now unto him that is able to do exceeding abundantly above all that we ask or think, according to the power that worketh in us, Unto him be glory in the church by Christ Jesus throughout all ages, world without end."*

— Ephesians 3:14-21.

Realize and use the Almighty Power that is within you . . . That Christ may dwell in your heart by FAITH. The Power that is able, exceeding, abundant, above, that worketh within us. Only then will you experience the FULLNESS of life and reach your FULL POTENTIAL.

TODAY

This is the beginning of a fresh new day,
    I greet it with HOPE.
Today comes only once, and never again returns,
    I must show my LOVE and be KIND.
God has given me this 24 hours to use as I will,
    I shall have a cheerful ATTITUDE.
I must do something GOOD with this day and
    not waste it.
This is my day of opportunity and duty, I expect something
    GOOD because I am going to help make it happen!

Today is a NEW DAY in my LIFE, a new piece of road to be
    travelled, I must ask God for directions.
Today I will be filled with courage and confidence,
    I must show my FAITH in God.
What I do today is very important because I am
    exchanging a day of MY LIFE for it.
The COST of a thing is the amount of MY LIFE
    I spend obtaining it.

When tomorrow comes, this day will be gone forever,
    leaving in its place something I have traded for it.
In order not to forget the price I paid for it, I shall
    do my best to make it USEFUL, PROFITABLE, JOYFUL.
The seeds I plant today determine my HARVEST in the future,
    my life will be RICHER OR POORER by the way I use today.
Thank you God for today, I shall not pass this way again . . .
    What I must do . . . I'll do today!

                         — *Alfred A. Montapert*

CHAPTER TEN

PRAYER MAINTAINS FELLOWSHIP WITH GOD

With this essay, I shall have only four more chapters to conclude the series of essays on prayer, which has occupied us for ten short chapters. Not that I have finished with the subject, for prayer is a subject with which one never does finish. I find, however, upon reviewing my notes that I have touched most of the salient points necessary to be understood in order to experience and develop a true prayer life. There are ramifications of the various points touched into which one must go for himself in order to make full use of what we have learned.

In the final analysis, all of these studies of mine are like acquiring an education . . . all a textbook, a classroom and a professor can do for a student is furnish the tools with which the student builds. Beyond a certain point the student is on his own. If he is too lazy, too careless or too self-satisfied to use what has been furnished him, he will become static. In the language of the colored preacher, "he done been whar he gwin." His "sheepskin" will soon become a dry, yellow thing which will serve to remind him only that he once attended school . . . a symbol of his own dry, useless mind. If, on the other hand, he uses what has been furnished, he will become dynamic and it will never be said of him that he has been where he is going. His command is to "GO FORWARD."

I feel constrained to emphasize again the one great objective of prayer . . . the truth which above all others I have tried to keep before us from first to last throughout this series of studies, namely: That prayer is not primarily an emergency provision . . . not merely something to be used in case of distress or when we need something. It is the vital life of a Christian which creates and maintains fellowship with God.

Prayer creates friendship . . . God becomes a friend to us and we become God's friend. Friendship is the word that Christ chose above all others to designate the highest spiritual relationship that both God and man experience. *"I call you friends,"* He said. In that realm, begging (and that is the cheap level to which most so-called prayer descends) is as unnecessary as words are to true prayer. Friends look out for each other's interests without being urged or even reminded. This is what the Bible calls "fellowship."

The objective of true prayer is to fellowship God and open the way for Him to fellowship us. The one true answer to prayer is God. When we have that answer all other answers are taken up into it.

"The Father knoweth what things ye have need of" and they are as certain to come as the Father's knowledge of our need. He does not even need to be reminded. The reminding is on our side. We need to remind ourselves to keep fellowship with God.

This accomplished, the flow of whatever things are necessary to us is constant. This, I say, is the one big thing that I have been trying to emphasize throughout this series. And this, alas, is exactly what most of you, it seems, have missed. Words, it seems, are more important to you than the true meaning of prayer. If there are plenty of words and your emotions are temporarily stirred, you seem content to accept counterfeit for "the coin of the realm."

Some of the most successful men whose names appear in the Hall of Fame and in the records of History, prayed and developed a close fellowship with God. No one can master living without knowing the Master. Jesus said, *"I am come that they might have life, and that they might have it more abundantly."* Prayer opens up "a new way of life" to you. *"And this is life eternal, that they might know thee the only true God, and Jesus Christ, whom thou hast sent."* In the long toil of life, in the quest for happiness and achievement, he who keeps expanding his faith in God learns that life can be beautiful and rewarding.

Apropos of the truth that God himself is the essential answer to prayer . . . *"He careth for you"* is, to me, the most momentous announcement in the Scriptures. It gives me a sense of security not experienced by reading any other passage of Scripture. It excites my imagination to the point of almost agitation. My mind conjures at once possibilities beyond the ken of thought . . . possibilities which, more than anything else, become the greatest of all incentives to keep fellowship with the "God of all grace" BY CULTIVATING A PRAYER LIFE that guarantees my friendship for and with Him and His friendship for and with me.

"GOD AND I ARE GOOD FRIENDS," said a good friend of mine. At the time it sounded just a little sacrilegious. I now see and understand what he meant. Questioned the Apostle Paul, *"He that spared not His own Son, but delivered Him up for us all, how shall He not with Him also freely give us all things?"* That is the truth that the old man, to whom I have just referred, had gotten hold of. To get hold of it is to experience the highest, deepest and broadest prayer life possible to a human being.

That may have been what was in the mind of the hymn writer when he wrote, "Simply trusting . . . that is all." The trouble is most of us trust in our prayers . . . or the prayers of others . . . instead of in God. Trust brings an answer before words . . . yours or the words of another . . . can be voiced. Our Lord's rebuke to His disciples. *"O ye of little faith,"* carries just that truth. They used words when they should have "simply trusted."

"Rest in the Lord," exhorted David in this same connection. Mark, rest . . . not "rassel." Sure, Jacob "wrestled with the Lord," but his wrestling was the result of his own stubbornness.

There are times when words in prayer are the evidence of unbelief. If you do not get what you want, pray louder and longer is the philosophy of the Prophets of Baal.

Elijah's prayer life took on the form of fellowship. He was GOD'S FRIEND, and He did not let his friend down . . . neither did His friend let him down.

SUCCESS IN PRAYER
IS NOT MEASURED BY "REMARKABLE ANSWERS TO PRAYER"
BUT BY THE NEW HAPPY SPIRITUAL LIFE
THAT WE EXPERIENCE IN PRAYER.

If it does not, you will never know a true prayer life. If it does, you are launched upon the most adventurous voyage of spiritual discovery that you have ever made . . . and may I simply add, to all of you who are minded to weigh anchor where you have been half-grounded in shallow water and "launch out into . . . the deep" . . . Bon voyage!

WHY PRAY?

Because God insistently commands it in the Bible. Because prayer is God's way to speak person to person and for you to know HE careth for you, and for you to have fullness and joy. Learn to know God, for He is your best friend.

WHY FAST AND PRAY?

The greatest saints of God throughout the Bible often fasted. Their prayers were answered when they waited on God in fasting and prayer. Jesus not only fasted, but he taught his disciples to fast. The spirit of fasting and praying simply means that one, for the time being, is willing to abstain from the otherwise normal and proper duties or pleasures that he may give himself wholly to the business of prayer. Fasting is really putting God first when one prays, wanting God more than one wants food. To abstain from other things in order to give the whole heart to prayer and waiting on God.

EVERYONE NEEDS AN IDEAL

Mankind's greatest ideal is to have God, Jesus Christ, and the Holy Spirit living in their heart. *"The kingdom of God is within,"* and mankind's greatest project is the development of his Spiritual Nature, so he knows God.

KNOW GOD

Some people have missed the most important thing in life . . . they don't know God:
"And this is life eternal, that they might know thee, the only true God, and Jesus Christ, whom Thou hast sent."
— *John 17:3*

To know is to experience.
To know is to fellowship.
To know is to enjoy.
To know is to appreciate.

This is the Summum Bonum of LIFE. This is the foundation for the life we were designed to live.

Mankind has a greater need of the IDEAL, THAN OF THE REAL. It is by the real that we exist; it is by the IDEAL that we live. The love of God is man's highest ideal. The difference is, some men merely exist, while others truly live.

Our ideals are
the blueprints of
our lives.

IDEALS give point to character and infuse purpose into life; what is the significance of ideals in life? What does it mean to a man to have great aspirations, hopes and ambitions in life? With great ideals . . . desire is aroused, a good defined, resolution taken, motive supplied, and will-power generated. And these are the things that release human energy and result in motion, action, and achievement in life. The reason why ideals determine achievement is because, more than any other influence, it is primarily our ideals which determine the direction and the extent of our growth and development in life.

JESUS CHRIST . . . MAN'S HIGHEST IDEAL

Lord Moynihan, the eminent British Surgeon of Leeds, England, was often invited to operate before groups of distinguished fellow surgeons. At the close of one of these operations, a younger doctor said, "It must be very difficult for you to operate with a group of brilliant surgeons watching your every move." "Well," said Lord Moynihan, "it is like this: there are just three people in the theatre when I operate . . . the patient and myself." "Three?" said his friend. "But that is only two, who is the other?" The surgeon answered, quietly, "God."

What could be more important than any unfailing awareness of the Divine Presence? Only as the light of God bears upon our work do we see its highest significance. How wonderful it would be if we could carry His name and the realization of His presence into every relationship of life!

I am confident that life for most of us would be transformed if before we commenced our duties in the home or the class-room or the bank or the store or the factory or on the farm, we paused for a brief moment and let the realization of the Divine Presence break in upon us, saying, *"Surely the Lord is in this place, and I knew it not."*

It would alter the tenor of the day for all of us, robbing it of its strain and tension, if we could keep even five minutes of it for fellowship with God. These occasional acts of prayer will one day deepen into a sense of habitual communion.

The only IDEAL you will find in this world is the ideal you carry in your heart. When we lose our ideal then we are ready for burial. Life knows no tragedy like the loss of an ideal. Disillusionment, certainly. Disappointment, surely. Failure in part, yes. But life knows no tragedy like the loss of an ideal. Without an ideal the soul dies. In a word, the secret of a man is the secret of his aspiration. Solomon had so well said, *"Where no vision is, the people perish."* AND THEY PERISH BECAUSE THERE IS NO LODESTONE TO PULL THEM UP TO WHAT THEY WERE MADE FOR AND TO INSPIRE THEM WITH THINGS BEYOND THEM.

CHAPTER ELEVEN

ALL PRAYER IS ANSWERED

Nothing is quite so gratifying to me as to discover a desire on the part of the reader to know what is knowable about the deeper phases of spiritual truth . . . and certainly there is no more important truth than PRAYER. It is, as the poet has well said, "THE CHRISTIAN'S VITAL BREATH."

Said an eminent physician, whose writings I was reading some time ago, "Let me watch a person breathe and I will, all things being equal, predict his physical future." Let me listen to a person pray and I will, all things being equal, tell you the quality of his spiritual life and predict his spiritual future. The catchword among physicians is: Shallow breathers, shallow life and short life; deep breathers, deep life and long life. The same catchword with different wording can be used with reference to spiritual life: Fitful, shallow praying means a fitful, shallow, unhealthy spiritual life. Deep, consistent praying means a deep, consistent spiritual life.

Those who specialize in physical fitness tell us, "You are what you eat." That also goes for spiritual life. And that is obviously what our Lord meant when He warned us, *"Take heed what ye hear"*, in Mark 4: 24. What you hear is the spiritual food you assimilate. A SPIRITUAL PERSON LIVES HIS LIFE BY INNER KNOWING. THE QUALITY OF HIS LIFE IS IN DIRECT PROPORTION TO HIS TRUST IN THE HIGHER POWER . . . the "KINGDOM OF GOD WITHIN". What YOU are, is revealed by your LIFE, your THOUGHTS, DEEDS, ACTION.

Truth is my passion and quality is my slogan. If, as a result of these essays, some develop an intelligent, scientifically balanced and spiritually poised prayer life, we shall feel amply rewarded for all the work that we have invested to "RIGHTLY DIVIDE THE WORD OF GOD."

Logically, in the further development of the subject of prayer, I think we should spend a moment with a statement I made some time ago: namely, that all prayer is answered. I mean that quite literally. There is no such thing as unanswered prayer. Unanswered prayer is a common phrase in common use.

Books are written on the subject, and most of us accept it as a fact. But there is no such thing as unanswered prayer. Prayer is always answered. I know exactly what some of you are thinking: That cannot be true, you're mentally saying. I've prayed for things I did not get. And that is the exact error on which so many books are written and tracts are printed.

The only answer to prayer we recognize is when we get what we want. That view of prayer does several things: First, it leaves God only one door of entrance. We virtually say to Him . . . come in by this door or stay out. Second, it leaves no place for wisdom above and beyond our own. We make up our minds and the Infinite must bow to the finite or else. In one breath we piously say, "God knows what is best," and in the next breath we peevishly complain, "He didn't give me what I prayed for."

We punish children because they will not accept the dictum, "Mama knows what's best," but we become pugnacious when we are reminded that we must accept our own dictum . . . Then too, our children squall and persist and we say, "Oh well, let the little fellow have it." The child by its persistence forces us to do what we know should not be done.

CONFESSION

Why does God require confession of sin before there is forgiveness? For the reason until we are ready to face and own up, that deviltry remains our own. Any psychologist will tell you that you can't get rid of what you won't face. That's why the Bible says, *"He that covereth his sins shall not prosper; but whoso confesseth and forsaketh them shall have mercy."*

— *Proverbs 28:13*

There is where Infinite Wisdom comes in and why it must have a large place in our prayer life. It may startle you, but it is actually possible to force God to give us what He knows is bad for us. We wear Him out with squalling and He gives us what we want . . . then is forced to stand by and watch us suffer the consequences of our stupid persistence.

I'll cite one very familiar example . . . there are others but this one will suffice. Exodus 16:12 reads . . . the Lord speaking . . . *"I have heard . . . the children of Israel."* "I have heard." He always does, whether our praying is in His will or out of it. At first He answered according to His wisdom. Later He was forced to give the Israelites what they wanted. And a good time they had "enjoying" their "answer to prayer." The record reads, *"the people stood up all that day, and all that night, and all the next day, and they gathered the quails"* . . . And the inference is they had a hilarious time recounting to each other their "marvelous answer to prayer." But the story is not fully told.

Their hilarity soon turned to intense mourning . . . their religious shouting died away in melancholy echoes among the dismal shadows of death-haunted caverns of spiritual loss. Ironically enough, they died because of an answer to prayer. Says David in Psalm 105:40 . . . *"The people asked, and He brought quails."* He HAD supplied what was best. Manna was the perfect food for that climate and under the circumstances. But they wanted meat! They got it . . . and died! And they were not the last to die because they made no place for Infinite Wisdom in their prayer life.

I know of some who are now walking spiritual corpses because they either did not know enough . . . or were too determined to have what they wanted . . . to pray in the will of God. That is the reason why John is careful to center all prayer in the will of God: *"if we ask anything according to His will."* The participial adjective "according" denotes complete adjustment to. That is, all prayer must be adjusted to the theme passage of all these essays: *"Your Father knoweth what things ye have need of."* Infinite Wisdom supplies on the basis of necessity . . . that is, if stubborn persistence on our part does not force the issue and compel God to give us what is not necessary.

How do we know then what to pray for? We do not. That is just the reason why I am pressing this issue. We are told plainly that we do not know . . . *"We know not what to pray for as we ought"* . . . Romans 8:26.

No matter how deeply spiritual you become you never will get beyond ignorance concerning prayer. Prayer is too deep for the deepest and yet it is the simplest of all spiritual exercises.

It is an attitude that can be cultivated by even a child. Rest, wait, confidently expect . . . and the Father who knows what things ye have need of will supply every need, *"according to His riches in glory by Christ Jesus."* How simple: How sublime! How restful! How common sense! *"Rest in the Lord"* . . . *"He shall bring it to pass."* Bring what to pass? Whatever you need! Thus ends one phase of our study of the proposition, all prayer is answered. We shall consider the other aspects of the proposition in the next chapter.

OUR LIMITATIONS

It seems GOD is limited by our prayer life. HE can do nothing for humanity unless someone asks HIM to do it.

— *John Westley*

The choice is yours. Your life will be what YOU make it. Therefore it is of utmost importance that believers know how to pray.

"Delight thyself in the Lord and He shall give thee the desires of thine heart."

— *Psalm 37:4*

GOD, grant me the serenity to accept the things I cannot change; the courage to change the things I can; and the wisdom to know the difference.

— *Rinehold Niebuhr*

BELIEVING prayer . . . sets into action a law as exact and infallible as the laws that govern the movements of the sun, moon and stars.

— *Russell A. Kemp*

THE WAY, THE TRUTH AND THE LIFE

The world never saw or heard anything like it. Kings, priests, emperors, philosophers, scholars and leaders stood aghast at the assumption that strength could come out of weakness; that might could be beaten down by a subtle principle called right; that he towers highest who stoops the lowest. But that is exactly the teaching of Jesus Christ.

He was regarded as a visionary and a radical. But centuries have demonstrated that His is the most practical message to which men have ever listened. Where are those who boasted their might and pomp and power? All passed and perished. But the Christ? He lives. He is the most disturbing factor in the world today. He is the greatest force in society everywhere. He has reappraised human values. His vision shall yet become universal. Who follows in His train? Do you? He who does shall win. He who will not shall ultimately lose all and perish.

Apart from the life and teaching of Jesus Christ life becomes an inexplicable enigma. No marvel then, that men who reject Jesus Christ find life "not worth living". There are no intellectual answers to the labyrinthian muddles, and illogical contradictions, which confront even those of ordinary ability to think, to say nothing of those who have risen a little in the scale of ability. But again I say, accept Jesus Christ as God's final revelation of Himself, and all the "mysteries of life" will vanish like summer mists from a meadow when the sun has risen. Or better still, re-center your life in Jesus Christ instead of in things and in self, and you will find His amazing words true, *"I am come that you might have life."*

Critics are often heard to complain that if after nineteen hundred years Christianity has not changed the world any more than it has it must not be a very good religion. Here is shallow thinking at its worst.

THE WAY, THE TRUTH AND THE LIFE
CONTINUED

In the first place, Christianity has never been accepted on a large scale. It has never been given a fair chance. In the second place, it can't change a world that rejects or neglects it! Were Christianity to fail where it is sincerely tried there would be grounds for complaint. A doctor's ability cannot be accurately judged when his diagnosis and prescribed remedy is rejected . . . or neglected.

In the third place, Christianity is not a grand social instrument for the reduction of crime, juvenile delinquency and the divorce rate. It will do all of these things if it wholeheartedly is accepted. It can do none of these things when it is rejected or neglected. The trouble with men is they try Christianity just far enough to find it a hard and demanding life. They prefer to live their own life. So they part with Christ. If Christianity fails it fails for the same reason that Christ failed; HE WAS AND IS REJECTED . . . OR WORSE STILL, ONLY HALF-HEARTEDLY ACCEPTED.

The truth taught by Jesus Christ is the right way to live. He is God's revelation of how life MUST be lived to be lived at its best. To misunderstand, or fail to grasp this truth, is to miss the whole purpose of God's revelation of Himself in Jesus Christ. To accept and believe it is at once to give us an intelligent conception of the whole scheme of things called life. Jesus said, *"I am the way, the truth, and the life."* To show us the way, God provides his inspired WORD, the BIBLE. The WORD OF GOD is the Way to PHYSICAL prosperity, MENTAL prosperity, SPIRITUAL prosperity. When you are walking in the WORD OF GOD, you will prosper and be in HEALTH.

We seek the blessings and the Power of God, the Power of Jesus, and the Power of the Holy Spirit. He sends His Power, His love, His nature, His wisdom to His own according to our FAITH.

> *But seek ye first the kingdom of God,*
> *and his righteousness;*
> *and all these things shall be added unto you.*
> *— Matthew 6:33*

CHAPTER TWELVE

REAL PRAYER . . . IS TO LIVE GOD-CONSCIOUS

The thesis of our last study demands more than a simple statement. There are, I am well aware, objections which, backed by certain scriptures, seem to furnish sound reasons for rejecting the thesis in toto. The sweeping statement that there is no such thing as unanswered prayer is open to debate.

On the basis of, as I have said, certain scriptures and human experience, it would seem that the statement cannot be successfully defended. Take, for example, one of the best known passages of scripture . . . and the passage which, I presume, came immediately to mind at once I made the statement, is in James 4:3 . . . *"Ye ask, and receive not, because ye ask amiss, that ye may consume it upon your lusts."* "Ye ask, and receive not," . . . that would seem to flatly contradict the statement that there is no such thing as unanswered prayer. But does it? Let's take the passage apart for microscopic study.

James is obviously dealing with the most popular and prevalent form of prayer, the form of prayer to which I have frequently referred throughout this series of studies: namely, the form of prayer that takes its rise in the realm of purely personal conveniences without respect to, or regard for, the larger, broader and deeper aspects of spiritual life itself. In other words, the form of prayer that is bounded by the limited horizon of an immediate present as it is related to our purely personal physical and material comforts, conveniences and gain . . . prayer that is bounded on the north, south, east and west by me, my and I . . . Lust "strong desire to possess and enjoy" . . . that is afflicted with chronic near-sightedness . . . Lust that is so lacking in essential spiritual quality that it insists upon having even though by having the larger spiritual future is jeopardized . . .

Lust that insists upon circumscribing Infinite Wisdom to the limits of selfish gain even though that gain may force God into second place and shrivel the soul to the size of a present that is as unsatisfactory as it is passing. That is the kind of praying, James is saying, which must be dealt with in one of two ways: Either God is finally forced to give what the petitioner is asking and by so doing stand by and see an answered prayer react to the eternal hurt of the petitioner (as in the case of the example cited in the last chapter), or refuse to answer and by so doing save the petitioner from the folly of his spiritual stupidity. In the case of refusal the answer is no . . . AND NO IS AS MUCH AN ANSWER AS YES. So the person who says, "I did not get what I prayed for", got an answer.

If you are spiritual enough to recognize God's no, you are well on your way to the fulfilling of one of the deepest and most essential of all spiritual laws . . . the law referred to by James in verse 7: *"Submit yourselves therefore to God."* The word "submit" takes up into itself all that I have been trying to impress upon us by frequently quoting Our Lord's reassurance, *"the Father knoweth what things ye have need of,"* and the assurance that every need will be supplied. *"Rest in the Lord"* is only another word for *"submit yourselves therefore to God."*

To sum up: two things, James says, are futile . . . First, to try to get things by our own method (verse 2) . . . Second, to force our desires upon God against His knowledge of us, our needs and the future. In both cases no is the answer . . . and no is an answer.

So much for the objection to my thesis that there is no such thing as unanswered prayer. There are other scriptures, but this one is sufficient since it is seemingly the most direct contradiction of my thesis to be found in either Testament. But there is another aspect of the same objection that must be considered.

The Apostle Paul . . . and none of us, I presume, will undertake to discredit either him or his prayer life . . . testifies one failure in prayer. In 2 Corinthians 12 he recounts his experience. Thrice, he says, he prayed for the removal of a thing which he considered detrimental to him and to his work. His prayer was unanswered. But was it? A closer look shows that his prayer was answered.

The answer is both yes and no. He did not get what he prayed for. In that case his prayer was unanswered. He did get a substitute for the thing for which he was praying. In that case his prayer was answered. Now, as in the case of the passage in James, let's put this passage under the microscope.

Volumes have been written and spoken on Paul's "Thorn In The Flesh." What it was no one knows. Others may guess and speculate where there is no positive evidence, but neither my theology nor my study of the Scriptures needs bolstering or defending by guesses and speculation. Since Paul does not choose to reveal exactly what his "thorn in the flesh" is, my answer to the question is, I do not know. All I know is, it was considered by Paul to be a detriment to both him and his work. There would, therefore, seem to be a good reason for asking to have it removed. This he did. God heard him, but the thing for which he asked was not forthcoming. And that brings us into head-on collision with the passage.

I John 5:15 reads, *"If we know that He hears us, whatsoever we ask, we know that we have the petitions that we desired of Him."* This passage I have heard isolated and quoted as a proof text many times. But like all Scripture, it cannot be isolated and understood. It must be read in its setting.

Prayer, like football, has its "safety zone." Verse 14 reveals that safety zone . . . *"If we ask anything according to His will."* His infinite wisdom is our safeguard against wrong answers to prayer. If we pray for wrong things . . . and wrong things may be perfectly right and legitimate things under certain circumstances.

Wrong things do not necessarily mean wicked or vicious things. It may mean good or desirable things which in the long run will militate against our largest spiritual development and usefulness. Unpleasant and undesirable things may, at times, be more profitable to us spiritually than pleasant and desirable things. MORE PEOPLE HAVE BEEN RUINED BY EASY PLACES THAN BY HARD PLACES.

Not all pleasant situations are profitable situations. All of us are naturally lazy and laziness is the shortcut to spiritual suicide. None of us are wise enough to always make right choices. Left to ourselves we would always choose pleasant situations, untroubled circumstances and happy environments. And there is nothing wrong per se with any of these choices . . . but it can be said . . . and must be said . . . that ease and comfort are seldom conducive to the building of sturdy character, strong faith and deep spiritual understanding.

I THINK IT IS PERFECTLY SAFE TO SAY THAT THE APOS-TLE PAUL COULD NEVER HAVE BEEN THE MAN HE WAS WITH HIS THORN REMOVED. Knowing that, God could only substitute an answer to his prayer. That He did. He gave *"more grace."* The point is, the substitute was an answer to prayer. Had Paul not prayed about his "thorn" he would not have gotten more grace.

To be conscious of a bad situation or condition frequently forces us to prayer. In that way "Satan's messenger" turns out to be our best spiritual ally. But only when we are wise enough and spiritual enough to leave the answer to prayer entirely to the Wisdom of God. Once we have learned that spiritual mood, all prayer is absolutely certain to be answered . . . either no, yes, or a substitute.

PRAYER . . . REAL PRAYER . . . IS TO LIVE GOD-CON-SCIOUS. When His will is the supreme desire of our lives, He knows it, and from the moment we attain that spiritual place, He takes over. His is the responsibility of seeing to it that our every need is supplied. So He says. So I believe.

GOD AND YOU

The soul is the bridge from MAN to GOD, and by the beautiful process of the world of the soul, we are able to go on to the next great step in our journey. Greater is the power that is in you, than the power that is in the world. God trusts everybody with the care of their own soul. Inside of you, down in that world of the spirit ... the world or realm where the real you lives ... the seat of your being, is the soul. None but God can satisfy the longings of the immortal soul; as the heart was made for Him, ONLY HE CAN FILL IT. *"For what is a man profited, if he shall gain the whole world, and lose his own soul?"* asks Jesus in Matthew 16:26.

The soul is, of course, the noblest part of man. It is the spiritual part of man as distinct from the physical. Steinmetz admonished, "The souls of men are the greatest undeveloped resource of men. Spiritual power is a force which history clearly teaches has been the greatest force in the development of men. Yet we have been merely playing with it and never have really studied it as we have the physical forces. Someday people will learn that material things do not bring happiness, and are of little use in making people creative and powerful. Then the scientists of the world will turn their laboratories over to the study of spiritual forces which have hardly been scratched."

It is this world of the soul that is ever-growing, which carries within it all of the aspects, attributes, qualities and powers which we associate with man's consciousness as a personal being. Here is the source of wisdom, love, faith, hope, charity, truth, believing, aspiring. Here are found the sum total of experience and knowledge. Here are the seeds of charity and compassion. Here are the incentives which cause the person to transform himself in the service of that which is greater than himself. This soul-body is the only instrument by means of which the soul can be known or sensed, and is the only dimension in which God can be experienced by man.

Man is God's agent on this earth. Man is here to GROW and DEVELOP HIMSELF and PREPARE HIMSELF FOR ETERNAL LIFE BY FELLOWSHIPPING and GLORIFYING GOD. Man is raw and wild. He needs the Scriptures, and the power of God's love to guide, tame, and mellow his wild nature.

I WONDER

Shall I ever live in a world:

Where every man will look every other man in the
eyes and mean exactly what he says?

Where men will search for faults in themselves as
diligently as they search for faults in others?

Where men have a greater sense of responsibility to
God than to anyone or anything else?

Where those entrusted with confidence and
responsibility will think of confidence and
responsibility as sacred trusts?

Where even the great will not feel themselves above
performing small duties with conscientious devotion?

Where everyone will mind his own business . . .

And give to others the same liberty they demand for
themselves . . .

And enjoy seeing others enjoy what they do not enjoy . . .

And think the best even though they fear the worst?

Shall I ever live in such a world?

I wonder.

— *Alfred A. Montapert*

CHAPTER THIRTEEN

THE RANGE OF PRAYER

Apropos of our last two chapters I want to discuss with you what I shall call, for the want of a better title, the range of prayer. It is commonly said that the range of prayer is limitless. That statement is both true and untrue, both partly true and partly untrue. As regards God's ability the statement is wholly true. As regards His Wisdom, the statement must be qualified.

In some matters He can do, but Infinite Wisdom dictates that He shall not do, lest by doing He jeopardize the highest spiritual interests of, not only an individual, but all with whom the individual may have contact. Too, God in answering prayer that is prayed on behalf of others is limited by the will of the person for whom prayer is made and frequently by a lack of cooperation on the part of both the petitioner and the individual for whom prayer is made. The part that cooperation plays in answers to prayer is in another study. At the moment we are concerned only with the range of prayer.

What may I, and what may I not, pray for with assurance that prayer will be answered? . . . and I am speaking now of affirmative answers to prayer. I have already pointed out that ALL PRAYER MUST BE SUBJECT TO THE WILL OF GOD. "According to His will" is the boundary set by Our Lord on prayer. Concerning some matters, the will of God is clearly revealed by direct statement. Some other matters cannot be so clearly stated, because they have to do with all the emergencies and needs that can possibly come into the ever changing pattern of life. The will of God in such matters must be revealed to the petitioner . . . either providentially or by "Inner Divine Guidance." But even in matters where the will of God is clearly stated there are factors entering into an answer to prayer which must be considered.

That brings us to a question that is very frequently raised with reference to prayer for the conversion of others. Here, the petitioner is clearly in the revealed will of God. It is not His will that any perish, *"but that all should come to repentance"* says Peter in 2 Peter 3:9. But here both God and the petitioner are subject to certain limitations.

Both God and the petitioner are dealing with a free agent. Neither can go further than the person involved is willing... and wills... to cooperate. God cannot... any more than you can... coerce a free agent. Both God and you can apply every known means, but neither He nor you can force a final decision. The question then is, of what value is prayer on behalf of unregenerated individuals?

It is not my purpose to shock and discourage you. On the contrary, it is my purpose to save you from shock and discouragement by pointing out where, when, how and why prayer is and is not effective. What I am about to say, may shock you, but, on the other hand, it may at some future time save you from a more severe and disastrous shock. I can find no warrant in the Scriptures for praying for the unconverted. I can find no single example that lends encouragement, much less sets a precedent. I have studied the prayers of both the Old and the New Testament and in no case can I find one that includes the unregenerate directly.

When first I made this discovery I must confess it was a shock to me. It was contrary to all I had heard and read. Having made this discovery, I went in search of God's method to reach and persuade the unregenerate. Before noting that method directly, I want to say another word about prayer. I do not say you shall not pray for the unconverted. There is a good reason why you shall. The value of such prayer is mostly to you. Several things are bound to be accomplished.

1. It will keep alive in you a desire for the salvation of others. You must feel before you can make others feel.

2. It will heap fuel on your own fire of faith. Faith without prayer is as impossible as life without breathing. Says James, *"Faith without works is dead"*, and he might have said without prayer there will not long be either faith or works.

The point is, prayer will put you to work to accomplish what you desire. And that is an important point. Many of your prayers will never be answered unless you answer them. The Holy Spirit is not your chore boy to be sent on missions while you conveniently sit and wait for Him to do the work. But all of this properly belongs to the study following this one . . . a study in which I shall take up the subject of how prayer is answered. At the moment the question is, how to bring the unregenerate to Christ?

I find in my New Testament a record of forty persons who were converted . . . other than the twelve Apostles themselves. In some cases the story is told in detail. In other cases there is just a simple statement. But in all cases, save one, one fact stands out clearly: They were brought to Christ by personal testimony. That is God's method.

Andrew found a spiritual experience. At once he was concerned about his brother. The story reads, *"He first findeth* (he did not send, or try to send, the Holy Spirit to hunt him up. He went after him) *his own brother Simon, and saith unto him, 'We have found the Messiah'* . . . *and he brought him to Jesus"* in John 1:40,41. Verse 45 reads, *"Philip findeth Nathanael, and saith unto him, 'We have found Him of whom Moses in the law, and the prophets, did write, Jesus of Nazareth'"* . . . These two examples are typical of all. A live, warm, personal testimony is the most persuasive method that can be used on the unconverted. You pray to keep your experience of Christ warm and persuasive. You testify that experience to win others.

It is worth-while to note the method used by these winners of others to Christ. There is no long argumentative preachment, just personal testimony. *"We have found Him!"* There is excitement, thrill and enthusiasm in these words. *"We have found him!"* And why not?

In a Central Western City a man drilled for oil on his little farm. A gusher came in. He filled his hat with the black stuff, slapped it on his head and came running wildly into town yelling, "I've got it! I've got it!" So Andrew and Philip felt when they found Christ! The trouble is, our enthusiasm runs to religion, our doctrines, our notions, our opinions. Few of us ever testify Christ. The woman at the well experienced Christ. She called a prayer meeting for all her friends . . . she did not! She rushed into town shouting, *"Come and see Him!"*

That, my friends, is the way you answer your own prayer for the unconverted . . . That is God's method. You go out and find them and bring them to Christ.

GOD'S VIEWPOINT

From time immemorial God's problem has been to get men to look from His viewpoint. Man's failure in this particular is the reason for the condition of the world today.

MEANING OF LIFE

A person has missed the whole meaning of LIFE . . . if they have not entered into an actual living relationship with God.

WHAT CAN PRAYER DO FOR US?

It can give us a new heart, a firmer spirit and a nobler attitude toward life. Like a divine prescription, prayer may be the one medicine that may cure our sick and stricken world. There is no substitute for prayer.

PRAYER PLUS WORK

When I pray, I pray like it all depends on GOD. But when I get through praying, I get up and work like it all depends on me.

— *Dwight L. Moody*

BELIEVE WITH THE HEART

For with the heart man believeth unto righteousness;
and with the mouth confession is made unto salvation.

— *Romans 10:10*

"*For*" . . . it is this word here in Romans 10:10 which intrigues me. "*FOR with the HEART man Believeth*" and note Paul adds quickly . . . "*unto righteousness*". And that's the ONLY THING you can SPIRITU-ALLY believe with your HEART! Everything else we believe mentally, with our intellect. The mind is the door to the heart, and it is in the heart that Spiritual things are Spiritually discerned. The heart, or soul, is the seat of being . . . the YOU of YOU. God reaches man through the HEART. Naturally, everything goes first to the mind, the intellect . . . BUT the Spiritual things of God go through the mind and into the heart, as God hath dealt to every person a measure of FAITH.

If you are not "born again" Spiritually into the family of God, you cannot understand the Spiritual language. No more than an Englishman can understand Chinese, or another foreign language.

With the heart man believeth, the seat of sensibility and emotion, that's where you exercise faith. And when it strikes that realm it has inherent transforming power. It releases within the individual a dynam-ic, capable of fully transforming him. With the heart man believeth. Not with the head. It is more than the accepting of facts. It is EXPERIENC-ING THE VERY LIFE OF JESUS CHRIST. Paul discusses that at some length throughout this entire chapter. He says, "*There is therefore now no condemnation to them which are in Christ Jesus, who walk not after the flesh, but after the Spirit . . . So then they that are in the flesh cannot please God. But ye are not in the Flesh, but in the Spirit, if so be that the Spirit of God dwell in you.*"

— *Romans 8:1,8-9*

Men can feel you when you have this Inner Power. God tells me I'm a man just like him. Living in the same world, under the same circumstance, in the same environment, all I need to do is climb to the high level where my fellowship with God is so full and complete that he will release His Power through me. "*With the HEART man BELIEVETH unto RIGHTEOUSNESS.*" The Christian experience to be "BORN AGAIN" is better felt than told. There is no way to become so revolutionary transformed as to be a brand new creature and NOT FEEL anything.

YOU!

The environment YOU fashion out of

. . . YOUR THOUGHTS . . . YOUR BELIEFS

. . . YOUR IDEALS . . . YOUR PHILOSOPHY

is . . . THE ONLY CLIMATE

YOU WILL EVER LIVE IN.

— Alfred A. Montapert

Why do some Positive Thinkers fail?

The real basis for positive thinking . . .

It is the Positive Force or Power that comes naturally from a person's Spiritual Development. Your "FAITH" in God is the Foundation for this Positive FORCE.

FAITH

FAITH IS A POSITIVE DYNAMIC FORCE

. . . THAT GIVES MEANING AND POWER

. . . TO THE BUSINESS OF LIVING.

— Alfred A. Montapert

CHAPTER FOURTEEN

THE OBJECT OF PRAYER
IS TO EXPERIENCE GOD

It has been my thought from the first of this series of chapters to conclude with several concrete examples of all that is embodied in the several studies. ABSTRACT TRUTH CAN ONLY BE MADE TO LIVE AS IT IS TRANSLATED INTO HUMAN EXPERIENCE. NO MATTER HOW TRUE A STATEMENT OF FACT OR DOCTRINE MAY BE IT IS ONLY A SKELETON UNTIL IT IS WROUGHT UPON BY THE MAGIC OF EXPERIENCE AND MADE TO LIVE.

For thirteen chapters we have been engaged with a general study of prayer. We have covered pretty nearly every phase of prayer life, going betimes very deeply into the more intimate aspects of prayer. I was anxious from the first to make one truth stand out. If I have succeeded in fastening that truth in your thinking, I shall be very happy with the results of these studies. The one truth to which I refer is, because it is so often spoken of: *"The Father knoweth what things ye have need of."*

And that being true, a great deal . . . shall I call it physical activity in which we have been engaged . . . a great deal of it, I am sure, misnomered prayer, is nonessential. Further, Our Lord tried in every way possible to impress upon us that the heavenly Father knows us. He is constantly aware of us. He is more deeply interested in us than we could possibly be in ourselves. And He is more deeply concerned about us than we could possibly be for ourselves.

Way back in the Old Testament it is announced that, *"He knows our downsittings and our uprisings."* That is pretty intimate knowledge, you know. And Our Lord added something to that when He said, *"The very hairs of your head are all numbered."* That's even more intimate knowledge. And something more is added to even that when Our Lord says, *"A sparrow shall not fall on the ground without the Father knoweth it."* That's exceedingly intimate knowledge of the world in which we live. Then He quickly adds, *"Ye are of more value than many sparrows."* Our Lord exhorted, *"Have faith in God."*

And how many, many times He tried to impress that truth upon us by the use of illustration. On one occasion, you recall, there was a storm sweeping over the Sea of Galilee. I take it that the boat in which He with His disciples was crossing was a comparatively small, frail boat. It seemed that Our Lord was tired after His day of ministry and contact with the mobs that were ever crowding in upon Him.

He wearied with His labors . . . and that ought to bring you very close to Him. People objected when I was discussing the intimate things of Jesus Christ, because I made Him too human . . . they say. Well, I am sure I didn't make Him any more human than He was and is. I read that He was weary, and so weary that He stretched out on the after-deck of the little boat and fell asleep. It was said that the disciples were battling the storm. Our Lord was asleep and comfortable throughout the storm. The disciples were battling the storm. The reason why many of us do not make more progress, we are battling the storm. When you ride with the storm, you weather the storm much better.

They speak about a boxer "riding with a punch." There is all the difference between riding the punch and being hit by the punch and being knocked out. Well, I say, when one remembers to ride with the storm, one weathers the storm much better. Have you learned that? If you have, you have learned a very valuable truth.

But Our Lord was sleeping soundly. You say, "Yes, but He was God." Yes, and He was a human being and He was just as human as you are . . . in every detail . . . and in everything. The difference between Him and the disciples was a little matter of something we call "faith," . . . and I remind you that Jesus Christ, in human form, had to exercise faith to live spiritually, just as you and I do. There was no other way of accounting for His prayer life.

He was sleeping soundly while the disciples were battling the storm. Finally, in their exhaustion . . . and that is about all battling is . . . exhaustion and desperation, they went to the after-deck and very fearfully demanded to know, *"Carest thou not that we perish?"* If you read that in the Greek text, you read it as an actual "snarl." I suppose they had said, one to the other, out there on the wind-swept deck, "Well, He pretends to care about us. Now look at Him. We could be swept overboard for all He cares . . . or seems to care." They went to Him and said, *"Carest thou not that we perish?"* I guess all of us have experienced that mood at some time. Some of you have probably said, "I guess the Lord has forgotten me." It was the same mood exactly . . . out of which grew the rebuke of the disciples. *"Carest thou not that we perish?"*

What the Lord really, truly said was: You should have had faith. That's the truth I have been trying to bring home. That's exactly what Our Lord was trying to impress upon them when He said, *"Have faith in God."* He had just performed an astounding miracle, and the disciples were wide-eyed and marveled. And He in His turn said in substance, Why, this is nothing, nothing astounding or marvelous about what I have just done. Why, He said, if you had just a wee little bit of faith, you too could say to the mountain, "Be removed."

ALL THROUGH THE BIBLE THE EXHORTATION IS: *"To TRUST God." "Have FAITH in God." "WAIT on God."* And you will notice in the 11th chapter of Hebrews, when the writer undertakes to pick out the high places in the life of those we call "ancient worthies," He puts His finger on the FAITH element every time.

By FAITH Abraham offered up Isaac. By FAITH Isaac blessed Jacob and Esau concerning things to come. By FAITH Jacob blessed both the sons of Joseph. By FAITH Moses was hid three months by his parents. By FAITH . . . by FAITH!

Now you may not know what you mean when you use that word. I know exactly what I mean. I mean the cultivation of a spiritual faculty and a spiritual mood. I mean the cultivation of a FAITH faculty and a spiritual mood which constantly needs an adjustment to God and His purpose and keeps steadily on its way without much questioning and without much talking. If you will cultivate that mood, you will be amazed at how many things you have wanted for a long time and didn't get by the method of prayer that you are in the habit of using.

In this whole series of fourteen chapters I have been trying to press home one truth, and one only, of having FAITH IN GOD. If you will carry with you this one truth, I assure you, you will have something that will be of eternal value, and you will have more answers to prayer than you have ever experienced in all your life.

THE OBJECT OF PRAYER IS TO EXPERIENCE GOD. When you carry with you every day the consciousness that *"your heavenly Father knoweth what things you have need of,"* you will have had a revolutionary experience and from this point on you will make more spiritual progress than you ever made in your whole life. You may be sure of that.

After all, abstract truth can only be made to live as it is translated into human experience. No matter how true a statement or fact or a doctrine may be, it is only a skeleton until wrought on by the magic of experience and made to live. It is by prayer that man reaches God and that God enters into him. Prayer appears to be indispensable to our highest development. Man needs God as he needs water and oxygen.

> *With GOD'S WORD in your heart . . .*
> *each day is a Victorious Day.*
>
> — *Evelyn W. Montapert*

POINTS TO REMEMBER

1. Prayer is a natural instinct of mankind.
2. Prayer is an ATTITUDE and a RELATIONSHIP powered by DESIRE.
3. Releasing life's greatest potential . . . Prayer.
4. We need PRAYER to raise us up to the LEVEL where all God's mercies and blessings flow in abundance.
5. Prayer is the Christian's vital breath.
6. No one should ignore prayer, the most profound and the most subtle need of our nature. The Spiritual shows itself just as indispensable to the success of life as the intellectual and the material.
7. The sense of the holy manifests itself chiefly by prayer.
8. Success in prayer is not measured by "remarkable anwers to prayer", but by the new happy spiritual life that we experience in prayer.
9. PRAYER . . . real prayer . . . is to live God-conscious.
10. "The Father knoweth what things ye have need of."
11. No one is a true Christian until he has learned to share the responsibility of life with God.
12. Man needs food for his SOUL. Here you will find a Banquet of Spiritual Food for your SOUL.
13. FAITH . . . what kind do you have . . . ETERNAL or TEMPORAL?
14. Faith, like PRAYER itself, can operate only where conditions are conducive to its operation.
15. A spiritual person lives their life by INNER KNOWING. The quality of their life is in direct proportion to his trust in the HIGHER POWER . . . "The Kingdom of God Within."
16. Elijah's prayer life took on the form of fellowship. He was God's friend and God was his friend. Man is built for fellowship with God.
17. Make God YOUR friend . . . YOUR partner. God seeks a partner.
18. "When you pray, enter your closet, close the door, and pray to your Father in that privacy."
19. It takes more than Positive Thinking . . . It takes the POWER of a Positive Faith in God to give you the Positive Outlook on Life.
20. Prayer is not words . . . it is an ATTITUDE and a RELATION-SHIP. Everything in your LIFE will depend upon your attitude.

POINTS TO REMEMBER

21. Try cultivating gratitude and watch your life grow in grace.
22. "Wait on the Lord." Friendship . . . God's deepest hunger.
23. Put your full LOVE and KINDNESS into your life.
24. The object of prayer is to experience God.
25. I will enjoy PEACE OF MIND which is more valuable than gold.
26. Prayer, an uplifting of the soul to God.
27. "He careth for you", how wonderful! By cultivating a prayer life, God and I are good friends . . . THE unbeatable combination.
28. We get what we expect. There is a law of life that brings to us what we expect.
29. Knowledge of yourself . . . "KNOW THYSELF."
30. REALIZE the Four Kingdoms, and enjoy them.
31. Man's Divine Dimensions . . . all three must be developed equally.
32. All prayer must be subject to the will of God.
33. All through the Bible the exhortation is: "To trust God." "Have Faith in God." "Wait on God."
34. The will of God is the Word of God.
35. Life is made or marred by Habitual Thinking.
36. All my sins are forgiven, except one. I must not shut God out of my life.
37. The secret and source of Power.
38. SUCCESSFUL LIVING FOR LIFE!
39. To build a MAN is the greatest project for each of us!
40. Man is overbuilt for this world.
41. How I discovered the secret of SUCCESSFUL LIVING.
42. What is TRUTH?
43. Protracted sorrow reveals a lack of vision. Why we should not grieve too long.
44. Definition of LIFE.
45. How to be a complete person, LEARN TO PRAY AND GROW HAPPY.
46. My Greatest Goal . . . to build a LIFE . . . MY LIFE.
47. My CHOICE, not CHANCE determines my future.
48. A set of VALUES that will make me a WINNER.
49. I will live with the far look . . . the BIG PICTURE . . . ETERNITY . . . for God hath set Eternity in my HEART.
50. Christianity . . . applied common sense, and SUCCESSFUL LIVING.

CHAPTER FIFTEEN

PRAYERS FOR ALL OCCASIONS

PETITION

A NURSE' S PRAYER

A FISHERMAN'S PRAYER

INTERCESSION

CONFESSION

HEALING

GRACE FOR FOOD

PRAYER AND PRAISE

POWER OF IMMORTALITY

FOR OTHERS

WORSHIP

PROBLEMS

ANSWERS TO PROBLEMS

AMERICA

NEW YEAR

PRAYER FOR NATION

PEACE

HEALTHY DISCONTENT

IN THE MORNING

EVENING

THE SPLENDOR OF OUR INNER BEING

IF, you abide in me, and my words abide in you . . . you shall ask what you will . . . and it shall be done!

— John 15:7

PRAYERS

Thank you for your prayers. These I consider as money in the bank, and will draw upon them to help meet the difficulties in my life.

— Alfred A. Montapert

PRAYER OF PETITION

Petition prayer is asking God to do something for us in our behalf or whatever our problem or concern is.

"And all things, whatsoever ye shall ask in prayer, believing, ye shall receive."

— *Matthew 21: 22*

The prayer of petition should be a prayer in faith believing. We are praying ourselves, not someone else praying with us or for us, and we must believe that we will receive.

God is interested in our daily well being, spiritually and physically and mentally, and about everything that touches our lives.

"Beloved, I wish above all things that thou mayest prosper and be in health, even as thy soul prospereth.

— *III John 1: 2*

> God, give me sympathy and sense,
> And help me keep my courage high;
> God, give me calm and confidence,
> And please . . . a twinkle in my eye.

Spread out your petition before God and then say, "Thy will, not mine, be done." The sweetest lesson I have learned in God's school is to let the Lord choose for me.

— *Dwight L. Moody*

A NURSE'S PRAYER

Dear Lord, thou great healer, may thy great strength and power flow through me and lend skill to my hand, vision and judgment to my mind and compassion to my heart. Grant me the strength to minister to my fellow man in his hours of suffering and travail. Make me worthy, O Lord, of this saintly task and may I faithfully discharge my duties in deep humility, worthy of the trust and faith placed in me. Amen.

A FISHERMAN'S PRAYER

Keep me, O my God, my boat is so small
and Thy Ocean is so wide.

INTERCESSION

The prayer of intercession is, of course, a prayer for others. An intercessor is one who takes the place of another or pleads another's case.

An example of intercessory prayer is found in Genesis 18:20-33 where we see Abraham's intercession for the cities of Sodom and Gomorrah.

Another example of intercession is when Moses pleaded with the Lord to spare the people of Israel when they had sinned against God and wanted to return to Egypt because of the "giants in the Promised land." See Numbers 14: 13-20.

We as Christians, are to intercede for our nation as set forth in I Timothy 2: 1-4. If the Christians would do this and pray for our leaders, things would not be as they are in our nation today.

We can change things by prayer. We can hold back judgment on the saved and unsaved. God told Abraham that if there were ten righteous people found in Sodom and Gomorrah, He would spare the cities. He would not destroy the cities because a man of God had interceded in their behalf.

PRAYER OF CONFESSION

Confession is to unburden one's sins or the state of one's conscience to God.

Have I been disobedient, unfaithful, careless?
If I have wounded any soul today,
If I have caused one foot to go astray,
If I have walked in my own sinful way,
Dear Lord, forgive.

"Confess your faults one to another, and pray for another, that ye may be healed. The effectual fervent prayer of a righteous man availeth much."

— *James 5: 16*

THE PRAYER OF HEALING IS FOUND
ALL THROUGH THE BIBLE

*Is any sick among you? let him call for the
elders of the church; and let them pray over
him, anointing him with oil in the name of
the Lord: And the prayer of faith shall save
the sick, and the Lord shall raise him up.*

— *James 5: 14-15*

It is the healing effects of Prayer which in all ages have chiefly
attracted the attention of men. Prayer has sometimes an explosive effect.
Patients have been cured almost instantaneously of afflictions. The
phenomenon produced is nearly always in the same way. Great pain,
then the feeling of being healed. In a few seconds the symptoms
disappear and the anatomic lesions mend. The miracle is characterized
by extreme acceleration of the normal process of healing. It is on the
FAITH, on the intensity and the quality of the prayer that its effect
seems to depend. Prayer produces tangible effects. Whosoever asks
receives, and the door is opened to him who knocks.

"There is an incredible power of healing in a prayer meeting,
infinitely greater than the power our greatest doctors can command. A
crowd, exalted and united by prayer, gives off some kind of fluid which
has tremendous effect on the nervous system. Never underestimate the
power emanating from thousands of people united in one fervent
purpose. Even the cry of one heart!"

— *Dr. Alexis Carrel*

A doctor who sees a patient give himself to prayer, can indeed
rejoice. The calm engendered by prayer is a powerful aid to healing. We
would simply like to draw attention to the fact that so-called phenomena
are very often natural facts, the causes of which we cannot determine.

DIVINE HEALING

You are healed by the Healing Law of GOD.
The SPIRIT OF GOD is LIFE and is the POWER in
the SPIRITUAL REALM. This POWER is always there . . .
You must mix your FAITH with the Higher Power
which releases this POWER OF GOD.

GRACE FOR FOOD

Father, we thank Thee for this fellowship. We thank Thee for this food. Bless and strengthen this food to our use. Keep each one of us in Thy will and help us to walk in Thy way. And may everything we say, and do, be pleasing in the sight of the Lord. Amen.

Great God, Thou giver of all good,
Accept our praise and bless our food.
Grace, health, and strength to us afford,
Through Jesus Christ, our risen Lord. Amen.

MORNING MEAL

O come, our Lord and Saviour,
And be our guest today,
That each may have a blessing
From Thee to take away. Amen.

NOON MEAL

Be present at our table, Lord;
Be here, as everywhere, adored;
These bounties bless and grant that we
May feast in Paradise with Thee. Amen.

EVENING MEAL

We thank Thee, Lord, for this food. May it strengthen our bodies, and feed our souls with the Bread of Life. Bless those who are gathered together here at our table. In Jesus' name we ask. Amen.

JEWISH

Lift up your hands toward the sanctuary and bless the Lord. Blessed art Thou, O Lord our God, King of the universe, Who bringest forth bread from the earth. Amen.

PROTESTANT

Bless, O Lord, this food to our use, and us to Thy service, and make us ever mindful of the needs of others, In Jesus' name.

ROMAN CATHOLIC

Bless us, O Lord, and these Thy gifts which we are about to receive from Thy bounty, through Christ our Lord. Amen.

PRAYER AND PRAISE

Two of the most important weapons in the Christian's arsenal are prayer and praise. These two must work as one. Where praise is lacking prayer is never effective. Where prayer is lacking praise is but an empty sound.

Both prayer and praise, in order to be effective must spring from conscious union with God. Without the consciousness of His indwelling presence both prayer and praise are so much wind blown against the naked masts of the ship of faith; they make a noise in the rigging, but they do not drive the ship.

Without prayer there may be ASPIRATION, but there will be no INSPIRATION. Prayer that inspires is the inner power that makes the Christian tick. It puts affirmation into our faith. What faith affirms grateful prayer and praise will soon confirm.

Thus we shall develop a tough faith for tough times . . . and the best shall be yours by right of conquest.

> *The LORD is my strength and my shield; my heart*
> *trusted in him, and I am helped; therefore my*
> *heart greatly rejoiceth; and with my song will*
> *I praise him.*
>
> *— Psalm 28:7*

Oh Lord, Our Lord, how excellent is thy name in all the earth. The heavens above us declare thy glory, the earth around us showeth Thy handiwork. We've long since learned that there is no speech or language where their voice is not heard. Thou art the creator of the world and all that is therein, of us, and the earth is so contrived, that day by day it speaks to the heart of us of God's amazing wisdom, and grace, and power. Every rock speaks of the rock of ages cleft, where we may hide and find a refuge from the storm. Every mountain brook that takes its rise on yonder slopes and leaps and roars and laughs its way to the meadows below, speaks to us of the washing of thy regeneration. The ocean tides that come and go to wash clean a thousand beaches speak to the heart of us of all the fullness of God which is ours for the taking. Every cloud that drifts overhead like white sailboats going out to sea talks to us constantly about the God who makes these clouds his chariot, who rides upon the heaven. All of this was revealed to us when the heart of us was made new. Amen.

POWER OF IMMORTALITY

Once again, Our Heavenly Father, we are aware of a deep sense of gratitude for the manifestation of Thyself in the Person of Jesus Christ . . . by whatsoever symbolism He appears to us, by whatsoever chronology, our hearts are at once captured and captivated. The old, old story it is, but it takes on newness with the passing years and every time it is called to our attention, we find some hidden beauty hitherto undisclosed. How marvelous it is that this oldest of all stories continues to hold its millions spellbound.

Other names have risen and they have flashed across the sky of Fame like a blazing meteor, leaving behind a trail of fire for a century and then disappear . . . but this Name, High over all, not only has risen but continues to blaze and burn more brightly with the passing of every century. And while the story of His Coming is the oldest of old stories, more people long to hear it today than ever since it began to be told. This, we doubt not, is because there is strange power in this thing . . . not only to capture the hearts of men but to transform them.

There is a strange power of immortality . . . not like the rose that blooms by the wayside to open its petals and spread its fragrance for a day, but like a rose . . . the bud that opens slowly and continues to open, and continues to open, and becomes more fragrant with the passing of the years and, finally, immortalizes itself in the splendor of its own endlessness.

Eye hath not seen, nor ear heard, neither have
entered into the heart of man, .the things which
God hath prepared for them that love him.
— I Corinthians 2:9

Let the words of my mouth
and the meditation of my heart,
be acceptable in thy sight, O LORD,
my strength and my redeemer.
— Psalm 19: 14

PRAYER FOR OTHERS

Bless those of whom we are thinking. Thy promise to them is, when thou passeth through the flood I will sustain thee, when thou goest through fire it shall not kindle upon thee. Lift their thinking to God. May they be aware of thy presence this moment while we pray, may their faith be lifted to the level of thine ability to do for them. Those who mourn, comfort them. Comfort them with that comfort which only thou can impart to the heart with such assurance of mind as will lift them entirely above the passing moment of the present. Make this an hour, a truly spiritual hour when we'll be more aware of God than we are of the man or the woman at our elbow. Let miracles be wrought on bodies, on minds, on circumstances this hour. As they will be if our faith rises to thy level. And in the name of Jesus Christ that name which is above every name, even in Heaven above, we come with our needs assured an infinite supply. Amen.

PRAYER FOR OTHERS

We, thy children, come to thee this hour believing our Father we may speak to thee, out of our hearts. And as we come, we do not come to a stranger, but we come to one who understands far beyond what we are even asking. And our Father while we do not know these needy hearts, especially these that need thy touch upon their physical bodies, we are so glad that thou dost know them. They are not strangers to thee. And our Father, we pray help us to come in confidence. Help us to believe, that God is able to do even what we ask him to do NOW. So we pray, our Father. We know that thou are here. Surely we feel thy presence, but we know likewise, that God can be everywhere. So we pray for a special visitation of God, the Holy Spirit, to go now while we pray and while we unite our faith together, believing that God is able. We pray for the divine visitation of God upon these needy ones now. Oh, God help us to believe that God would delight to reveal his grace and power if we would only prepare our minds and hearts, ready for God to do it. So we pray to bless these individuals, and grant Lord, there may come into their hearts a sense of thy presence, and God's divine touch will open their physical bodies and heal them and restore them even while we pray today. In Jesus' name, we pray. Amen.

WORSHIP

We are always glad when they say unto us let us go up into the house of the Lord. Here in thy presence we have experienced our finest hours. We have caught glimpses of things unforgettable. Thou has demonstrated thine ability to remake men so that we have become new creatures in Jesus Christ.

We no longer think our thoughts and speak our words. We have been lifted to a new plane of life. We are grateful for all thy mercies. They come to our daily lives so abundantly that they are innumerable. Day by day they keep oncoming a constant flow. Thy goodness should have long ago lead men to repentance. But at last the heart of us is so set upon its own ways, that many of us never rise above the level of mere animal living.

We thank thee for a group of people who know the truth and having experienced the truth rise to these sublime heights. We thank thee for the dawning of a new day which is near to come. In that new day are all our hopes, the fulfillment of all our dreams. The amazing privileges which are ours because of the redemption of Jesus Christ. Now we pray that thou wilt help us to so use this hour of worship that we shall be lifted infinitely above the level on which we have lived.

So many of us find ourselves so cluttered up with mundane things, little things. Oh God, give us vision this hour which will raise us infinitely above the common little level on which we have been living. Help us to see and appreciate these words of thine. What assurance, what confidence, what strength, they carry to the heart that is open to receive them. Grant that this hour shall be more than merely coming and going. It shall be an unforgettable transforming hour. And we pray that thou wilt once again bless those whom thou in thine providence has placed in positions of such tremendous responsibility. Make this a day when they shall look from God's viewpoint. For Jesus' sake, Amen.

SOMETIMES WHEN YOU SING
IT IS ALMOST LIKE A PRAYER.

PROBLEMS

With our problems, God grant that we shall by faith be able to hook on and solve these problems. Thou didst question Thy servant Moses, *"Is anything too hard for the Lord?"* The answer is, *"NO!"* And Our Lord said, *"All things are possible to those who believe."* Fact is, there is nothing impossible . . . if we doubt not; there is nothing possible if we doubt. How slow the world is to learn that doubt is the most death-dealing thing in the universe. The most powerful guns known to men, the most powerful inventions of destruction are child's play beside this destructive force released by doubt. When faith is operative, God is abroad in His World. There is nothing impossible with Thee . . . this, with all our hearts, we believe. In the name of the Christ, who assured us that all power is His . . . in heaven and in earth . . . and our hearts respond with this assurance, with a deep and unearthly "Hallelujah!" Amen.

ANSWERS TO PROBLEMS

Bless those of us who have experienced trouble and distress and bewilderment. Make this time when in a new inspiration our problems shall be dissolved. Worry shall be displaced by an awareness of God. He who said to me and to all of us, let not your heart be troubled. We have but to believe in God. The God who at the beginning spoke to darkness and there was light. The God who at the conception of his infinite purpose brought worlds into being and are just as mighty now as in the ages past when Elijah felt thy power; when Moses endured as seeing him who was invisible. When Abraham kept steadily on his way, not looking on circumstances, but in spite of every unfavorable circumstance believed God. And as always God was there with the answer to his problem, so He will be in our day. Amen.

GOD IS GREATER than any problem I have.

There is a missing dimension to our human knowledge.
MOST OF OUR DEFICIENCIES STEM FROM
OUR SPIRITUAL INADEQUACIES.

AMERICA ON ITS KNEES

OUR FATHER IN HEAVEN:

We pray that you save us from ourselves.
The world that you have made for us, to
live in peace, we have made into an
armed camp. We live in fear of war to
come.

We are afraid of the terror that flies by
night, the arrow that flies by day, the
pestilence that walks in darkness, the
destruction that wastes at noonday.

We have turned from you to go our selfish
way. We have broken your commandments
and denied your truth. We have left
your altars to serve the false gods of
money and pleasure and power.

Forgive us and help us.
Now, darkness gathers around us and we are
confused in all our counsels. Losing
faith in you, we lose faith in ourselves.

Inspire us with wisdom, all of us of every
color, race, and creed, to use our
wealth, our strength, to help our
brother, instead of destroying him.

Help us to do your will as it is done in
heaven, and to be worthy of your promise
of peace on earth.

Fill us with new faith, new strength, and
new courage, that we may win the
Battle for Peace.

Be swift to save us, dear God, before the
darkness falls. Amen.

— From "The Battle for Peace"
An Address by Conrad Hilton

A PRAYER FOR THE NEW YEAR

Dear Lord: Let us walk into the future, clasping Thy hand with heads and hearts filled with high hopes and the kind of warm faith that will enable us to face all problems courageously and constructively.

Let us try to create a better world by first improving ourselves. Let us grow in culture and in the appreciation of beauty, truth and goodness which constitute the real values of life. Let us share our blessings with others irrespective of race or creed.

Bless us with the sensitivity that will enable us to look down deep into the hearts and souls of human beings and thus understand them. Let us always remember that every one of us has virtues and weaknesses.

Let there be peace on earth and elimination of war which is man's greatest enemy. Let peace reign within our country and within our hearts. Amen.

— *Rabbi Magnin*

THE NEW YEAR

Another year is dawning,
    Dear Father, let it be,
In working or in waiting,
    Another year with Thee;
Another year of progress,
    Another year of praise,
Another year of proving
    Thy presence all the days.

Another year of service,
    Of witness for Thy love;
Another year of training
    For holier work above.
Another year is dawning,
    Dear Father, let it be,
On earth, or else in heaven,
    Another year for Thee.

— *Frances Rider Havergal*

PRAYER FOR A NATION

Almighty God: We make our earnest prayer that Thou wilt keep the United States in Thy holy protection; that Thou wilt incline the hearts of the citizens to cultivate a spirit of subordination and obedience to government; and entertain a brotherly affection and love for one another and for their fellow citizens of the United States at large. And, finally, that Thou wilt most graciously be pleased to dispose us all to do justice, to love mercy and to demean ourselves with charity, humility, and pacific temper of mind which were the characteristics of the Divine Author of our blessed religion, and without an humble imitation of whose example in these things we can never hope to be a happy nation. Grant our supplication, we beseech Thee, through Jesus Christ our Lord, Amen.

— George Washington's
Inaugural Prayer

A PRAYER FOR OUR COUNTRY

Oh, God, our Father, we pray that the people of America
who have made such progress in material things,
may now seek to grow
in spiritual understanding.

— Alfred A. Montapert

PRAYER FOR PEACE

"We sit here, thirty minutes away from some missiles in the middle of Siberia . . . targeted on Los Angeles," the speaker warned. This illustrates the uncertain condition of our times. I would strongly recommend prayer, reciting the rosary, chanting a mantrum or whatever you know of that will bring divine help.

Our Father God, in a "NUCLEAR SURVIVAL" world, there is no place else for us to go but to You. The world is full of evil doers but our trust is in You. In You we live, breathe and have our being. Expand our faith so we may become one with Thee. Amen.

HEALTHY DISCONTENT

Sometimes I sit and wonder
    Looking out the window at the vast city below.
Discontent of the little place I fill
    In this great scheme of things.

I had a part in building this great city
    And that brings back some wonderful memories;
But what I have done does not seem to satisfy now.
    It's what is ahead that greatly concerns me.

When a lad . . . I loved to dream . . . and dream
    That someday I would live in a big castle,
And that I would live forever, and be a great
    And good man like King Alfred.
Have riches, power, fame, family and friends.
    Perhaps I would even build a great edifice
Like the Statue of Liberty.
    At such a time I felt almost content.

The years have come and gone, my hair is now white,
    Friends and family one by one like phantoms go,
Riches can also take wing and fame will always evaporate.
    But I keep on keeping on, praying that God
Will lead and guide in this rough and tumble world.
    Hoping there is time left for me to do some worthy work.

Something that will live forever . . .
    So that my soul will be satisfied and content.
Then, and only then, will I know that I have filled
    My little place in this great scheme of things.

I have no time now for things that do not count.
    The purpose of life is to bear fruit
And the unfolding of the inner man.
    The best and most satisfying thing in the heart is God.

What will ABIDE? My knowledge? No. My wealth? No.
    Now ABIDETH . . . FAITH . . . HOPE . . . and LOVE.
May our hearts experience a sense of ABIDING reality
    In these great spiritual powers with ETERNAL VALUES.

— Alfred A. Montapert

IN THE MORNING

I met God in the morning,
        When my day was at its best
And His presence came like sunrise
        Like a glory in my breast.

All day long the Presence lingered.
        All day long He stayed with me.
And we sailed with perfect calmness
        O'er a very troubled sea.

Other ships were blown and battered
        Other ships were sore distressed.
But the winds that seemed to drive them
        Brought to us a peace and rest.

Then I thought of other mornings
        When a keen remorse of mind,
When I, too, had loosed the moorings
        With the Presence left behind.

So I think I know the secret
        Learned from many a troubled way.
You must seek God in the morning
        If you want Him through the day.

— *Ralph Cushman*

EVENING PRAYER

We thank thee our Heavenly Father for this good day. Our hearts have responded to God from early morning until this hour. Thy mercies have fallen like the raindrops. Goodness and mercy have followed us all the days of our lives. So it shall continue until the end we are assured. We thank thee for these words of thine, they find us where we live, and we are highly resolved by thy grace to live on a higher thought level than we ever thought or lived on. And as we do we shall experience the transforming power of the incoming of the Holy Spirit who will make our bodies the temple, His temple. All things being equal we shall have better health, more success and especially at this business of spiritual living. Hallelujah, Amen.

THE SPLENDOR OF OUR INNER BEING

An incomparable spark of divinity is to be found in the heart of each human being, waiting to radiate love and wisdom everywhere, because that is its nature. However, the task of refining this gold is up to us. We must remove the dross . . . that which is petty, destructive and self-seeking. Or like removing the weeds from our garden, we cultivate the good.

Ordinary people like you and me have taken on the immense challenge of the spiritual life and have made this supreme discovery. They have found out who awaits them within the body, within the mind, within the spirit of man. *"The kingdom of God is within"* IF, and a big IF, you BELIEVE in your heart and CONFESS with your mouth your oneness with God. HE is your creator, your hope, your joy, your redeemer, your life, your all. The same power, force, that cast Paul to the earth and made him cry out . . . *"Not I, not I, But Christ liveth in me."* This same Power is in you and me, if we are ready for it.

Saint Francis of Assisi received this power and heard the irrestible voice of God calling to him . . . "Francis, Francis rebuild my church." Not only did he rebuild the Church, but that which was closest of all . . . the man himself. Whenever we repeat the Prayer of St. Francis we are immersing ourselves in the spiritual wisdom and blessings of a holy lifetime. As one grows spiritually, these words will mean more and more to you . . .

> "Lord, make me an instrument of thy peace.
> Where there is hatred, let me sow love;
> Where there is injury, pardon;
> Where there is doubt, faith;
> Where there is despair, hope;
> Where there is darkness, light;
> Where there is sadness, joy.
> O Divine Master, grant that I may not so much seek
> To be consoled as to console,
> To be understood as to understand,
> To be loved as to love;
> For it is in giving that we receive;
> It is in pardoning that we are pardoned;
> It is in dying that we are born to eternal life."

CHAPTER SIXTEEN

PRAYERS FOR MY NEEDS

NEEDS SUPPLIED

We are here with as many needs as there are individuals. And with the Apostle Paul we are thinking, _"My God shall supply ALL your needs according to HIS riches in glory, by Christ Jesus."_ Not according to thy riches in glory. Thou hast literally opened the vaults of eternal worlds and bidden us come in and help ourselves. Help us to believe that. Amen.

SPECIAL NEEDS

And our Father for this hour, possibly some of us have a special need. Some of us need, our Father, a moral spiritual touch. O God, do not pass us by, but may each of us open our minds and our hearts for the recipience of God's best. We pray our Father to bless every one that is here. O God somehow speak to us, speak in terms that we will understand. We are so ignorant and sometimes so dull in understanding. O God, speak to us so that we will understand, then, help us to yield, to say yes to God. We ask it in the name of Christ. Amen.

KEEP IN TUNE WITH THEE

Our heavenly Father, tune our hearts to the pitch of heaven, this we ask. We are so sorely in need. Our lives need to be tuned to thee. Make the heart of us be so responsive to God he'll have his best unhindered opportunity to do for each one of us what he sees needs to be done. We can't be left to our own choices. We do not know how to live, not only hath thou warned us of that, but experience with the years has taught us. When the poet sang, "I must have the Saviour with me", that is more than sentiment to some of us. We dare not walk alone. Much apart from being cowardice, that is the highest type of courage. Amen.

INDIVIDUAL NEEDS

So bless each individual that we shall take out of the hour something definitely appropriate to our needs. Now there are many needs represented as there are individuals. We pray that thou wilt help us to so worship as though we were the only person present in the sanctuary and we recall that thou didst give to an individual thy best ministry when thou were upon the earth. Thou dost deal with us as individuals as though we were the only one. And we are, as far as our individual lives are concerned. Thou art saying to me, and saying to all of us as thou didst say in the days of thy earthly ministry to one concerned with everything, but not enough concerned with one thing . . . what is that to thee. What is this and that to the other one does . . . FOLLOW ME.

Thou art saying that to each one of us. When we become aware that we are so committed to God, and he pays attention to us as individuals, then will we come into the bold knowledge of this uttermost salvation of thine. This amazing gift which thou hast offered to each one of us. Save us from presuming that we as a Christian are out to sell somebody something. We're not salesmen, we are laborers together with God. How deeply the heart of us resents the idea that we're trying to sell somebody something, or sell somebody on an idea of ours. Oh God, make very clear to the heart of us that we were built for Thee, to this end thou hast offered us the free gift of the fellowship. Amen.

CONSCIOUSNESS OF GOD

Now we pray that each heart in this present will be aware of Him. We shall be more conscious of God than we are of any human being. And may that consciousness of His presence be the source from which will flow every need. Some are present who need the physical touch, may Thy hand be upon them for Good. Thou can do what no human power can do for us. This is the place, above all places, where thou art pleased to work miracles. In Jesus' name we pray, Amen.

OVERCOMING HARDSHIPS

We shall fellowship, appreciate and enjoy God through the days of this earthly life of ours. At best, at best it is bound to be a life full of the vicissitudes incident to the business of living. Thou hast said to Thine own, Fear not I have overcome the world therefore you may overcome the world. And the victory that overcomes the world is our FAITH. Inspire our hearts to believe as it has never been INSPIRED. That's the urgent need of the hour. All around us the clouds drop lower and lower and grow blacker and blacker. Worry and fear and fret are on our right hand and on our left hand. But from all of this we shall be saved. Thy peace, thou dost give unto thine own. Not peace of mind, but Thy peace. That extreme confidence which Thou dost know. The same father that was Thine is ours. We may say to him as Thou didst say . . . we know that Thou dost always hear us. Thou has not left us to ourselves. WE ARE NOT SUPPOSED TO FIGHT OUR BATTLES BY THE STRENGTH OF OUR WILL, BY WHAT FORTITUDE WE CAN MUSTER, BUT BY THE FAITH OF GOD, LODGED IN THE HEART OF US. Amen.

"Thus saith the Lord unto you, Be not afraid nor dismayed by reason of this great multitude; for the battle is not yours, but God's . . . set yourselves, stand ye still, and see the salvation of the Lord with you . . . for the Lord will be with you . . . Believe in the Lord your God, so shall ye prosper."

— *II Chronicles 20:15,17,20*

ACCORDING TO OUR FAITH

We remind ourselves once again Heavenly Father, it's a great thing to be a Christian. Thou dost say to us as Christians you are co-laborers together with Me. What I am able to do is unlimited. Thou dost question each one of us . . . *"Is anything too hard for the Lord?"* The answer is NO, provided you can find a heart in cooperation with Him. The only thing that puts restriction on Him and His ability to do is lack of faith. He chided his disciples, so he chides us, *"Oh ye of little faith."* He is saying to us, *"according to your Faith be it unto you."* Little faith, little results . . . Big faith, results unlimited.

THE PROBLEMS OF LIFE

Oh Lord, the problems of life are entirely beyond us . . . we can't fathom it mentally. Nor can we learn all the answers by experience. Even the schools do not come within sight of adequate answers. Only Thou can do what must be done. We're not infinite, we're not able to fathom the mysteries of thy deep, far reaching purpose. We don't know when it is time for a man to go, when it is time for him to linger, but we're certain thou dost know and WE REPOSE OUR CONFIDENCE UNRESERVEDLY IN THEE. The longer we live and the more we observe, the more certain we are that this is the only wise thing for human beings to do. Amen.

THE POWER OF THE HOLY SPIRIT

Oh Lord, Oh Lord, the heart of us is speaking to thee, a language which our lips can't shape into words. Oh God, look on my heart and in answer to its cry let this baptism of the Holy Ghost come upon me, afresh. Come upon all of us afresh. Here are young men who could be used to shape a nation. Here are young women if they are wholly dedicated to God, could be heard all around the world. Unless we are so dedicated, unless we do become so baptized in the Holy Spirit, so dominated with a deep conviction nobody will ever hear from us. We'll die in anonymity. Thou didst say to these men of whom we've been thinking, *"You shall be baptized with the Holy Ghost not many days hence, and you shall be Witnesses unto me."*

They were comparatively unknown men. They were unsung outside their own neighborhood. Their names had never appeared in print. Nobody outside of the little circle had heard of them. Yet so dominated, so baptized with the Holy Ghost the entire world heard them. Even the Caesars in their might and with their power could not stand up against them. So it could easily be again. Oh God, Oh God come upon us. Come upon me. Let my heart be so responsive to thee that thou can speak to me. Let us become so filled with God that our dynamic influence will be felt all around our home, our business, and lives. Oh God, for Jesus' sake, we pray. Amen.

WORDS OF THINE

Now Lord, we approach thy word humbly as becomes men. We are always aware that we are listening to God speak . . . intimately, personally. And these words of thine are eternal words. Other things having to do with time, they are transitory, they are passing, they are like a fleeing shadow, they are like a dream. They are like a tale which is soon told. These words of thine, they will remain the same when the heavens have waxed old and folded up like a well worn garment. When these stars shining so brightly in the blue dome of the heavens tonight shall have fallen from their sockets like raindrops of fire. When that day comes when everything will be shaken, which is shakeable, this word of thine will remain the same . . . yesterday, today, and forever. Amen.

VALUE OF THY WORD

These words of thine, Oh God, are sweeter to some of us than honey in the honeycomb. More to be desired today than gold, yea and much fine gold. This word of thine is right concerning all things. We have seen it so. It is settled forever in the heavens. Like thy throne it is unmovable, unchanged and unchanging. Help us then to pay heed to these words of thine that they may be hidden in our hearts. That our feet may take fast hold on the ways of life. In Jesus' name, we pray. Amen.

RICHNESS OF THY WORD

How rich and full, Our Lord, are these words of thine, help us to read, and re-read until they grapple with our hearts and lift us up to thy level. May we not just read this word of thine, may we read it with a complete understanding. It is the revelation of thy purpose to usward, and to the world. Help us once again we pray, to hide this word of thine in our hearts, that we may not sin against thee, but be lifted up to the full height of thine eternal purpose. Amen.

WORSHIP

We come again, Our Heavenly Father, gratefully, to this hour of worship, profoundly grateful that we are privileged to share the hour with these, Thy People, who earnestly desire Thy Word. We pray Thy very special blessing upon us now as we read Thy Word. Grant to us that spiritual discernment which we must have in order to discover the full meaning of Thy Word. It is impossible to go into these inspired realms by intellectual processes. Some have tried it and they have succeeded only in bewildering themselves. There are those of us who have learned that in order to inherit the things of the Kingdom of God, we must become as little children. Amen.

SPIRITUAL WORSHIP

Put us in the mood to truly worship our Heavenly Father. We've long since learned thou art a spirit and desirest such to worship thee, as worship in spirit and in truth. A mere coming to the house of the Lord does not guarantee the benefits which accrue to those who do worship in spirit and in truth. We have long since learned that SPIRITUAL WORSHIP IS THE HIGHEST FUNCTION OF WHICH WE ARE CAPABLE. It involves our entire being. It is the fountain from which flows all the streams of living. And if the fountain is pure all the streams will flow pure. If that fountain is muddied by selfishness and indifference, and a lack of concern, all the streams are bound to flow muddy. It is literally true we become like the God or gods that we worship. A low unworthy conception of Thee is bound to produce a life that is low and unworthy. Our lives can never rise higher than our best thinking, and they are bound to sink as low as our worst thinking. Put us in the mood then, we pray once again, for the true worship. If the heart of us becomes so involved we are bound to take out of this hour an uplifting, stimulating, strengthening power that can be known in no other way. Amen.

NO ONE ELSE'S PRAYER CAN BE YOUR PRAYER,
YOU HAVE TO DISCOVER YOUR OWN.

NEED

Again, our Heavenly Father, our hearts are bowed before thee in gratitude for the coming of this another day of worship and for the privilege of thy house. This place where thy honor dwelleth. The place above all places in the universe where Thou art pleased to reveal thyself to the heart of thy people as Thou canst not reveal thyself anywhere else. It is here that we are reminded with the coming of this beautiful morning that we are built for God. Things here do not because they cannot satisfy us. We are contrived on too vast a scale to be content with a handful of things. WE MUST HAVE CLOSE CONTACT WITH THE ETERNAL, FOR THIS ALONE WE WERE MADE.

We're assembled here from our various walks in life, and to walk through the day in which we live is so confusing and so confused, so bewildering and so bewildered. We need Thee, more perhaps, than any single generation who have ever lived upon the face of the earth. We've insisted on building up our world, and we have built a world in which none of us know how to live.

We pray God to so lift us up that we'll catch a new vision of thy ultimate purpose. It is this purpose that gives us heart. It is this purpose that gives us courage to carry on. There is no future only as we see thy future. We've said for years that time is short but it is so short now, we have but five minutes, four minutes, three minutes, in which to finish the task assigned to us.

There may have been a day in which men could live carelessly and indolently, and disregarding God's purpose but this is not the day. Time is almost up. If we had ears to hear we would doubtless hear the clock of destiny on time's great tower striking off the first strokes of midnight. But thy people look forward to the dawning of a new day, and the sunrise on a new day. A new beginning, as thou didst say in Genesis, *"In the beginning God . . . "* So thou wilt say once again, in the beginning God. Not this or that man, but GOD. Thy word to us is that you will supply our every need, according to our FAITH. Amen.

HELP US TO BE STRONG IN OUR FAITH

Make us aware constantly, like thy servant of old, that the mountain where we are, is filled with the horses and chariots of fire, and thy chariots we're told were ten thousand times ten thousand. With David, may the heart of us grow so confident that we will boldly say, *"Tho a host shall be encamped against me, in this will I be confident . . . by my God I shall run through a troop and leap over walls, I shall be strong and do exploits."* Save us from being weaklings in our faith, and in our actions. Help us to so live momentarily that internally we shall feel like a strong man girded to run a race. Help us to so run that we may at long last seize the prize. This is the ambition of our lives. Amen.

THE BIBLE

Oh God, we thank thee for this letter of thine, written and posted and addressed to us at such terrific expense. Don't let the heart of us rest day or night until we have set the watch of our daily living to this infinite chronometer. Help us everyone to see that this and this alone is what we shall eventually need. Not more than we need it through this immediate hour, but in a new and in a broader, and in a vastly infinite sense. GOD'S LETTER ADDRESSED TO ME. Amen.

THE BIBLE — THY WORD

Help us as we approach it to be always mindful of this . . . Save us from picking up this word of thine and just casually reading a passage. Help us always, as we open it, to reverently recall that God is speaking to me. And we've long since learned that there is no exigency, no emergency that can possibly come to our lives of which this Book does not speak, and for which this book does not give direction. It is thy word. We handle it as such, reverently. WE ASK THE ASSISTANCE OF THE HOLY SPIRIT, WHO INSPIRED HOLY MEN TO WRITE AS WE UNDERTAKE TO SPEAK AND THINK. CONDITION OUR HEARTS TO HEAR WHAT GOD THE LORD WOULD SPEAK. Amen.

The Bible is
God's letter to YOU!

FELLOWSHIP WITH GOD

Send us out, our Heavenly Father, with a steadier confidence in Thy Word, that it will fulfill our faith more than we have ever had. Thou art not working behind the clouds, Thou are working here on earth. All this Thou hast been doing is for the purpose of bringing to man, ultimately all that he has ever dreamed or hoped for.

And once again we pray Thou wilt give us the good sense, not only to come into fellowship with Thee but . . . to make it our supreme business to stay in fellowship with Thee until the time when we shall know, when the cry shall be heard, *"Behold, He cometh."* And Thy Word says, *"They who are ready shall go in,"* and *"They who are ready shall go in with Him."* Help us to make it our first business to be ready. In His name we ask it. Amen.

EXPERIENCE GOD

Oh Lord, we thank thee that such a possibility lies within our reach. We human beings, living in this mundane today, may experience God, and walk with Him and talk with Him, and fellowship Him day by day. And we know, as commented one in the long ago, we were built for this and the heart of us will never experience a moment's satisfaction until we experience what we were built for. For Jesus' sake, we pray. Amen.

FOLLOW ME

What is this and that to what the other one does . . . FOLLOW ME . . . Thou are saying that to each one of us. When we become aware that we are so committed to God, and He pays attention to us as individuals, then will we come into the bold knowledge of this uttermost salvation of thine. This amazing gift which thou hast offered to each one of us. SAVE US FROM PRESUMING THAT WE AS A CHRISTIAN ARE OUT TO SELL SOMEBODY SOMETHING. WE'RE NOT SALESMAN, WE ARE LABORERS TOGETHER WITH GOD. OH GOD MAKE VERY CLEAR TO THE HEART OF US THAT WE WERE BUILT FOR THEE. To this end thou hast offered us the free gift of the fellowship in the family of God, Amen.

BUILDING A LIFE

Oh Lord, if put to serious choice we'd rather have fellowship with thee than all the world has to offer and we mean that. We mean it because it has dawned on us long since that THERE IS BUT A SHORT DAY IN WHICH TO LIVE . And I CAN ILL AFFORD TO GIVE MY UNDIVIDED ATTENTION TO THE BUSINESS OF MAKING A LIVING. I must find a place somewhere to enter God's workshop and COOPERATE WITH HIM WHILE HE MAKES FOR ME A LIFE, an enduring life. Sad, sad in the extreme, that the day in which we have to build a life has devoted itself so almost unreservedly to the business of making a living that we can hardly find time to foundation our lives to these abiding things that endure.

May thy word come to us with new force and new meaning, not because the preacher has eloquently put into words. Speak to us infinitely deeper so that we'll hear Him say, *"It is my meat and drink to do the Father's will."* Possess us with such passion as can truthfully testify, *"the zeal of thine house is the controlling passion of my life."* Bless these dear young people. Give them a vision of these eternal things as shall be abiding. Spoil them for cheap content. Create in them an ambition to be rated double AA by God instead of by Dun & Bradstreet, important as it may be. Help us that these really important matters may take precedent. Amen.

NEW DAY

Life has been made glorious because of thy manifested presence. We glory in the fact that God leads on, ultimate triumph will be the result of all His planning and thought and power. A new day shall dawn. A new day when the earth shall be flooded with light as the waters cover the sea. When righteousness shall prevail. When thy best thoughts will be more than words to us. When thy plan shall be fully consummated. We'll have no need then to say the one to the other . . . *"Knowest thou the Lord"* . . . *for all shall know Him . . . from the least to the greatest."* When we shall sit once again under the vine and fig tree of thy creation. When each of us shall experience a life for which we were built. We feel the surge of this life within us. We have believed on thy Son, and to believe on Him is to have life eternal. We know that to be true. It is not a creed, it is not a doctrine, it is not a mere empty saying with some of us. In His name, we pray. Amen.

GOD KNOWS US INDIVIDUALLY

For the multitude of mercies which have attended our lives during the week agone, we are grateful. Each one of these mercies reminds us again of thy care and thy concern. Our lives are not one of a great mass, we are individuals with thee. So individual are we that thou hast said, *"the hairs of our head are numbered."* Thou knowest our down sittings and our uprisings. The simplest things we do have thine attention. Thou knowest our comings and our goings. Our secret thoughts are revealed to thee. Lo, thou art with us day by day and night unto night. Those of us who have made our fellowship with thee see thee everywhere, in everything. Nothing HAPPENS to us, all things come to pass in thy purpose. Each of us have our niche to fill. A definite task assigned to us by God. The accomplishment of this task is our life's ambition. The fact is, we have no business but thy business.

It is impossible for us to escape thy notice and one day we are aware thou wouldst reckon with us as individuals. Then shall we receive, we are told, according to that which we have done, whether it be good, or whether it be bad. There are no indifferent things with Thee. It is impossible for any of us to remain neutral. Thou has warned us, he that gathereth not with Thee, scattereth abroad. It is not a question of a choice between this and that, it is a question of actual participation with God in His ultimate purpose. Or a question of being the enemy of God. And as far as we are concerned the frustration of His purpose. Amen.

SPIRITUAL REGENERATION

Christ is asking me and asking you, show me your heart. Give to the heart of me, Oh God and to the heart of all of us the sense, burning sense, of the urgent necessity of spiritual regeneration that will so change us at the source of our being, that we shall from this day forward be controlled by the operation of the Holy Spirit indwelling. Amen.

> What you are is Spirit,
> and can never die!

GOD IS THE MIRACLE OF LIGHT IN DARKNESS

Our Heavenly Father, the heart of us is full of praise to thy great and excellent name. That thy mercy endures forever, we are the witness. Goodness and mercy have followed us all the days of our lives. In retrospective view, we find God constantly in the shadows keeping watch above his own. Help us above all things to remind ourselves that it is ours through Jesus Christ to always have a victorious faith. Thou hast not left us to ourselves to become victims of circumstances and crises. We have more than ability to endure or to spend our days whistling through the dark. THOU DIDST BRING TO US THE MIRACLE OF LIGHT IN DARKNESS. Out there in the world they may stumble and grope and fumble and bungle, but it is given to us thy people, to walk in the light. Today we have as many problems as there are individuals. God's word to us is, *"the steps of good men are ordered by the Lord."* Thou dost direct thy people in their goings. Amen.

THE HOLY SPIRIT AND FIRE

Oh God we thank thee once again that this Word of Thine, it calls us very drastically to heroic decision. We thank thee for the privilege of knowing what Elijah meant when he said, *"The God who answers by fire, let him be God."* Of the Christ it is said, *"He shall baptize you with the Holy Ghost and fire."* We have found him true to His word.

May the heart of these young people be so stirred by meditating on this Word of Thine that they will never, never, never, think of any decision but the decision to worship the God, to serve the God, to devote themselves wholly to the God who answers by fire.

May thy great grace and amazing love and the communion and the fellowship of the Holy Spirit, so real to some of us, abide in our hearts tonight, tomorrow, day after tomorrow, and to the outer most rim of the eternal. Amen.

GOD is saying "I LOVE YOU"
to the whole human race.

ETERNITY

Our profoundest pity goes out to men and women whose lives are blinded, who try to live, and serve, and work, and love, in this immediate present. Thou hast set eternity in our hearts. We are built for two worlds. It is impossible for any of us to live within the narrow confines of this immediate materialistic present. We were not built for fifty years, but for fifty million. In Jesus' name, we pray. Amen.

KEEPING IN TOUCH WITH THEE

O Lord, We thank thee for these words of thine, they are searching, they are probing, they find us out, they unravel us. In their light we stand stripped of all pretense, all sham, all professions. Naked and open for what we are. Help us as Christian men and Christian women, to incorporate, to so incorporate this truth of thine that we shall not be particular about hobnobbing with this present, for it is a passing present. WE SHALL BE PARTICULAR, VERY PARTICULAR, ABOUT KEEPING IN TOUCH WITH THINGS INFINITE. In His name, we pray. Amen.

SPIRITUAL VISTA

We thank thee for these words of Thine, Lord. These assurances, and they are so numerous. When we are born again, when we are supernaturally regenerated, and become a Christian, thou dost open to us a whole new vista. Eternal years but glow and glitter as filled with rare promises as the sky is filled with stars. Oh God, grant to me, and grant to all of us that the heart of us shall be so involved with God, we shall have no misgivings. We'll begin at long last to say what we mean, and mean what we say and sing. With the Apostle Paul, we shall be enabled to say, *"For me to live is Christ, not money, not fame, nor getting ahead, nor finding my place in the sun. For me to live is Christ. Then to die is gain."* And it isn't such a fearsome thing, to exchange mud pies, for a gold mine. For Jesus' sake, we pray. Amen.

BENEFITS

IF, only all people would pray daily we would have a different loving world.

IF, all men's hearts were Christ-centered we would have NO more wars. Brotherly love would blanket the Earth.

IF, we taught TRUE BIOLOGY in our schools the child would learn there is a Spiritual Kingdom which is the guide to the Highest and Best life known to mankind.

The Spiritual Realm is the only place that I know of where morals, goodness, character and the generous qualities are taught.

LIFE

When man understands that the aim of life is not material profit but life itself, he ceases to fix his attention on the external world. He considers more attentively his own existence and the existence of those around him. He realizes that he depends on others and that others depend on him. Just as your physical body needs oxygen, water and food . . . your soul needs spiritual food.

What good is all our technical progress if it doesn't make us happier and better people? The truth is we have neglected the science of life and have done nothing to improve the soul of mankind. We are unhappy, we are degenerating morally. It's past time to improve ourselves. The only possible remedy for this evil is a much more profound knowledge of ourselves. In the past 100 years we have lost the art of tracing an effect to the prime first cause, that is why we never get anything fixed. We also have lost the art of developing our spiritual dimensions. We rarely pray and we rarely help our fellowman. Crass materialism, sheer greed, has blinded our common sense and goodness. Some have both hands full of money yet are miserable.

We are the victims of things not worth-while. It is past time to return to our true nature, that thrives on the things worth-while. Our VALUES help us to enjoy our spiritual development and the blessings of our beneficial Spiritual activities. We need food for our soul just as much as we need air and water. We need the INNER JOY and BLESSINGS of GOD. We need to learn to pray and to grow happy!

CHAPTER SEVENTEEN

WORTH REMEMBERING AND REPEATING

GOODNESS
Let the words of my mouth and the meditatian of my heart, be acceptable in thy sight, O LORD, my strength, and my redeemer.
— Psalm 19:14

GOD
God is God, whether we believe in him or not . . . Whether we serve HIM or not. We need to worship GOD. Our humanness depends upon it. It is not God who suffers when we do not worship . . . it is WE WHO SUFFER! *— Richard C. Halverson*

IF YOU ARE WISE . . . BE MERRY
A merry heart doeth good like a medicine . . . But a broken spirit drieth the bones. *— Proverbs 17:22*

CHARACTER
Character is something each one of us must build for himself, out of the laws of God and Nature, the examples of others, and most of all . . . out of the trials and errors of daily life. Character is the total of thousands of small daily strivings to live up to the best that is in us.
— Lt. General A. G. Trudeau

ETERNAL
Jesus Christ the same yesterday, and to day, and for ever.
— Hebrews 13:8

EVER INCREASING FAITH
Form the life-long habit of carrying a New Testament or some portion of Scripture in your pocket. The BIBLE . . . the WORD OF GOD, is our DEPENDABLE GUIDE and GREAT COMFORTER on Life's Journey.
— Frederick K. C. Price

INNER MAN
What lies behind us and what lies before us are small matters compared to what lies within us. *— Ralph Waldo Emerson*

TIME . . .
An earthly trust which if invested wisely, will produce eternal treasures.
"So teach us to number our days, that we may apply our hearts unto wisdom."

— Psalm 90:12

CHEERFUL
A cheerful friend is like a sunny day, which sheds its brightness on all around; and most of us can, as we choose, make of this world either a palace . . . or a prison. — *John Lubbock*

FUTURE
Don't let the FUTURE scare you. It will be just as shaky as you are. *"According to your FAITH . . . be it unto you."*
— *Matthew 9:29*

SELF-DEVELOPMENT
Unfortunately, governments cannot legislate decency or integrity or goodness. Each individual must develop this power within himself. Man is raw and wild and it takes the Spiritual Development to temper his nature and to make him a whole person. We overlook the natural fact that we are here primarily to overcome the weakness of our own character. — *Personal Planning Manual*

FAITH
"Pray for a good harvest . . . BUT keep on plowing and planting."
— *Old Adage*. Here you have two forces working . . . The Spiritual Forces of the HIGHER POWER . . . GOD . . . plus the Natural Forces and Skills of Man. This is the unbeatable combination. GOD works through MEN . . . always has . . . always will. — *Distilled Wisdom*

SPIRIT
I believe that man will not merely endure, he will prevail. He is immortal, not because he alone among creatures has an inexhaustible voice, but because he has a soul, a spirit capable of compassion and sacrifice and endurance. — *William Faulkner*

THE SUPREME POWER
We are in the presence of an Infinite Power . . . God. The eternal element in man is SPIRIT. It is through Prayer the Spirit of man connects up to God, the Holy Spirit. God has given man all the faculties, and responsibility for man to use his efforts to become the best that he can be.
— *The Supreme Philosophy of Man*

THE WHOLE BALL OF WAX
This book distills the lessons I have learned in more than sixty years of observation, experience, personal study, triumph and failure.
— *Alfred A. Montapert*

"Jesus is Lord!" — *E. Stanley Jones*

BELIEF
A man without solid beliefs is a man who merely Exists, not Lives. To put MORE LIFE into your LIVING you have to develop HEALTHY BELIEFS . . . To chart your course through LIFE.

— Inspiration & Motivation

LIMITS
Man is great or small in the way he limits himself, by his PERSONAL BELIEF. Man limits God, by his FAITH IN GOD.

— Distilled Wisdom

RESULT
Before every action ask yourself . . . Will this bring more monkeys on my back? Will the result of my action be a Blessing or a Heavy Burden?

— Alfred A. Montapert

HUMANITY is never so beautiful as when praying for forgiveness, or else forgiving another. *— Jean Paul Richter*

WISHFUL THINKING
Be not angry . . . that you cannot make OTHERS as you wish them to be . . . since you cannot even make YOURSELF as you wish to be.

— Thomas a Kempis

CAUSE AND EFFECT
Things don't just happen. They come to pass by our own . . . Thoughts . . . Actions . . . Deeds. *— Inspiration & Motivation*

GOD'S POWER
Study to obey GOD'S WORD in everything and keep in HIS WILL and HIS WAY. This is your DUTY and your WISDOM. This is the TRUTH and the SECRET of genuine JOY and SOLID PEACE within. *"I am the WAY, the TRUTH, and the LIFE."* *— The Way To Happiness*

SILENCE
Speaking dilutes your thinking. Keep silent and concentrate in order to get your most sublime ideas. Be SILENT until finally you begin to hear what the silence tells you. The small voice of silence often contains the greatest wisdom. To DREAM . . . to THINK . . . to KNOW . . . that is everything. *— Alfred A. Montapert*

HUMAN NATURE
Our problem is NOT the Atomic Power . . . it is the NATURE of the men who discovered it . . . and the NATURE of those who will use it.

— Alfred A. Montapert

FAMILY
When youngsters get into serious trouble, it is generally the parents
who are delinquent, not the children. If you will look a little deeper,
when some unpleasant incident occurs, you'll find that there's usually
something wrong in the domestic menage. In too many cases, the
parents are the ones who are in trouble and the parents are the ones
who need help.   — *Walt Disney*

THE POWER OF LAUGHTER
Few people realize that health actually varies according to the amount of
laughter. People who laugh actually live longer than those who don't
laugh.   — *Dr. James J. Walsh*

WORKING IN GOD'S VINEYARD
We live a simple happy life . . . and take God into everything we do.
We work on our books every day and enjoy creative work and even take
our work with us when we go on a vacation. Of course, it is just a fine
line and really hard to tell whether we are working or on a vacation.
                                    — *Alfred & Evelyn Montapert*

TODAY'S WORLD
There is no need to lament the modern world. The TODAY it offers is
the only one we have and we must learn to make the most of it. We
must learn TO LIVE with the problems and absurdities that we now
face; even use them to make a good living for ourselves and our families.
                                        — *William D. Montapert*

GLAD DAY
*This is the day which the Lord hath made; we will rejoice and be glad in
it.*   — *Psalm 118:24*

REAL WEALTH
True wealth is what we become as persons . . . what we are. What we
possess is outside of us. WHAT WE ARE is an inner condition better
than money. God gave everyone a bundle of gifts, and we are to
develop these human resources, for that is where our real wealth lies.
Goodness, Character, Confidence, are the generous qualities. FOR TO
BUILD A MAN OR WOMAN IS LIFE'S GREATEST PROJECT . . .
FOR EACH OF US!
                                — *The Supreme Philosophy of Man*

POISE
What happens to YOU and around YOU is not nearly as important . . .
as HOW YOU REACT to what happens to you and around you . . . HE
WHO MAINTAINS HIS CENTER ENDURES.
                                          — *Louis Charbonneau*

GENIUS VS. INTEGRITY

Far more important than what a man achieves is WHAT HE IS. Men of genius are not nearly as important to civilization as men of GOOD-NESS. What men ARE is what makes them superior or inferior. It frequently happens that great intellectual ability is a curse because it is NOT accompanied by great INTEGRITY.

— Alfred A. Montapert

TRAGEDY

There are NO tragedies . . . Just FACTS NOT RECOGNIZED IN TIME. *— William D. Montapert*

EVIDENCE

Upon every face is written the record of the life the man has led; the prayers, the aspirations, the disappointments, all he hoped to be and was not . . . all are written there, nothing is hidden, nor indeed can be.

— Elbert Hubbard

SACRIFICE

On the Cross of Calvary, Christ gave His life to redeem the world. The life of Christ was a life of sacrifice. The life of a Christian must be a life of sacrifice. We can imitate the sacrifice of Christ on Calvary . . . by trying to give all we can.

— Genevieve W. Sampson

YOUR RECORD

No matter what else you are doing,
    From cradle days through to the end,
You're writing your life's secret story . . .
    Each night sees another page penned.
Each month ends a thirty-page chapter,
    Each year means the end of a part,
And never an act is misstated
    Nor ever one wish of the heart.

Each day when you wake, the book opens,
    Revealing a page clean and white.
What thoughts and what words and what doings
    Will cover its surface by night?
God leaves that to you . . . you're the writer,
    And never one word shall grow dim,
Till someday you write the word "Finis,"
    And give back your life book to Him.

— Wallace Dunbar Vincent

CHRISTIANITY
Christianity is NOT a doctrine. It is not a creed that we commit and live by rule and rote. CHRISTIANITY IS A WAY OF LIFE. "FOLLOW ME" is the command.
— John L. Smart

THE GIFT OF LOVE
Our love is the greatest gift we can give one another.
> "A bell is not a bell till you ring it.
> A song is not a song till you sing it.
> Love in your heart is not put there to stay.
> Love is not yours . . . till you give it away."
— Oscar Hammerstein

LIFE
For when the One Great Scorer comes
To write against your name,
He marks . . . not that you won or lost . . .
But how you played the game.
— Grantland Rice

GRADUATE
There is more to graduating than getting a diploma . . . you have to be able to cope with LIFE, too!
— Alfred A. Montapert

UNPARDONABLE
The UNPARDONABLE SIN is to shut God out of your life.
— Inspiration & Motivation

PRAYER
It isn't the words that we utter in prayer that count . . . it is the FAITH which the heart of us exercises that gets results.
— The Way To Happiness

RESPONSIBILITY
God gives us three score and ten years . . . All over is PROFIT . . . IF we don't "Screw Up" or "Burn Out".
— Words of Wisdom To Live By

EXPECTANCY
Whatever other habits we form, let us form the habit of expectancy. An expectant frame of mind attracts what we expect. Expectancy is prayer at its best. *"What things soever ye desire, when ye pray, believe that ye receive them, and ye shall have them,"* said Jesus Christ. And He never opened a more clear road to God's abundance.
— Alfred A. Montapert

HUMAN NATURE
Our basic conflict is between man and himself.

— Distilled Wisdom

THE TRUE JOY OF LIFE
Is being used for a PURPOSE that is only mine to fulfill. A PURPOSE which I recognize and BELIEVE to be a mighty one. To give my best and be truly used in doing some good. My greatest passion is to be a creative force of Nature. I must do my noblest and walk hand in hand with God into the future . . . into the forever. This is my duty for the Gift of Life.

— Personal Planning Manual

BIBLE
The truth taught by the Bible is the right way to live. Apart from the LIFE and TEACHINGS of JESUS, life becomes an inexplicable mystery. No marvel, then, that men who reject JESUS CHRIST find life "not worth living."

— Distilled Wisdom

UNIVERSE
Let shallow minds reject and ridicule as they may, the fact remains that there is NO explanation of the universe, nor of man, apart from the creative genius of GOD. Remove GOD from the scene and there is neither sense nor reason in the UNIVERSE. Remove MAN and there is neither sense nor reason in CREATION.

— Alfred A. Montapert

CHRISTIANITY
Christianity is a Power, a Spirit, a Person. It is not a philosophy, not a doctrine, not a creed. Christianity is a Person. It is Christ. *"Christ in you,"* said the Apostle Paul, *"is the hope of glory."* When the hard moment comes to die, you need a Person. No man can face the future courageously without the awareness of HIS Presence.

— The Supreme Philosophy of Man

HEALING
"Attend to My Words, incline thine ear to My sayings for they are LIFE . . . " GOD'S WORD is GOD'S MEDICINE. God heals by HIS WORD. FAITH comes by hearing, and hearing by the WORD OF GOD. According to your FAITH be it done unto you!

— Alfred A. Montapert

LOVE IS ETERNAL
The man or woman you really love will never grow old to you. Through the wrinkles of time, through the bowed frame of years, you will always see the dear face and feel the warm heart union of your eternal love.
— *Alfred A. Montapert*

CONTENT
Happiness and contentment are not commodities which we import; neither do they depend upon "the abundance of things" which we possess. It is not where we are, what we have, or what we possess, that makes us happy or unhappy. WHAT WE ARE determines our state. A very poor man can be immensely wealthy, and a very rich man can be abjectly miserable. The most blessed kind of happiness is a state of basic contentment. St. Paul said, "*in whatsoever state I am, therewith to be content.*"
— *The Supreme Philosophy of Man*

SECRET LOVE
There is a name
Hidden in the shadow
Of my soul,
Where I read it
Night and day
And no other eye
Sees it.
— *Lamartine*

WORK
Thank God every morning when you get up that you have something to do that day which must be done, whether you like it or not. Being forced to work and forced to do your best will breed in you temperance and self-control, diligence and strength of will, cheerfulness, and content, and a hundred virtues which the idle will never know.
— *Charles Kingsley*

WRITER
To the thousands of students who wrote to a famous writer asking how to become a writer . . . here is the reply: "Solitude and Prayer . . . then go on from there."
— *Carl Sandburg*

LIFE
An important thing in life is to act according to your conscience. I place my money and my actions where my heart is.
— *Jacques Cousteau*

THE WORD OF GOD
My people are destroyed by lack of knowledge of the Word of God.
— *Hosea 4:6*

LOVE
Love is demonstration . . . NOT declaration.
— *The Way to Happiness*

THE LAWS OF GOD
. . . are unseen forces which pervade and govern the UNIVERSE and all therein. They are never fully defined . . . only EXPERIENCED!
— *Alfred A. Montapert*

SUCCESS . . . in its broadest definition . . . OBEY GOD!
— *Personal Planning Manual*

BIBLE
There is no EMERGENCY or NEED that can possibly come into our lives for which the BIBLE does not give DIRECTIONS.
— *Inspiration & Motivation*

PURPOSEFUL LIVING
What is the use of living if it be not to strive for noble causes and to make this muddled world a better place to live in after we are gone.
— *Winston Churchill*

OBSERVATION AND EXPERIENCE
See everything . . . Overlook a great deal . . . Correct a little.
— *Pope John XXIII*

THOUGHTS
Nothing is more important to YOU than this: YOU . . . are the sole master of your Thought Process! *"As a man thinketh in his HEART so is he."* This is a Law as real as The Law of Gravity.
— *Personal Planning Manual*

SELF-DISCIPLINE
The control of the sexual desire is one of the greatest factors in determining a person's success.   — *Alfred A. Montapert*

FAME
The constant pursuit of success and fame can eat up your whole life. Most celebrities come to believe that they are more important than they really are. It is destructive to a person's existence.
— *Albert Musso*

WHAT YOU ARE

Remember that WHAT YOU POSSESS in the world . . . will be found at the day of your death to belong to someone else, but WHAT YOU ARE will be yours forever. — *Henry Van Dyke*

WATCH YOUR WORDS

"LIFE and DEATH are in the power of the tongue." — *Proverbs 18:21*. The words of YOUR MOUTH can be YOUR FRIEND or YOUR ENEMY. You get what you ORDER! — *Alfred A. Montapert*

SAFEGUARD

The greatest safeguard to this nation or any other nation, is the teaching of THE WORD OF GOD. REAL SECURITY IS HAVING A SENSE OF GOD. A PERSON CAN NO MORE BUILD A LIFE WITHOUT SOLID BELIEFS AND IDEALS THAN HE CAN BUILD A BUILD-ING WITHOUT A SOLID FOUNDATION.

— *Inspiration & Motivation*

PRAYER

Prayer is a force as real as terrestrial gravity. As a physician, I have seen men, after all other therapy had failed, lifted out of disease and melancholy by the serene effort of prayer. Only in prayer do we achieve that complete and harmonious assembly of body, mind and spirit which gives the frail human reed its unshakable strength.

— *Dr. Alexis Carrel*

LIFE

The longer I live the more beautiful life becomes.

— *Frank Lloyd Wright*

PRAYER is the contemplation of the facts of life from the highest point of view. It is the soliloquy of a beholding and jubilant soul. It is the spirit of God pronouncing his works good.

— *Ralph Waldo Emerson*

NATURE'S LAWS

We know there is a Higher Power greater than we are. We see it every day in the daily law and order of the sun, the stars, the constellations, Nature and Nature's Laws. Man lives in Nature's Laws as fish live in water. This is the secret of the wise. Nature is the handiwork of God.

— *The Supreme Philosophy of Man*

NATURE

In Nature, we recognize an infinite power. — *Goethe*

I PRAY thee, O God, that I may be beautiful within.   — *Socrates*

DYNAMIC FAITH

FAITH IS THE WHOLE ESSENCE... THE HEART OF THE BIBLE. FAITH is produced by knowledge and use of GOD'S WORD. FAITH is to BELIEVE and ACT according to GOD'S WORD. FAITH IS BELIEVING BEFORE RECEIVING. FAITH is a life-style... God's Way of Living. You limit GOD'S POWER in your life by your FAITH. A Victorious Life depends upon YOUR FAITH!

— *Distilled Wisdom*

LIFE

"I am come that you may have life." — *Jesus.* Not a philosophy about life, not a set of do's and don'ts: *"I am come that they might have life."* This is His entire Gospel in epitome. Everything He did and said centers here.

— *The Way To Happiness*

FAITH UNLIMITED

What I am able to do is UNLIMITED. Is there anything too hard for God? The answer is NO, provided you can find a heart in cooperation with Him. The only thing that puts restriction on Him and His ability to do is our lack of FAITH: *"According to your FAITH be it done unto you."* Little faith... little results. Big FAITH... results unlimited.

— *Alfred A. Montapert*

FAITH

MIGHTY FAITH makes the heart full of the POWER OF GOD. The heart knows for CERTAIN that there is... *"Nothing impossible to him that BELIEVETH."* Great FAITH, like muscles, develop with use.

— *The Supreme Philosophy of Man*

PATIENCE is the Companion of Wisdom.   — *St. Augustine*

HELP

I will lift up mine eyes unto the hills, from whence cometh my help. My help cometh from the Lord, which made heaven and earth.

— *Psalm 121:1,2*

PROSPERITY

The old saying was KNOWLEDGE IS POWER. Today it has changed to MONEY IS POWER. So the bottom line is... MONEY IS MATERIAL PROSPERITY... JOY IS SPIRITUAL PROSPERITY. To have both is the unbeatable combination, the ULTIMATE.

— *Alfred A. Montapert*

POWER OF PRAYER
One of the most effective means of substituting positive conscious thoughts for the negative "emotional thinking" which destroys us, is prayer.

— *Walter M. Germain*

POWER OF PRAYER
One of the most important things to get across to the modern world is an understanding of the power of prayer. Prayer is thought contact with the Holy Spirit. It is the greatest power in the world.

— *Cecil B. DeMille*

PRAYER joins the finite (man) with the infinite (God) and makes the finite man omnipotent. The mysteries in this realm I don't pretend to know. What I do know is, that prayer releases a mysterious force that sets in motion omnipotent forces. He is a fool who tries to live in a world like this without prayer.

— *Distilled Wisdom*

BLESSING
May the Light of Heaven shine through each day, To warm your life and show The Way.

— *The Way To Happiness*

WHAT man is before God, that he is and no more.

— *St. Francis of Assisi*

LAWS OF LIFE
Everyone in the Universe . . . as well as the Universe itself, including the Constellations, Nature, and every Beast and Fowl, and every form of life including Man . . . is governed by Nature's Laws. Man lives in Law as fish live in water. To know and obey is the secret of the wise.

— *Alfred A. Montapert*

WE should pray for:
Health enough to make work a pleasure; Strength enough to battle with difficulties and overcome them; Patience enough to toil until the most worth-while good is accomplished; Love enough to make them most useful to others; Faith enough to make real the things of God; And hope enough to remove all anxieties concerning the future.

— *Goethe*

THE only basic principle of authority in the American nation is GOD.

— *H.R. Luce*

THE HIGHER POWER
"I can do all things through Christ which strengtheneth me."
— *Philippians 4:13*. We thank you, our Father, for a Gospel such as this. We have hold of the greatest force in the universe for mankind.

— *Distilled Wisdom*

HOW BIG IS YOUR GOD?
How free we are to exalt ourselves entirely above the Infinite God, aren't we? Most of us can't handle the simple affairs of our lives. And yet we claim the prerogative of ordering all the affairs of all men, for all time. How easily we toss it off our tongue! Some talk against God like they knew more than God.

— *Inspiration & Motivatian*

GOD DIRECTS
"In all thy ways acknowledge Him, and He shall direct thy paths."
— *Proverbs 3:6*. There is no such thing as highest and best living . . . only as we walk on the level of God's thinking, and God's saying. It is not in ANY man to direct his own way. If we keep up the egotistical assumption that we are wholly sufficient unto ourselves, we end up bankrupt.

— *The Supreme Philosophy of Man*

VALUES
God's *"Well done!"* is more important to me than the passing approbation of men who themselves have never known the true meaning of life.

— *Alfred A. Montapert*

ALL men instinctively pray. — *Rex*

ONE prays as one loves, with one's whole being.

— *Alexis Carrel*

PRESENT CONDITIONS
God have mercy on a world so ignorant of essential truth. Going blythfully on their way. Alas, to stumble over the precipice into outer darkness. Oh God, have mercy on the world. So full of men and women who have their own plans, so they think, and are bent on their own way, so they think. Thoughtless of the truth that their neglect of God will finally catch up. Oh God, save us from the utter folly of presuming that we can go into head-on collision with these inexorable laws of right without coming to tragedy.

— *A. P. Gouthey*

LET the Divine Mind flow through your own mind, and you will be happier. I have found the greatest power in the world is the power of prayer. There is no shadow of doubt of that. I speak from my own experience.

— *Cecil B. DeMille*

PRAYER covers the whole of a man's life. There is no thought, feeling, yearning, or desire, however low, trifling, or vulgar we may deem it, which, if it affects our real interest or happiness, we may not lay before God and be sure of sympathy. His nature is such that our often coming does not tire him. The whole burden of the whole life of every man may be rolled on to God and not weary him, though it has wearied the man.

— *Henry Ward Beecher*

THE very act of prayer honors God and gives glory to God, for it confesses that God is what he is.

— *Charles Kingsley*

SPREAD out your petition before God, and then say, "Thy will, not mine, be done." The sweetest lesson I have learned in God's school is to let the Lord choose for me.

— *Dwight L. Moody*

PRAYER is conversation with God.   — *Clement of Alexandria*

TELL God all that is in your heart, as one unloads one's heart to a dear friend. People who have no secrets from each other never want for subjects of conversation; they do not weigh their words, because there is nothing to be kept back. Neither do they seek for something to say; they talk out of the abundance of their hearts, just what they think. Blessed are they who attain to such familiar, unreserved intercourse with God.

— *Francois de la Mothe Fenelon*

PRAYER is the highest use to which speech can be put.

— *P. T. Forsyth*

IN the physical world releasing the greatest power would be Atomic energy. In the spiritual world releasing man's greatest power would be PRAYER. Releasing life's greatest potential . . . PRAYER.

Jesus said:
"Come unto me, all ye that labour and are heavy laden, and I will give you rest. Take my yoke upon you, and learn of me; for I am meek and lowly in heart and ye shall find rest unto your souls."

— *Matthew 11:28*

DON'T expect a thousand-dollar answer to a ten cent prayer.

— *Sunshine Magazine*

"If ye abide in me, and my words abide in you, ye shall ask what ye will, and it shall be done unto you." — *John 15:7*

EVERY man wants to pray the day before he dies. As he does not know when his time will come, he must pray every day in order to be safe.

— *Jewish Proverb*

LORD, make me wiser every year, and better every day.

— *Charles Lamb*

I HAVE been driven many times to my knees by the overwhelming conviction that I had nowhere else to go. — *Abraham Lincoln*

THE spectacle of a nation praying is more awe-inspiring than the explosion of an atomic bomb. The force of prayer is greater than any possible combination of man-controlled powers, because prayer is man's greatest means of trapping the infinite resources of God.

— *J. Edgar Hoover*

CERTAIN thoughts are prayers. There are moments when, whatever be the attitude of the body, the soul is on its knees.

— *Victor Hugo*

PRAYER is the opening of the heart to God as to a friend. Not that it is necessary, in order to make known to God what we are, but in order to enable us to receive Him. Prayer does not bring God down to us, but brings us up to Him. — *Ellen G. White*

PRAYER, is talking to God. MEDITATION, is listening for his answer.

MIGHTY FAITH makes the heart full of the POWER OF GOD. The heart knows for CERTAIN that there is . . . "Nothing impossible to him that BELIEVETH." Great FAITH, like muscles, develops with use.

— *Frederick K. C. Price*

THE value of Knowledge is measured by the return it generates.

— *Alfred A. Montapert*

EDUCATION
Some day Science will get around to admitting that God is the measure of the Universe, and that man at his best is an elemental and potential measure and revelation of God. Then, for the first time in several thousand years, we shall have education worthy of the name.

— *Alfred A. Montapert*

HE who has learned to pray has learned the greatest secret of a holy and happy life.

— *William Law*

TO be with God, there is no need to be continually in church. We may make an oratory of our heart wherein to retire from time to time to converse with Him in meekness, humility and love. There is not in the world a kind of life more sweet and delightful than that of a continual conversation with God.

— *Brother Lawrence*

WHERE God is concerned the only language open to us is prayer.

— *J.H. Oldham*

IF God is going to do it, it has to be by prayer.

— *Armin Gesswein*

KEEP praying, but be thankful that God's answers are wiser than your prayers!   — *William Culbertson*

IF you don't have faith, pray anyway. If you don't understand or believe the words you are saying, pray anyway. Prayer can start faith, particularly if you pray aloud. And even the most imperfect prayer is an attempt to reach God.   — *Cary Grant*

PRAYER is the mortar that holds our house together.

— *Sister Theresa*

PRAYER should be the key of the day and the lock of the night.

— *George Herbert*

CALL on God, but row away from the rocks.

— *Indian Proverb*

DO not pray for easy lives; pray to be stronger men. Do not pray for tasks equal to your powers; pray for powers equal to your tasks. Then the doing of your work shall be no miracle, but you shall be a miracle.

— *Phillips Brooks*

PRAYER'S real purpose is to put God at the center of our lives.

THE success of any man depends upon his character, motives and ideals.

— *Alfred A. Montapert*

TO LIVE is the rarest thing in the world. Most people exist, that is all.

EVERY human mind has access to the greater mind of God, where wisdom, love, forgiveness, and all the divine attributes abound in limitless measure. It is through prayer that we are quickened with understanding of ourselves, of our fellowman, of the world we live in. Through prayer we learn how to have peace of mind within ourselves and how to have peaceable relations with the persons in the world about us. — *Cleda Reyner*

WHEN you must deal with some frightening or unpleasant situation, you can temper your reactions by employing the technique of prayer.
— *Hazel Joy*

ALL IN GOD'S TIME
A prayer unanswered may be only a delay. The answer is waiting for a future day. — *Diana Rankin*

HE prayeth best who loveth best. — *Samuel Coleridge*

PRAYER can work miracles, but it should not be considered only in terms of miracles. And let us not think that it is concerned solely with spiritual salvation. That is a common error, perhaps the commonest, and if we fall into it we have lost a good part of the meaning that prayer should have for us. It brings us an awareness of God, yes, but also it nourishes the one who prays, both mentally and physically.
— *Mahatma Gandhi*

YOU pray in your distress and in your need; would that you might pray also in the fullness of your joy and in your days of abundance.
— *Kahlil Gibran*

NATURE
We are technological giants... we create space ships, computers, engines and machines. BUT, suffering goes on because the individual has not been taught the mystery of his own nature. WHY SHOULD NOT MAN, WHO HAS CONQUERED ENERGY AND MATTER, ESTABLISH THIS SAME MASTERY OVER HIMSELF?
— *Personal Planning Manual*

PROMISE
But it is written, Eye hath not seen, nor ear heard, neither have entered into the heart of man, the things which God hath prepared for them that love him. — *I Corinthians 2:9*

LOVE produces a certain flowering of the whole personality which nothing else can achieve.

MANY famous people know that they have God to thank for their success.
— *Pat Boone*

VERY few of us have learned how to fully develop the awesome power of prayer.
— *Rev. Billy Graham*

PRAY as if everything depended on God, and work as if everything depended upon man.
— *St. Augustine*

PRAYER is not a substitute for work, it is a desperate effort to work further and to be efficient beyond the range of one's powers.
— *George Santayana*

PRAYER is the guage by which we test the quality of life.
— *Distilled Wisdom*

PRESCRIPTIONS TO WIN . . .
Today, Man's relationship with GOD is wrong, when MANKIND really sees and realizes that they just CANNOT deal with EVIL, GREED and SELFISHNESS in human hearts, they will WAKE UP to find . . . what has really wrecked all their schemes. For from within . . . out of the HEART proceed all GOOD . . . and all EVIL. We must REALIZE how important it is to have our heart filled with the AWESOME POWER OF GOD. Instead of the DESTRUCTIVE POWER of the DEVIL. ONLY GOD HAS THE POWER TO CHANGE THE HEART. Mankind today is dealing with EFFECTS . . . more burglar alarms, more policemen, more laws, more jails. NOT dealing with FIRST CAUSES! . . . GOODNESS and HUMAN BETTERMENT . . . like changing people's hearts so they will act NOBLE, have PRIDE and not do the lowly destructive things. That is why Mankind NEVER gets anything fixed. Herein lies the SAFEGUARD of the INDIVIDUAL and the NATION.
— *Alfred A. Montapert*

IF you are going to soar with the eagles in the morning, you can't hoot with the owls all night.
— *Dail West*

GREED, is one of the most difficult of all human emotions to control, right up there with sex.
— *Personal Planning Manual*

SELF CONTROL
He who reigns within HIMSELF . . . and rules PASSIONS . . . DESIRES and FEARS . . . is more than a KING.
— *Milton*

DOING WRONG
You can fool people . . . but you can't fool your own autonomic nervous system.
— *Dr. Max Levine*

HUMAN nature being as it is, the average person's thoughts turn to God only when he is in some trouble, seriously ill, financially despondent, suffering the loss of a loved one, lost in the mountains, buckling on a life preserver, or worshipping in a church service.

— _Dani Unick_

JUST as a candle cannot burn without a fire, men cannot live without a spiritual life. The spirit dwells in all men, but not all men are aware of this. Happy is the life of him who knows this, and unhappy his life who does not know it.

— _Buddha_

OBSERVATION and experience has taught me that every man must go through the fire. This means that during your lifetime you will experience great suffering or great sorrow, and you will need the help of God to win over your problems.

— _Alfred A. Montapert_

THE Bible tells us how to secure the good things . . . _"Seek ye first the kingdom of God, and his righteousness; and all these things shall be added unto you."_ Can you live according to God's plan for us? Can we place our love for God and our fellowmen first in our hearts? If we can, then good things are in store for us.

— _Grenville Kleiser_

MAN'S true aim is to glorify God and enjoy Him forever.

— _Westminster Catechism_

ALL purely human ideas of God are necessarily imperfect. Our ideas are qualified and limited by what we have seen and known. He is the way of life that we were created to live. With Him life has meaning; without Him men exist in a meaningless discord.

— _A. P. Gouthey_

MODERN society has committed the fundamental error of disobeying the law of spiritual development. It has arbitrarily reduced spirit to mere intellect. It has cultivated the intellect because, thanks to science, the intellect gives it mastery of the physical world, but has ignored those other activities of the spirit which can never be more than partially represented in scientific language and which are only expressed in action, art and prayer.

— _Alexis Carrel_

ACT
Put feet on your prayers. If the widow needs food, pray for her, then go
and buy her two bags of groceries. — *Alfred A. Montapert*

FAITH
Why pray if you have no FAITH? In true prayer it is the FAITH, the
BELIEF that the heart exercises that brings results.

WISDOM
All knowledge exists only that man shall discover his own Divine
Nature. — *Plato*

MY OBSERVATION
Man kills himself by his "WAY OF LIFE". I can give you examples and
names of the individuals, who like Absalom in the Bible, died like a
fool. — *Inspiration & Motivation*

PRAYER
More things are wrought by prayer . . . than this world dreams of.
— *Alfred Lord Tennyson*

PRAYER is the power on earth that commands the power in heaven.

IN VAIN WE BUILD
We are blind until we see,
That in the human plan
Nothing is worth the making if
It does not make the man.
Why build these cities glorious
If man unbuilded goes?
In vain we build the world, unless
The builder also grows.

— *Edwin Markham*

INFINITE POWER
Among the mysteries which become more mysterious the more they are
thought about, there will remain the one absolute certainty that we are
ever in the presence of an Infinite Power from which all things proceed.
— *Herbert Spencer*
World's Great Scientist

MOTIVATION
The most impelling urge in our life should be our motivation and drive
to self-fulfillment and self-realization. To be and do our BEST.
— *Personal Planning Manual*

CHAPTER EIGHTEEN

HOW PRAYER HELPS ME

SUCCESS THROUGH GOD'S HELP

I have never for a minute believed that any success of mine could have been attained without God's help, nor have I ever embarked on any undertaking without asking His help. I would feel very lonely indeed if I didn't know He was within the sound of my voice.

— *President Ronald Reagan*

PRAY EVERY DAY

I am proud to say that I pray every day. Our Forefathers who founded this country, prayed . . . and if we want to keep our wonderful country free from the darkness that threatens us, we'd better all pray . . . and pray hard.

— *Roy Rogers*

PRAY FOR, AND PROTECT, PEACE

In the Great Tomorrow men shall learn that to give abundantly is the only way to reap abundantly. The super-man of Tomorrow's history shall be he who is the servant of all.

— *R.S. Reynolds*

THE VALUE OF PRAYER TO ME

When Abraham Lincoln left his home town of Springfield Illinois, for Washington, to become President of the United States, he asked but one thing of those old and tried Springfield friends who went to the station to see him off . . . "Pray for me". Perhaps the most we should ask of God when we pray is for His help in living our lives in such a way that we will deserve the best He has to offer. Today our nation and our world are in a very grave condition. Never was there a time . . . and our country has faced many a crisis . . . when universal prayer was more badly needed. Prayer is powerful.

— *Johnston Murray*

GOD'S POWER AT YOUR COMMAND

Prayer is as needful in our lives as the air we breathe. No matter what the circumstances, it is a pillar of strength. It helps to solve the problems where education, science, technology and skill fail. It lightens the burden of grief. It becomes the means of expressing to Divine Providence the gratitude of a happy heart.

— Harvey S. Firestone, Jr.

PSALM OF THANKSGIVING

We rarely ever pray, truly pray, until we are in peril. A tight place is the shrine where we plead our plight. That's what David is saying . . . *"In my distress I called upon the Lord, and cried to my God: and he did hear my voice out of his temple, and my cry did enter into his ears."*

— 2 Samuel 22:7

PRAYER
AS NECESSARY AS BREATHING

I know that if I let one night slip by without saying my prayers, I wake up the next morning kinda disturbed, thinking how selfish I've been that I did not give a few minutes to prayer. Prayer and going to church regular gives me a feeling of satisfaction and a feeling inside of me that I can't describe . . . it's as necessary as breathing.

— Jimmy Durante

MY FAITH

I have a strong personal belief and reliance on the power of prayer for Divine inspiration.

Every person has his own ideas of the act of praying for God's guidance, tolerance and mercy to fulfill his duties and responsibilities. My own concept of prayer is not as a plea for special favors or as a quick palliation for wrongs knowingly committed. A PRAYER, IT SEEMS TO ME, IMPLIES A PROMISE, AS WELL AS A REQUEST.

All prayer, by the humble or the highly placed, has one thing in common, as I see it; a supplication for strength and inspiration to carry on the best human impulses which should bind us all together for a better world. Without such inspiration, we would rapidly deteriorate and finally perish.

— Walt Disney

LET US PRAY AS LINCOLN PRAYED

Even though America from the beginning of its settlement has been motivated by religious faith, it is doubtful whether our people ever have had greater need for Divine help and guidance than they do today.

In reaction against the crass materialism which is at the bottom of the disasters that threaten us, the American people increasingly are turning to a belief in prayer to God as the surest means of peace of mind and salvation.

— Robert G. Dunlop

MY CLOSEST COMPANION

Prayer is described by the poet as "The soul's sincere desire, uttered or unexpressed." It does express an attitude and a conscious dependence upon some higher power beyond self.

To me, prayer is a personal communion with a personal God, who is my Creator and who always seeks to develop in me those attributes which contribute to my highest good.

God abides within my soul, a real personality which we call "The Holy Spirit". My communion with God, my prayer to God is what I say to this Holy Spirit and what I hear in response.

I find prayer to be a simple and natural thing. God is my closest companion, always ready to hear my plea and give immediate help, guidance and counsel. I am always conscious of God's presence and his loving care. He hears my expressions of gratitude as well as my request for counsel and guidance in making decisions.

Prayer is then an attitude of mind, an emotion of the heart, a companionship of spirit with spirit. When I exercise my own judgment and forget to ask God's counsel, then I often make grievous errors.

When God's Holy Spirit and my spirit tread life's pathway together in loving companionship, there are no mistakes. It is then easy to "trust and obey". Prayer helps me forget the errors of yesterday . . . live right today and have no worries about tomorrow.

— W. C. Coleman

OUR STRENGTH IS IN GOD

We have great reserves of spiritual strength from which to draw courage for the tasks ahead. The familiar words of Paul can be a stirring inspiration:

> *"Wherefore,"* said Paul, *"take unto you the whole armor of God, that ye may be able to stand in the evil day, and having done all, to stand. Stand, therefore, having your loins girt about with truth, and having on the breastplate of righteousness. And your feet shod with the preparation of the gospel of peace. Above all, taking the shield of faith wherewith ye shall be able to quench all the fiery darts of the wicked."*

> — *Ephesians 6:13-16*

In these ancient words of truth and inspiration, we find the "wholeness" we seek. The shield of our faith is inscribed with the help of God, we shall direct our endeavors to this end.

— *Dean Acheson*

WITHOUT PRAYER, NO MAN HAS STRENGTH

These are turbulent days. They are days of uncertainty and of difficult decision. These are days, in a certain sense, of the wrath of God, who seems disposed to release man into his own custody, and abandon him to the devices of his own making. This would be a terrible fate. It is perhaps the most fearsome to which human nature can be given over. Because man without God is man without any measure by which to live.

Those of us who devote our lives to the maintaining of that modern Holy Grail, the Moral Law, are every day being made increasingly aware of the desperate decline in spiritual standards in our beloved country. It is like a great shadow of sickness across the nation, and can only be the result of neglect of prayer, and gradual disassociation with the Creator of Heaven and earth.

Prayer may not make our problems vanish, or even conveniently solve themselves. But it certainly will serve to put man back into proper proportion with his Maker, and thus rekindle the sense of decency and respect for morality which we stand in danger of forfeiting. Only then will our great nation, under God, continue to flourish, for generations yet to come.

— *Joseph I. Breen*

OUR ONLY SURE FOUNDATION

I have just come from the National Cemetery at Arlington, where I laid a wreath on the grave of an American hero. No American knows, no real American cares, whether that man was a Catholic, a Jew or a Protestant, or what his origin or color were. That grave . . . the Grave of the Unknown Solider . . . symbolizes our faith in unity.

I am trying to get all those people who look up and who know that there is a greater power than man in the universe to organize themselves to meet those who look down and who are strictly materialistic. It is only the people of religious faith throughout the world who have the power to overcome the force of tyranny. It is in their beliefs that the path can be found to justice and freedom. Their religious concepts are the only sure foundation of the democratic ideal.

Sustained and strengthened by one another, we can go forward, under God, to meet and overcome the difficulties which confront us. With His help, mankind will come at last to a world where peace, freedom and justice will be enjoyed by all people everywhere.

— *President Harry S. Truman*

NECESSITY OF PRAYER

No one ever won complete victory over his temptations or obtained satisfying light on his religious perplexities apart from the practice of looking to God in prayer. God is our heavenly Father; and prayer is simply talking with Him. Even if a man does not believe in prayer he should pray . . . for the simple reason that prayer is one thing which can be verified only by praying. The harder it is for a man to pray, the more he needs to pray.

Wherever possible, we should get alone at least once each day for solitary prayer. If there is no room to which we can retire for this purpose, we might pray as we walk along at night under the open heavens, or in some secluded place during the day. This suggests the value and necessity of acquiring the habit of looking to God many, many times during the day, wherever we are and in whatever circumstances. If a man is tempted at four o'clock he should not wait until just before he lies down to sleep before he calls upon God for a help greater than his own.

— *John R. Mott*

REFRESH EACH DAY WITH RELIGIOUS DEVOTION

For six thousand years, since recorded time, every civilized race has believed in a Supreme Being. The Sermon on the Mount established the transcendent concept of compassion and good will among men. The great documents of our heritage: the Bible, the Declaration of Independence, and the Constitution of the United States . . . Within them alone can the safeguards of freedom survive.

— President Herbert Hoover

BE NOT FORGETFUL OF PRAYER

Dostoyevsky said, "Be not forgetful of prayer. Every time you pray, if your prayer is sincere, there will be new feelings and new meanings in it, which will give you fresh courage and you will understand that prayer is an education." I believe that learning to pray is an important process in the growth of a Christian life. In personal tribulation, in the hour of temptation, in the struggle against injustice, in every human crisis, the source of Power is available for us through prayer.

— Brooks Hays

HEARTFELT PRAYER

We can pray in a modest house of worship or a magnificent architectural gem. It's the same God and we are the same people. What counts is neither the impressiveness of the church nor synagogue building, but what is in our hearts. If we are deeply religious we can pray anywhere. The truth is that God dwells in the sanctuary only when we bring Him with us.

The advantage of public worship is a sense of belonging to a community . . . a feeling that we are not alone in our religious convictions. The music and the atmosphere should add to the feeling of sanctity. This in no way should interfere with private devotions, which should be carried on every day of the week.

A prayer before we rest at night should add to our peace of mind and it's good to greet the dawn with a blessing. It can make the day so much more meaningful.

— Rabbi Magnin

Prayer is a very personal business,
however, we can learn a lot about prayer
from others.

SUCCESSFUL LIVING

What good is our present progress through technology and science if we fail to become better people? The fact is, that EACH OF US IS RESPONSIBLE FOR WHAT WE MAKE OF OUR OWN LIFE. The Government cannot play God and create people who are identical in ability. This development is an INDIVIDUAL RESPONSIBILITY.

— Personal Planning Manual

CONFIDENT LIVING

What is God's answer to this turmoil, this struggle, this life, this perplexity in which we live?

"Let not your heart be troubled."

Believe in God . . . center your life in God. Times have changed, but here is a TRUTH that does not change . . . The man who is centered in God is weaponed against any and every foe.

— The Way To Happiness

DREAMS

We grow great by dreams. All big men are dreamers. They see things in the soft haze of a spring day or in the red fire of a long winter's evening. Some of us let these great dreams die, but others nourish and protect them; nurse them through bad days till they bring them to the sunshine and light which comes always to those who sincerely hope that their dreams will come true.

— President Woodrow Wilson

OPPORTUNITY

There is a tide in the affairs of men, which, taken at the flood, leads on to fortune; omitted, all the voyage of their life is bound in shallows and in miseries. On such a full sea are we now afloat, and we must take the current when it serves, or we lose our ventures.

— William Shakespeare

ABILITY

The severest test of a businessman's ACUMEN and ABILITY sometimes lies in the SPEED and MANNER with which he RECOGNIZES, and GRASPS, the OPPORTUNITIES presented by the vagaries of fate.

— J. Paul Getty

THE WAY TO PEACE

The way to peace is an UNTRODDEN PATH, but it is NOT UNKNOWN. It is the WAY Jesus gave us. Jesus came with LOVE, *"Love thy neighbor as thyself."* This LOVE was the cement to bind all people together in brotherly LOVE.

We have failed to use the mighty energies which prayer can release. We have failed, and we have overlooked the greatest resource (PRAYER) of all. We have pursued scientific inquiry in other directions with enormous results.

"Lord, what a change within us one short hour
Spent in Thy presence will avail to make;
What heavy burdens from our bosoms take!
What parched ground refreshes as with a shower,
We kneel and all around us seems to lower;
We rise, and all, the distant and the near,
Stands forth in sunny outline, brave and clear.
We kneel, how weak! We rise, how full of power!"

— *Unknown*

MANTRUM

The East Indians have a practice to quiet the mind, relieve tension and praise a higher power like God or Nature. They repeat the mantra over and over, such as Rama... Rama... Rama. They say it works. The Catholics say Hail Mary, Hail Mary, over and over. Some say Jesus, Jesus, Jesus or Jesus is Lord. This has a beneficial effect on the chanter.

Mahatma Gandhi wrote:

"The mantram becomes one's staff of life and carries one through every ordeal. It is not repeated for the sake of repetition, but for the sake of purification, as an aid to effort... It is no empty repetition. For each repetition has a new meaning, carrying you nearer and nearer to God."

A medical friend once told me, "I know it works... we don't even know how aspirin works, but that doesn't keep it from relieving pain." Similarly, with the mantrum, no explanation I can give can take the place of your own personal verification.

CHAPTER NINETEEN

THE SCIENCE OF LIVING

Science, Belief and Faith have one thing in common: they deal in facts, and they are concerned exclusively with evidence. There is only one thing that establishes a truth as scientific, and that is when it can be so completely demonstrated that you can prove that the Law never deviates. Then you have science. In this sense PRAY TO WIN! based on the Laws of human nature, could be called THE SCIENCE OF SUCCESSFUL LIVING, for all the Laws of Life are documented by people's lives throughout history.

Even though the Laws of our nature are ABSTRACT, they are still facts. We cannot define or explain any of the real values of life, such as love, beauty, truth, friendship, creation, God. They are the most stable things in our lives, and yet we can only EXPERIENCE them. We do not explain, we can only state. And this is all we can do with a large proportion of all the most important truths we know. ABSTRACT TRUTH CAN ONLY BE MADE TO LIVE AS IT IS TRANSLATED INTO HUMAN EXPERIENCE. No matter how true a statement of fact or doctrine may be, it is only a skeleton until wrought on by the magic of EXPERIENCE and made to live.

The conclusions we come to in PRAY TO WIN! are the result of PRACTICAL HUMAN EXPERIENCE. In what ways do we arrive at true knowledge? By the law of logic, by the findings of science, and by close observation in the realm of human experience. Of these three realms, human experience is the most conclusive. LIVING EXPERIENCE HAS THE POWER TO COMPEL BELIEF. Experience is the most scientific of all evidence, the most positive of all knowledge. Man's laws are a way of dividing things. By contrast, in the words of Luther Burbank, "Nature's laws affirm instead of prohibit. If you violate her laws you are your own prosecuting attorney, judge, jury and hangman." To be able to weather the "storms of life" man must "return to nature" and Nature's Laws.

The whole universe is pervaded (actually governed) by immutable Laws, or unseen forces, whether we know them or not, and the unknown is just as lawful as the known. There are Laws of Chemistry, Mathematics, Electricity, Physics, etc. These Laws are inherent in the physical universe, and we are continually discovering new ones.

As an apple tree has a Law within itself that governs its actions so that it produces apples, not oranges, just so man has a combination of Laws within himself which determine what he should do to live the life for which he was created to live. This nature within man and the universe is the NATURE OF GOD, and is known as the NATURAL LAW or LAW OF NATURE, which is the handiwork of the Creator. Only by obeying these Laws, which are inborn in man's nature, can man reach perfection and fulfill himself.

No one doubts the operation of Natural Laws in the growth of life around us. We see these Laws at work and accept them. We look at the miracle of seed sown in the ground, at growth and harvest, and say it is "the Laws of Nature," and work with them. We look at the stars, observe sunset and sunrise, and mark the coming of an eclipse without fear for we know that dependable Laws of Nature also govern these things. But when we come to our mental and spiritual world, in spite of evidence to the contrary, we stop short, frightened, and doubt the existence of its Laws. And we attempt to pattern our lives on the doubt instead of the fact.

Today man is ignorant of the Laws of his nature, his body, soul, spirit. One hundred years ago the Laws of Electricity existed but man had not discovered them. Seventy years ago the Laws of Radio existed but man had not discovered them. Forty years ago the Laws of Television existed but man had not discovered them. It is time now for man to discover and develop the LAWS OF HIS OWN NATURE. What is more important to every man than developing his own personal human resources? INDIVIDUAL BETTERMENT is what PRAY TO WIN! is all about.

Every individual has more real wealth INSIDE of him or her that has not been developed, and only each individual can develop their own inner resources. We have developed the material things and have not given proper consideration to the INNER MAN, which is where we really live, and what we really are. Our real potential is far more valuable than money, and must be developed first.

If to build a man is our biggest project . . . and it is . . . then we must not be ignorant of our full potential, which lies in the development of our body and soul.

CHARACTER is the keystone of the good life. Character means the quality of the stuff of which anything is made. Success depends more upon character than upon either intellect or fortune. Your character will be what you yourself choose to make it.

We cannot erect a building or even a house without a knowledge of the Law of Gravity. Neither can we live the way we were designed to live without knowing and obeying the Laws of man's nature and the Natural Laws.

Man is endowed with certain powers, faculties and abilities. Each man is responsible for their proper use, misuse or neglect. It is each man's responsibility and duty to himself, to his world, and to the Eternal Power to which he owes his existence, to develop these talents in keeping with the Laws of his nature. In doing so, he will learn to govern his temper, subdue his appetites, refine his emotions, inform his mind, increase his understanding, and safeguard himself and his fellow man.

It is natural for man to overlook the obvious. Goethe said, "The last law man will learn will be the laws of his own nature." Yet to discover the nature of man, and the laws of that nature, marks the highest of human enterprises. Most of man's problems stem from the nature of man. To solve this problem is to open the way to everything which can be of importance to the individual, to human welfare and happiness.

Twenty-four hundred years ago Socrates admonished, "Man, know thyself!" Man does not truly live unless he knows, understands and obeys the Laws of his own nature. Here is man's Waterloo . . . his downfall. Man is more than one-hundred-seventy pounds of meat. Man has a mind, a soul, thought processes, feelings, emotions. The REAL MAN is his thoughts, feelings, emotions, love, joy, anxiety, fears, anger, motives. He has THREE DIVINE DIMENSIONS . . . Physical . . . Mental . . . Spiritual.

Every person's heart cries out for a better life. Each of us should ask, "How can I develop my full potential and live a useful, constructive, enjoyable life? How can I render a service to my fellow man, and live for the purpose and the way I am designed to live?"

The answers to these questions are the heart of this book which is a guide to SUCCESSFUL LIVING. Each reader will know and understand that there is a natural order in all things . . . first we understand the Law, next we obey it. When we obey the Natural Laws we are rewarded with health, with happiness and with success. This is Nature's effort to induce us to obey her Laws. When we violate the Universal Laws, the result is pain, disease, discontent, lack of harmony, and material failure.

> "I will follow nature as the surest guide,
> and resign myself with implicit obedience,
> to her sacred ordinances."
>
> — *Cicero*

The purpose of PRAY TO WIN! is to explain how the Laws of man's nature are the best guide to our spiritual development and to successful living. Underneath the surface of our highly polished, sophisticated and proud personal lives there exists inborn, unseen forces called THE LAWS OF OUR NATURE. These Laws are universal; they are the same for all men, in all countries, at all times. Knowledge of these Laws, and obedience to these Laws is the KEY to the highest and best life known. It is also the highest and most beneficial study that every person can aspire to.

SELF-FULFILLMENT

What a man CAN be, he MUST be. This is what self-fulfillment means. A person becomes uncomfortable with himself if he is not doing what he is suited for. Man has strayed further and further away from nature and is now deteriorating. The root cause of all our trouble is man's ignorance of his body and soul; man's ignorance of his own nature.

In the heart of every person there is a HUNGER, a longing for something that you cannot find in this world. It is the soul that longs for a comforting spirit, a fellowship with God, the Supreme Power. Apart from God, man exists, but does not live. Apart from God and His Word, man only guesses and theorizes and gropes and stumbles along in the blindness of his own finite understanding.

A great and wise man has well said, "It is absolutely essential that I know God." Essential because time will pass, things will perish, human relationships will cease and the brightest prospects of our most exciting hopes will become blank and barren. Nor do we need better evidence of this truth than the fact that we so soon outgrow the "delights that thrill our little selves." To experience the Infinite is my one hope of finding the inexhaustible God, and God alone is THE ANSWER TO THE INFINITE ME OF ME.

MAN TODAY HAS MASTERED THE
MATERIAL WORLD (TECHNOLOGY) WITHOUT
ANY CONSIDERATION OF HIS OWN NATURE.

Religious education, including the basis for morality and the ways in which we distinguish between right and wrong, is the basic foundation of all useful education. Our relationship to God is the most important thing we can learn. The great central fact in human life is the coming into a conscious, vital realization of our oneness with Infinite Power, and the opening of ourselves to this divine inflow. The important thing for us is not so much a comprehension of the totality of God as it is to discover the necessity for our own spiritual development. Spiritual life is the emancipation of what we are.

Greater is He that is in me,
than he that is in
the world.

— I John 4:4

THE SCHOOL OF LIFE

Life has been likened to a school. All things considered, it is a good simile.

The school bell rings at birth. It need never be rung again. School is never out. Nor are there any vacations or holidays. The curriculum is exacting. The lessons are hard. The course is prescribed. There are no elective subjects. Professor Time plays no favorites. The Superintendent is concerned only with eternal values. He is determined that all shall graduate with honors.

While we may not elect a course in the School of Life, we may SPECIALIZE in certain subjects. I have chosen for myself certain subjects in which you may be interested also.

I want to know:

— How to keep the symphony of my life in tune with the Infinite.

— How to gain the wisdom to order my life in such a way as to achieve my own highest good while keeping due regard for the opinions, rights, and privacies of others.

— How to obtain the highest legitimate reward for myself, without robbing others by failing to always give value received.

— How to capitalize my own disappointments and weaknesses so that I shall be able to enrich others with understanding, encouragement, and helpfulness.

— How, when wounded in life's battle, to draw the water of hope and courage from the deep wells of quiet meditation and prayer, and return to the conflict undaunted and unafraid.

THE SCHOOL OF LIFE
CONTINUED

— How to keep a due appreciation of myself, my abilities, and whatever of value I may have accomplished without becoming egotistical, arrogant, and boastful . . . knowing that self-depreciation is a cardinal sin and egotism is a cancerous growth.

— How to gracefully say, "I do not know," rather than attempt to bluff in the name of wisdom, and by so doing reveal my ignorance the more clearly to those who do know; and thus become an object of pity and contempt when I might have kept their respect and confidence by being honest.

— How to use several languages when the occasion requires it, but how to keep silent in all several languages most of the time.

— How to occasionally let others have the last word even though I know they are wrong.

— How to wear a victor's laurels gracefully; and how to accept defeat just as gracefully.

— How to acquire wisdom and yet keep my place in the kingdom of God with the faith and simplicity of a little child.

And finally, how to keep constantly before me the truth that God's "well done" is more important than the passing approbation of men who themselves have never known the true meaning of life.

These are the subjects in which I am most interested, and which I conceive to be of paramount importance.

IMITATE JESUS

A friend went to hear a lecture by Will Durant, the great scholar and philosopher, author of "The Story of Philosophy," and with his able and distinguished wife, the ten volume "Story of Civilization." Here is a man who is said to possess more knowledge than can be found in any one library. But on the day in question, this world renowned scholar and historian said, THAT IF HE WERE BEGINNING LIFE AGAIN, HE WOULD NOT PLAN TO WRITE 20 BOOKS, TO ACHIEVE WEALTH OR FAME, BUT WOULD TRY TO LIVE AS NEARLY AS HE COULD IN ACCORDANCE WITH THE TEACHINGS OF JESUS CHRIST.

Arnold Toynbee, the most eminent historian of our day, has allotted more space to Jesus Christ than to any other six great men who have ever lived combined. This included Mohammed, Buddha, Caesar, Napoleon, George Washington, Abraham Lincoln. All thinking men, of all lands and religions, who have had the opportunity to investigate the evidence will agree that JESUS CHRIST IS THE GREATEST PERSONALITY THAT THIS WORLD HAS EVER KNOWN. THAT HE HAS HAD THE GREATEST INFLUENCE FOR GOOD THIS WORLD HAS EVER KNOWN, EVEN THOUGH SOME OF THESE MEN DO NOT ACCEPT HIS DEITY!

CHOOSE WHOM YOU WILL SERVE

To the seriously thoughtful person the existence of Jesus Christ is the pivotal point in the history and destiny of the world. What He said and did continues to influence the thinking and affairs of men and nations. Of no other can that be said. Nor will men and nations experience their highest and best until they take Him and what He taught as chart and compass by which to set their course.

Nor is that a mere preachment. It is demonstrated fact. Our present mess and muddle but further confirms this truth. Our political decisions will have but little lasting influence upon our future. But our decisions concerning Christ and His teachings will determine our destiny. You are the United States of America. Choose for YOURSELF and YOUR COUNTRY and YOUR FUTURE.

CHAPTER TWENTY

PRAYER LIFE IN ACTION

PROSPERITY

The surest way to prosperity is to put and keep God first. NOW is possibly the best opportunity any of us have ever had to test that. To you who are testing it, my heartiest congratulations and my best thanks. There are good days ahead. Let's not miss them by failing to share these days with God by investing largely in His work.

"Thy Word is truth" — *John 17:17.* For a clearer meaning substitute "the Word" for "truth" as follows:

"Beloved, I wish above all things that thou mayest prosper and be in health, even as thy soul prospereth. For I rejoiced greatly when the brethren came and testified of the truth (The Word) *that is in thee, even as thou walkest in the truth* (The Word). *I have no greater joy than to hear that my children walk in truth* (The Word)."

— *III John 2-4*

Through our traditional ideas we have been led to believe that prosperity is bad or ungodly. However, John writes that we should prosper and be in health and then says in verse 11, *"Beloved, follow not that which is evil, but that which is good. He that doeth good is of God, but he that doeth evil hath not seen God."* If prosperity is evil why would he want us to prosper? You see, there is nothing wrong with prosperity in itself. Money is not the root of all evil. The LOVE OF MONEY is the root of all evil. (See I Timothy 6:10), and there are people commiting this sin who don't have a dime!

I want you to realize, however, that prosperity covers much more than the finances. When John said we should prosper and be in health he added the phrase . . . *"even as thy soul prospereth."* Man is a spirit, he has a soul consisting of the mind, the will, and the emotions; and he lives in the body. Thus, there is SPIRITUAL PROSPERITY, THERE IS MENTAL PROSPERITY, AND THERE IS PHYSICAL PROSPERITY. What brings all these areas together? THE WORD OF GOD. The Bible says in Hebrews 4:12, *"the word of God is quick* (alive), *and powerful, and sharper than any two edged sword, piercing even to the dividing asunder of soul and spirit, and of the joints and marrow, and is a discerner of the thoughts and intents of the heart."*

WHAT REALLY MATTERS?

There is a famous cathedral in Milan, Italy, which is one of the most beautiful churches in the entire world. It has three large front entrance doors. Over each entrance are inscriptions that contain a profound message for us all.

Over the first doorway and beneath a carving of a beautiful wreath of roses are found these words: "All that which pleases is but for a moment." The other outside doorway is decorated with a lovely sculptured cross, beneath which one reads: "All that which troubles is but for a moment." Inscribed over the central doorway are the words: "That only is important which is eternal."

Do you have the far look? Do you see the real values in life? If so, congratulations, little things won't bother you, you won't sweat the small stuff. So little really matters.

With most people the preoccupation with secondary things and secondary matters has pushed what is primary and eternal into the corners of our lives. We have become masters of small talk, advocates of small causes, thinkers of small thoughts, and pursuers of small goals.

What we can buy is often fleeting. We are not material beings at heart. We are created with the longing for spiritual fulfillment and possess the capacity for its satisfaction. That capacity can be filled only in relation to the God who made us, who loves us, and has given his son for our salvation. David said, *"God has placed eternity in our hearts,"* and we won't be satisfied unless we satisfy this eternal longing which we possess.

Jesus admonished: *"Lay not up for yourselves treasures upon earth, where moth and rust doth corrupt, and where thieves break through and steal: BUT lay up for yourselves treasures in heaven, where neither moth or rust doth corrupt, and where thieves do not break through nor steal; for where your treasure is, there will your heart be also."* Let us live from this day on in the knowledge, "that only is important which is eternal."

VALUES

We need a new sense of values, a new definition of success. As Jesus said, *"Take heed, and beware of covetousness: for a man's life consisteth not in the abundance of the things which he possesseth."* Success is not measured in things, it is to be measured in relationships to God and to man.

The Bible is not against material things, it is against material goods. For example, in Luke 12:16-31, the rich farmer was a fool because he forgot God. His materialism was killing him and it did.

The solution is found in the simpler life. It begins with a new perspective. The greatest adventure in life is to know God. To know is to experience, to fellowship, to enjoy, to appreciate God. Living for God is man's greatest adventure.

People sometimes try for great accomplishments, this is natural, but is secondary . . . living for God is the most satisfying. In fact, your chance for great accomplishment increases tenfold if you put God first in your life. The Bible is full of examples. Abraham, Solomon, Moses, and many others obeyed God and were rewarded by pursuing the greatest adventure of living and obeying God.

Listen to the words that have echoed down through the centuries: *"Therefore I say unto you, take no thought for your life, what ye shall eat; neither for the body, what ye shall put on . . . For all these things do the nations of the world seek after: and your Father knoweth that ye have need of these things. But rather seek ye the kingdom of God; and all these things shall be added unto you."*

Our mad scramble for things has become the bandit that has looted us clean of the wealth of goodness and with the loss of genuine goodness has gone our greatness. Our quest for gold has robbed us of our sense of God. Our boasted largeness is rapidly becoming our littleness. Even our "religious life" has deteriorated into a shallow pretense. I repeat, we need a revival of the sense of individual worth. Both the church and society need to specialize on the production of worthy manhood.

The values taught by Jesus Christ produce worthy people.

WHAT IS THE KEY TO
TRUE HAPPINESS?

Someone has said, "ALL THE WORLD IS SEEKING HAPPI-NESS." Actually, all the world is in search of something infinitely deeper and more abiding than mere happiness. THAT SOMETHING IS JOY. Joy is contentment that fills the soul, A STATE OF HEART.

The difference between happiness and joy is more than a mere play on words. JOY IS THE ABIDING FELLOWSHIP WITH GOD, WHICH EXPERIENCES NO CHANGE AMID THE VICISSITUDES OF LIFE. Happiness can be a superficial happiness which depends upon an abundance of things one possesses which evaporate. JOY IS DEEP, ABIDING SPIRITUAL UNION WITH THE UNCHANGING GOD.

"A man's life," said Jesus Christ, "is not fulfilled, nor is it filled full of, nor by, the abundance of things which he possesses." Here is one of the most important statements ever given a bewildered, heart hungry world. The shallowness and futility of superficial happiness is its dependence upon things . . . congenial companions, good clothes, a bank balance, a comfortable home. These things, of course, contribute to the sum of life, but the point is THEY ARE NOT THE FIRST NEEDS OF LIFE. JOY IS A LIVING SPRING HIDDEN DEEP IN THE INNER LIFE that is not dependent upon things. We live in a rough-and-tumble world. "In the world," Christ said, "ye shall have tribulation," but He further added, "Be of good cheer."

WHAT IS THE PRACTICAL VALUE OF SEEKING JOY AS WELL AS HAPPINESS? Joy is strength. The Old Testament writer said, "The joy of the Lord is your strength." The joyful person will surpass all others in spiritual strength, poise, and usefulness. Joy is content, and contentment is the positive, constructive, creative force on which life depends for both health and happiness. JOY IS SPIRITUAL PROSPERITY. "Rest in the Lord," and lo, joy will come out of its hiding and if you will live quietly and confidently, in prayerful fellowship with God, it will abide with you forever.

Happiness consists in being perfectly satisfied not only with what we have, but also with what we do not have. IT IS NOT HOW MUCH WE HAVE, BUT HOW MUCH WE ENJOY THAT CREATES HAPPINESS.

THE GOOD WAYS TO LIVE

Look for all the good ways to live that are still possible.

You can give fifty women the same ingredients to make a cake and the cakes will all taste different. What makes the difference? It is all in the mix.

The difference in the quality of life between people is the mix. And by mix, in the human sense, I mean a person's attributes, thoughts, attitudes, beliefs, values, ideals, philosophy and quality.

I would be dishonest if I did not tell you that the Christian teachings of the Bible are the foundation of my life. I have made many errors in my life but you soon learn not to fall in the same hole more than once. The advantages of knowing and living the teachings of God is that you have the KINGDOM and the POWER OF GOD within you. The benefits are many:

You eliminate FEAR . . . because you put your TRUST in GOD.
　You have high ideals . . .
　　You have self-respect . . .
　　　You have high spirit and morale . . .
　　　　You have a confident and happy attitude.

WHY? Because you are using the natural inherent spiritual qualities of your being. Your spiritual dimensions. This is your natural environment, just as a fish is built for water, a bird is built for air, a man is built for God. Develop your spiritual dimension and live the life you were designed to live. The ultimate in living is to develop the God-like quality in self. This is our number one NEED. You could have all the money in the world and not get your needs met. God wants you to live out your days in health and happiness. God is our source . . . our light. You need a MIRACLE from God and you need them every day.

"YOU are made for God, just like your eye is made for light. You cannot see in the dark. You cannot find peace except in the will of God for 'thy will is my peace.' With all the sincerity of my eighty years, I say, God is the answer to the modern confusion that dogs us."

— *Frank Buchman*

FAITH OR FRENZY

In a kind of frenzy too many of us rush through our days, not living life, but consuming it. We are mere machines . . . the victims of our high-pressure age. Our nervous excesses are responsible for more unhappiness than any other one cause.

The haste of modern living is waste in the truest, deepest sense. We are so busy reaching for things beyond us that we miss eternal values which are near at hand. In our hurry and fret we have forgotten how to walk and talk with God. We sing on Sunday, "Take time to be holy," and straightway go out to fall prey to, what a great physician calls, Americanitis.

We have forgotten that solitude and growth are synonymous. There is no royal road to development. Rush is the enemy of growth. Leaf by leaf the great oak grows into a sturdy tree. Forty years alone in the desert produced a Moses. Three years alone in the Arabian desert perfected Paul's vision. Christ spent thirty years getting ready for three years of ministry.

A healthy mind must be housed in an unhurried body. Professor Beecher used to tell the students at Yale, "the first requisite is to take time." Thomas Jefferson once said, "Most men spend their time at nothing, other than hurrying about and never arriving anywhere."

Happy is the man who has learned how to substitute faith for frenzy, and rest for rush.

HAVE courage for the great sorrows of life, and patience for the small ones, and when you have accomplished your daily tasks, go to sleep in peace. GOD IS AWAKE.

— *Victor Hugo*

THE BENEFITS OF TRUE LIVING

Life consists of much more than mere existence . . . more than breathing, eating, wearing a few clothes, and taking up space. The most important thing has not been learned . . . How to conduct ourselves so that we may truly live.

True living is to ENJOY each day. Happiness depends not on the things around us, but on our ATTITUDE. Everything in our life will depend on our ATTITUDE. Here is the crux, the core of life: *"As a man thinketh in his heart, so is he."* So simple, but how true, how profound. How few understand and practice this natural law.

True living means self-development. The first and most important thing in this world for every individual to understand is HIMSELF. This is the greatest problem in life. Knowledge of self requires study. The greatest responsibility given to every person is the development of self. Which means the EQUAL development of our PHYSICAL . . . MENTAL . . . and SPIRITUAL faculties.

True living means doing your best every day, being a blessing to others as well as to ourselves. You are living only when you are useful, constructive, and accomplishing things worth-while. Accomplishment brings happiness.

True living means THINKING, OBSERVING, and LEARNING. It recognizes the difference between TRUTH and TRASH, and that the QUALITY of life is more important than life itself. Our BODY must be fed, but much more important . . . so must our MINDS and SOULS. For to build a MAN is life's greatest project . . . for each of us!

True living is life lived quietly, CONFIDENTLY, and in prayerful fellowship with the God of the fields and the valleys, the mountains and the sunshine. Living such a life is the end of the rainbow, where is hidden the pot of gold for which we are in search.

LOVE

Jesus Christ came to this earth to bring LOVE and his life demonstrated this fact. This CHRISTIAN LOVE was the cement to bind all men together in Brotherly Love and Kindness. But few men practice HIS WAY.

"Alexander, Caesar, Charlemagne, and myself founded empires. But upon what did we rest the creation of our genius? Upon sheer force. Jesus Christ alone founded his empire upon LOVE, and at this hour, millions of men would die for Him."

— *Napoleon*

"Things go much better when you love God. For staying close to Him you will do right things. And only right things turn out right. As you love God, you will grow in spiritual insights and understanding. Judgments and decisions will be rightly motivated. As guidance passes from God's mind to yours, things will indeed work together for good."

— *Norman Vincent Peale*

"Though I speak with the tongues of men and of angels, and have not charity, I am become as sounding brass, or a tinkling cymbal. And though I have the gift of prophecy, and understand all mysteries, and all knowledge; and though I have all faith, so that I could remove mountains, and have not charity, I am nothing. And though I bestow all my goods to feed the poor, and though I give my body to be burned, and have not charity, it profiteth me nothing . . . And now abideth faith, hope, charity, these three; but the greatest of these is charity."

— *I Corinthians 13:1-3,13*

Love is by far the most important thing of all. It is the Golden Gate of Paradise. Pray for the understanding of love, and meditate upon it daily. It casts out fear. It is the fulfilling of the Law. It covers a multitude of sins. Love is absolutely invincible.

There is no difficulty that enough love will not conquer; no disease that enough love will not heal; no door that enough love will not open; no gulf that enough love will not bridge; no wall that enough love will not throw down; no sin that enough love will not redeem.

"It makes no difference how deeply seated may be the trouble, how hopeless the outlook, how muddled the tangle, how great the mistake; a sufficient realization of love will dissolve it all. If only you could love enough you would be the happiest and most powerful being in the world."

— *Emmet Fox*

CHAPTER TWENTY-ONE

THE SPIRITUAL DIMENSION

A CHRISTIAN

It is a great thing to be a Christian. The most exalted privilege we shall ever experience is to Walk with God. To have, handle and enjoy free access to His Word is the best possible means of developing the finest type of character in the universe.

If we must make a resolution, let us highly resolve to spend some time each day reading the Bible. The Bible is exactly what it claims to be . . . The Word of God. It is historically accurate, inerrantly correct and indispensably essential. It reveals the best way to live, and the safe way to die, and the only sure way to secure us for time and eternity. It is God's Word. It will never fail, or fail us. Whatever the crises or emergency it will shine light upon an otherwise totally dark night of despair, strengthen us against a day of battle and turn defeat into a triumphant victory.

Read it! Believe it! Trust it! Incorporate it! If you do, this is sure to be an eventful year!

Above all things else, the Christian is a man of decision. That's a Christian. He knows what he believes and why he believes it and he is prepared to believe it all the time. Popular or unpopular, welcome or unwelcome. A Christian is a man who knows what he believes because he has experienced something.

We are a new creature in Christ Jesus. For this our heart is constantly rapturous in praise. Christianity is not a word to us, it's not a doctrine, nor a creed . . . it is the life of God imparted to men. We've been warned, not alone by the hearing of the ear, that this is life and life eternal, that we experience Thee. Neither art Thou a word in our vocabulary. Thou art truly to us the God with whom we have fellowship by a supernatural experience.

THE SPIRITUAL REALM

MAN LIVES IN TWO WORLDS. One in the material or PHYSICAL world, one in the SPIRITUAL world. MAN IS BOTH A PHYSICAL BEING AND A SPIRITUAL BEING.

The first need is my spiritual development. This is the foundation stone of my life. With this I can cope with life and handle anything that comes my way. Spiritual development is the number one need of man.

Man is basically a spiritual being . . . his equipment for living far surpasses any visible resources available in his environment. His spirit calls out for a greater destiny. It demands a greater satisfaction than is ever possible within the confines of the visible universe. This longing is spiritual. And God has provided man with the resources he needs in the spiritual realm to satisfy the longing of his heart and to fulfill his destiny to a far greater extent than we would dream.

The spiritual dimension of man must be developed in order to make him whole or complete. It is here he develops morals, goodness, character and the generous qualities.

MAN is indivisible, he is a whole . . . body, mind, spirit . . . but with the only real, fully representative voice . . . the voice of the heart, sometimes called the soul or the seat of being . . . the YOU of you.

YOU RECEIVE THE POWER OF GOD THROUGH YOUR SPIRIT . . . YOUR HEART . . . YOUR INNER MAN. We shall make our best contribution to the world if we cultivate a DEEPER SENSE OF GOD, a firmer conviction, a stronger FAITH.

MOTIVES are invisible, but they are the TRUE test of character, they operate in the realm of the SPIRIT. The greatest contribution any of us will make to the world is . . . TO LIVE AT OUR SPIRITUAL BEST!

The Old Testament writer said, *"The joy of the Lord is your strength."* The joyful person will surpass all others in spiritual strength, poise, and usefulness. Joy is content and contentment is the positive, constructive, creative force on which life depends for both health and happiness. MONEY IS MATERIAL PROSPERITY . . . JOY IS SPIRITUAL PROSPERITY!

CHRISTIANITY

A Sing-Sing warden once said, "We have enough Ph.D's behind bars to staff a modern college." Why? Because we are separated from God, and without God we are restless, we cannot control our passions, and that's the reason, if America forgets God, we are going to become even more violent.

The Duke of Wellington once said, "Education without religion gives us only a lot of smart devils." Only for "religion", I would substitute Christianity. Christianity is the one thing that involves the heart and that is the urgent need of men. To be transformed is the one thing that will save us from being conformed to the way the world lives, and the way the world lives is too low a standard to lift us to God's level. We must be raised to His level or tomorrow will be our undoing.

When Roger W. Babson asked Thomas Edison what he thought the next great scientific discovery would be, he answered: "There is a great moving spirit in the Universe. We must discover Him in order that our souls may keep pace with our brains or our brains will destroy us." Men who do not experience Jesus Christ in their hearts will become so clever in their brains that they will destroy us with their undisciplined genius.

A world famous physician recently said that the modern medical scientist must know more than the physical realms; he must know how to relate the physical to the spiritual; men need peace more than they need pills. Security and safety are more a matter of soul than of brains and scientific genius. Our day is too busy teaching us how to make a living rather than how to make a life. As General MacArthur well said, "The only way to save the flesh is to save the spirit." It's time, past time, for us to get first things in first place.

THE MAJESTY OF MAN! You are an emissary of the Infinite. You are God's agent on earth. You are God's representative. You are made in the image of God. THINK: these are the hands that DO the work of God in the world of man! When man awakens and realizes he is truly a Son of God, and that all the powers of God are within himself, it is then that he will begin to achieve his true mastership. It is then he will function in the full majesty of which he is capable.

IT TAKES MORE THAN POSITIVE THINKING

We can be positive in our mental processes and at the same time wholly shallow and inadequate deep down in the realm where FAITH operates. This is why many positive thinkers FAIL.

MOST PEOPLE HAVE THE CART BEFORE THE HORSE. If you have FAITH, it GIVES YOU THE POSITIVE OUTLOOK. It is infinitely more important to have our faith foundationed than anything else. Now FAITH means putting our full confidence in the things we hope for. FAITH comes by believing, and believing comes by the Word of God. It is the Word of God which lays the foundation on which we build our spiritual superstructure. FAITH is the substance, the foundation word, that stands under the superstructure. It is the evidence of things not seen. Your senses will take you further than your intellect. You can EXPERIENCE, infinitely more than you can master, by a mental process. By the intellect men do not come ever to know God. God is entirely beyond a mental process. What we know about God must be revealed to the senses, because your senses walk abroad throughout a vast realm where your intellect cannot go.

First have Faith in God and you will automatically have FAITH. The foundation for your faith is with the heart . . . the seat of being. Men believe not from the intellect but . . . *"with the heart man believeth."* It is important to be a Christian . . . BUT it is more important to be an obedient Christian. And, nothing is more important than having FAITH in God . . . Trust in God. The greatest work any of us will ever do is to BELIEVE GOD WITHOUT QUESTIONING. This is what gives vitality to life. TRUST IN GOD, is the positive and major force, if we will but use it. Jesus Christ had more to say about FAITH and FEAR than any other subject. Why do we think God is limited? ONLY BECAUSE OF OUR LACK OF FAITH.

You ask me, "What is the matter with my life, I don't seem to be getting ahead?" I can answer you. And I could answer you without knowing a thing in the world about it. You need to get some positive force in action, and the positive force to get into action is not a mere mental statement of certain facts. You need to get a positive force at the seat and source of your being that will so clean out the streams of life that they will literally be freighted with power . . . PRAYER OF A POSITIVE FAITH. You don't believe that will work? I challenge you to try it.

WHAT DO YOU WANT FROM LIFE?

Just what do you want personally from life? This is one of the most important questions you will ever consider. Try the plan of writing out in definite statements the things you really desire to BE and to DO and to HAVE. What will you achieve with your life: business or professional success? A substantial income? Friends? Influence in your community? Standing in your chosen field? FAME? POWER? POSITION? SECURITY? SPIRITUAL SATISFACTIONS? What?

You can have just about whatever you want . . . if you want it badly enough, and are willing to sacrifice for it. The world will give you nothing without extracting its price. By your nature as well as the laws of the universe, you cannot receive or be given something for nothing. That is not the scheme of things. Take what you need and want. But pay for it you must, in one way or another.

The plain truth is this: First, you have to make up your mind what you really want. Second, are you willing to pay the price of attainment in study, work, sweat, effort, and money? If the price of attainment is too great for you to pay, your desire is not strong enough for you to have it. DESIRE is the POWER behind your effort. Little effort . . . little results; big effort . . . big results. It's as simple as that.

How can I discover myself and live a rich full life that I was designed to live, and how can I best serve my fellow man? And if possible do some work that would live after I die? I HAVE FOUND OUT REAL FULFILLMENT IS MY ONENESS WITH GOD. This is the only thing that will ever satisfy man's spiritual nature, and this spiritual nature is in fact, the FOUNDATION for my other dimensions which are my physical being, and my mental being. I have never met a great man who had not developed his spiritual nature.

There is plenty of money in the world, and if you know and practice the basic Christian principles the money will follow. Through prayer I find God and God finds me. Prayer is the key to Successful Living. PRAYER IS UNION WITH THE POWER BY WHICH WE LIVE. Prayer is the tie between the individual and the Great Spirit. It is the human soul searching for its relationship. Men cannot live greatly without it. God abides within my soul . . . *"the Kingdom of God is within."* He is my best friend. SUCCESS is my heritage IF I obey the Word of God.

THE WAY TO HAPPINESS

THE MOST IMPORTANT THING TO LEARN IN LIFE IS HOW TO LIVE. MAKE UP YOUR MIND TO BE HAPPY. Learn to find happiness in simple things. When the famous French writer, Colette, was dying of cancer and was being interviewed by a newsman, she exclaimed, "What a wonderful life I've had! Those were my happiest days!" Then after a sigh of remorse she added, "I only wish I'd realized it sooner."

The capacity to enjoy life is inborn in all living beings, but JOY, like LIFE, does not sustain itself. It must be cultivated. The noxious weeds of worry and strife, rush and rumpus, must be constantly rooted out. Each of us must be the gardener who labors together with God, if the finest things of life are to come to full flower and fruit. ENJOY LIFE . . . FEEL GOOD!

There are two levels of happiness, and the human heart is designed to live on both. One level is MUNDANE HAPPINESS. The other is DIVINE HAPPINESS. Mundane happiness grows thin and quickly loses its glow. Genuine happiness, or JOY, has its source in God and is the Summum Bonum or Supreme Good. It will never lose its luster. St. Augustine said, "We are made for God and will be dissatisfied until we have God in our Hearts." Happiness is a spiritual quality.

FORGET GOING OUT AND CONQUERING THE WORLD, GO IN AND CONQUER YOURSELF! Then you will have mastered the universe within you. Men are going to learn sometime that this inner world of man is very much bigger than we have ever suspected. We are going to realize that the INNER MAN, the real you of you . . . the heart, the mind, the soul, spirit, is a UNIVERSE in itself!

Develop a kind, loving, Christian nature and you will be looking at the world through rose colored glasses. How often a careless, unkind word spoken can spoil your day, wreck some big job or deal, hurt a loved one, lose a friend. Many of us through ignorance, thoughtlessness, or want of judgment, hurt those we love best and wish to help. IF YOUR HEART HAS FOUND HAPPINESS, DON'T LET YOUR TONGUE LOSE IT FOR YOU.

MAN WORSHIPS OVER 3000 GODS

No man is an atheist. He worships some god or gods. If he does not subscribe to the Biblical statement of the Eternal God, he will create a god to which he will render his undivided allegiance. He may not "go to church" but he will, nevertheless, attend a church of his own making. He may call himself an atheist but he is, in reality, a devout believer. He may flatter himself that he does not "believe in prayer" but he is, finally, a devout man of faith.

He must worship SOMETHING. He is built that way. If not the God revealed in the Bible, then the gods of the State, Success, Money, Power, Fame, Education, Sex, Work, Laziness, Pleasure, Possessions, Gambling, Narcotics, Idols, Drunkenness, Gluttony, Pride. Of course, he does not call them "God", but they command the same devotion that a believer renders to the True God . . . and, alas, sometimes even more and better devotion. But the final hour of life will bring disillusionment. He will find that his god is too small and altogether inadequate.

Dr. Wernher von Braun, the leading space scientist, says, "Only if God is reinstated in the heart of the world will He furnish mankind and its leaders with ethical guidance through the dangers and pitfalls of the space age." This is the foundation for a rich dynamic life. It equips us with positive personal values as anchors against the storms of life.

St. Francis desired that men should go through life giving thanks to God for His gifts. Pray for a more peaceful and just society, where it is easier for people to be good. We have taken religion out of everything and have put commercialism into everything.

Man is more than an individual with individual rights, he is a person with personal duties toward God, himself, and his fellow man. As a person he cannot serve God without serving the common good.

"Happy is the man who has learned the secret of coming to God daily in prayer. Fifteen minutes alone with God every morning before you start the day can change circumstances and remove mountains."

— *Billy Graham*

KNOW THYSELF

The next big step man should take is not on the moon. We are well advanced in technology. The next step should be the HUMAN SCIENCES ... "MAN, KNOW THYSELF." We should go inside man, show all man's Powers and let every man know how wonderfully he is made and stop this epidemic of human destruction by drugs.

God will possibly give his people the protection against evil doers with "Star Wars." But the biggest problem man always has is with himself. A true Christian will not destroy or harm his body, which is the Temple of the Holy Spirit. Do you have a purpose for living greater than yourself, and does that purpose revolve around God?

The quality of your life is dependent upon your inner attitude. Therefore, get rid of ANGER ... FEAR ... GREED ... and all your bad qualities. Cultivate the God-like qualities and you will radiate GOODNESS, LOVE, and JOY! Only when the spiritual dimension is awakened, do we realize our true potential as human beings.

We recommend large portions of LOVE and KINDNESS in your life, but that does not mean you can assassinate your brains and throw DISCIPLINE out the window. The Christian life gives you freedom but you can't do everything you please. You must do what is right.

The awakening or baptism of the inner Holy Spirit is the true beginning of the Spiritual Journey. It is only when the Holy Spirit within us is awakened that we become aware of our true nature, of our greatness, of the fact that not only do we belong to God, we come to know God.

Man is born a long way from himself. It takes a long time to "Know Thyself," some never do. Man needs to see the end (eternal life) toward which he moves. The immediate is so small it must be absorbed by the future. The measure of his strength must be revealed by a vision of his highest faculty, which is from the higher Divine Power of God. He must see the unseen, and work in the realm of the invisible (spiritual)! Happy is the man who learns that the present is but the challenge of his future. His FAITH in the Divine Power and future helps him to overcome situations. THIS IS THE BIG PICTURE ... THE FAR LOOK ... LIFE AT ITS BEST!

DISCIPLINE

You have to LEARN it and PRACTICE it.

"For years we have listened to some quack theorists and pseudo-psychologists who have preached that discipline and control were bad for children . . . that they should be left uninhibited to work out their own life patterns, their own self-discipline. But you don't acquire self-discipline if you never learn what discipline is.

Now we are reaping the harvest." — *J. Edgar Hoover*

The greatest need of the United States is DISCIPLINE and PRIDE. The greatest need of any individual is SPIRITUAL DEVELOPMENT . . . oneness with God, the HIGHER POWER.

THE LAW OF SELF-DISCIPLINE

MAN IS MADE OR UNMADE BY HIMSELF. Man controls his own passions, emotions, future. He does so by channeling his physical drives to produce mental achievement. Any animal can dissipate his strength by expending his physical drives every time he feels them. Man's job is to channel them to more productive ends than self-indulgence.

No man ever became great doing as he pleased. Little men do as they please . . . little nobodies. Great men submit themselves to the laws governing the realm of their greatness.

SELF-DISCIPLINE IS ALWAYS REWARDED BY A STRENGTH WHICH BRINGS AN INEXPRESSIBLE, SILENT INNER JOY WHICH BECOMES THE DOMINANT TONE OF LIFE. Self-control is the quality that distinguishes the fittest to survive.

"The most important attribute of man as a moral being is the faculty of self-control," wrote Herbert Spencer. "There never has been, and cannot be, a good life without self-control; apart from self-control, no good life is imaginable. FOR MAN TO CONQUER HIMSELF IS THE FIRST AND NOBLEST VICTORY."

THE END OF ALL DISCIPLINE IS THAT MAN SHOULD BE TRULY HIMSELF AND ATTAIN PEACE IN HIS OWN SOUL. Happy indeed is the person who learns early in life to subordinate his animal impulses to the finer things of high spiritual sentiments. THRICE HAPPY ARE THEY WHO CARRY THEIR FACULTIES AND POWERS UP TO THE LEVEL OF GOD'S BEST THOUGHTS.

TRUE EDUCATION

The true purpose of education is the harmonious development of all our faculties; and the first object of any learning is that it should serve us in the future. We can become wise in many ways, yet all too often our learning does not directly contribute to the improvement of character or peace of mind, or gain us a basic understanding of values.

If we believe these statements, why don't we acknowledge and develop the spiritual kingdom as part of our education process? We recognize three kingdoms now: mineral, vegetable and animal. A fourth one should be added: the spiritual kingdom. When we do this we shall have education at its best.

True education is the harmonious development of all our faculties. Reading, writing, arithmetic, and grammar do not constitute education anymore than a knife, a fork and spoon constitute a dinner. It seems that we can develop a kind of philosophy which enables us to gain some distinction or knowledge, but does not enable us to cope with the daily issues of living. Many well informed persons are in a constant state of inner agitation, and fail to enjoy inner peace and happiness. The most important thing has not been learned . . . how to conduct ourselves so that we may truly live.

Religious education, including the basis for morality and the ways in which we distinguish between right and wrong, is the basic foundation of all useful education. Our relationship to God is the most important thing we can learn. The great central fact in human life is the coming into a conscious vital realization of our oneness with Infinite Power, and the opening of ourselves to this Divine inflow.

The important thing for us is not so much a comprehension of the totality of God, as it is to discover the necessity for our own spiritual development. Spiritual life is the emancipation of what we are. Through a spiritual life we become responsive to God. On that level, and on that level only, do we find release for our highest powers and qualities. Jesus taught that life must be centered in God . . . that our happiness is dependent upon our holiness, that our union with God is our hope of fulfilling the ultimate purpose of life.

TRUE EDUCATION
CONTINUED

This way of life teaches us to rule our passions and impulses by reason and right. It teaches us to think God's thoughts, speak His language, and how to live the life we were created to live. By so doing, we safeguard ourselves and the society of which we are a part.

Modern society has committed the fundamental error of disobeying the law of spiritual development. Our greatest need now is to develop the soul. Never were we more in need of being made whole. With this development, we are free to enjoy to the highest degree the beauty, order and permanence of the universe; we are free to dedicate ourselves in service to others; we are free to commune with nature and find in that communion the ties to the universe that we have always sought. THIS IS EDUCATION AT ITS BEST!

We teach our children that they descended from lower forms of animals and they are nothing but a sophisticated animal with a brain, that our impulses and emotions stem from jungle situations and are not authentic human experiences. We neglect to teach them the truth that man is a spiritual being, born of God, in His image. That our true potential for life accomplishment and meaning is in the development of our spiritual dimension. Until we see life from this viewpoint, there is nothing worth living for except creature comforts.

Most of our present day personal and national problems stem from our spiritual inadequacies. The key to any problem is to get at its root cause. The lack of spiritual development IS the root cause of our present conditions. Someday we will have the opportunity to repudiate this whole anti-God setup in this nation. Then it will be possible for God to do for this nation and us individually what He cannot do under present circumstances.

True education is the total development of the total man . . . body, mind, spirit. The wholesome development of his ambitions, aspirations and emotions. The mature application of these qualities to his work, his play, his home life, his community life. To be mature, adjusted, contributing vital personalities should be the goal of all true education.

Dear Reader . . . You have heard much about evolution,
do you know anything which you have evolved from?

WHAT ARE MY POWERS?

Do you realize the awesome POWERS you have? Very few people have systematically thought about all their marvelous POWERS. How wonderfully you are made? Life is a challenge to develop these POWERS for Good. You have ALL the POWERS . . . it's all up to YOU . . . to LIVE . . . BE . . . and HAVE . . . the BEST! Will you be a winner? . . . or will you settle for mediocrity?

POWER OF:

Attitude	Love	Achievement	Living
Thoughts	Work	Motivation	Choice
Courage	Money	Reasoning	Beauty
Character	Poise	Mental Power	Change
Integrity	Hunger	Expectancy	Beliefs
Suffering	Rest	Creativity	Old Age
Eternity	Habit	Human Nature	Growth
Happiness	Death	Confidence	Memory
Appetite	Sex	Imagination	Success
Tact and Skill	Joy	Spirit, Soul	Responsibility
Radiant Health	Mind	Your Culture	Being Negative

Visualization
Self-discovery
Physical Power
Spiritual Power
Self-discipline
Acting and Taking Action
Moderation in ALL Things
Peace, Freedom, Security
Heredity and Environment
Realizing Your Limitations
SERVICE You Can Render

Establishing Values
Realizing Mysteries
Meditation and Prayer
Becoming Materialistic
Your Creative Powers
Being Yourself, Naturalness
Realizing the Value of Time
Standards, Morality, Ethics
Human Relations, Friendship
Adjustment and Adaptability
Excessive Appetites

Your Conduct and Correct Use of Yourself
Realizing You Have Only So much Energy

You have all these powers, but if you do not know how to use them correctly or conduct yourself properly, acceptably, or in good taste . . . you "FOUL UP" or "SCREW UP", which means you are subject to the whole spectrum of troubles, problems, illness and diseases from nervousness, anxiety, worry, stress, depression, sad, bitter, wretched, dejected, heartsick, distress, suicide, or death.

TROUBLE

One does not travel very far in the pathway of life without encountering what we call trouble. Trouble is a relative term in that it does not mean the same thing to all people. Some of the human experiences we are accustomed to call "trouble" have to do with bodily affliction. To another it may be a great sorrow brought about by the death of a loved one or a friend. To another it may take the form of failure or disappointment.

Some folk seem to think that the best way to deal with trouble is simply to "Laugh it off" . . . "Keep smiling!" . . . "Chins up!" . . . etc. That philosophy is good as far as it goes, but how inadequate is this advice of laughing off one's trouble when we have to deal with stark reality. The really decisive question is not what happens TO US, but what happens IN US. Not what kind of troubles come to us; but OUR ATTITUDE toward them that counts most. Self pity and resentment is all wrong and un-Christian. So many interpret trouble and sorrow in this manner. God so often enables us to triumph over our troubles. This is always true when we let Him have His way with us.

The Christian way is to transform our troubles into triumph. Just as the oyster must put up with the irritable grain of sand and suffer the long process of spinning a gummy substance around the trouble spot to produce a pearl, our suffering can be transformed into a blessing. The liability can be changed into an asset. The adversity and disappointment can beget victory. Shall we not try hard to transform our troubles into triumph?

> For every hill I've had to climb,
> For every stone that bruised my feet,
> For all the blood and sweat and grime,
> For blinding storms and burning heat,
> My heart sings but a grateful song . . .
> These were the things that made me strong.
>
> For all the heartaches and the tears,
> For all the anguish and all pain,
> For gloomy days and fruitless years,
> And for the hopes that lived in vain,
> I do give thanks, for now I know
> These were the things that helped me grow!
>
> — *Author Unknown*

THE LAWS OF LIFE

The universe is governed (pervaded) by LAW. These LAWS are the Nature of God. The Laws of Gravity, Electricity, Light, Chemistry, Physics, etc... these are the physical Laws. The Law of Cause and Effect is built into the nature of the entire Universe.

THE LAWS OF HUMAN NATURE

Man's Nature is under LAW, which is the NATURE of GOD Himself. The Laws of thought, work, belief, attitude, survival, growth, learning, choice, supreme power, self-discovery, habit, use, health, prayer, responsibility, service, old age, death, etc., are but a few of the imperatives programmed into man's very nature. (In "THE SUPREME PHILOSOPHY OF MAN" I have discussed at much greater length the 47 Laws of Life.) These laws are invisible (abstract), but they come to life when put to human experience.

Education has failed to teach that every man is brought to true knowledge by the refinement and discipline of his own nature. In these so-called days of enlightenment, very few people know or understand the laws of man's nature. Yet nature's laws are SUPREME. We cannot change them. Ignorance of these laws is responsible for one man's foot on another man's neck. WITH THE TRUE KNOWLEDGE OF NATURE'S LAWS YOU HAVE THE BASIS FOR ALL REAL SUCCESS AND THE KEY TO WISDOM. THE KNOW-HOW FOR BETTER LIVING.

The QUALITY of every person's life is DETERMINED by the KNOWLEDGE OF, and USE OF, the Laws of God which are built into the very structure of man's nature. To discover and obey these laws is the highest of human enterprises.

Spiritual life is the emancipation of what we are. Through spiritual life we become responsible to God. On that level, and on that level only, does man find release for his highest powers and qualities.

We live in a world of Natural Laws... such as the Law of Cause and Effect... Action and Reaction. Things don't just happen by chance, they come to pass by our or others'... thoughts, actions and deeds.

> As we learn to distill the salt of wisdom
> from the vast ocean of man's experience
> I believe we will discover patterns that are clues
> to the natural laws governing human affairs.
>
> — *Bernard Baruch*

DON'T LET THE GOOD LIFE PASS YOU BY

Everybody looks outside themselves when their real treasures are within. GO WITHIN. *"From within, out of the heart of men"* proceeds all good and bad. Understand yourself, or as the ancient Greeks used to say, "Know thyself," and you will eliminate 90% of the emotionally induced illnesses and you will have peace of mind, and contentment in your heart.

We of this day have classified, arranged and pigeon-holed a vast amount of knowledge to almost every conceivable subject except the BASIC question of life. What is my TRUE nature? Where did I COME FROM? Where am I GOING? What is the TRUE MEANING of life? The fact is, the average one of us knows very little about ourselves.

We know more about the physical world AROUND us than we know about the spiritual world WITHIN us. We hear and talk much about the "conflict between nations," but fail utterly to understand that our basic conflict is between man and himself. We do not know how to adjust ourselves to ourselves. We suffer from the senselessness and emptiness of our lives. We have all the little answers, but we never ask the really big questions. Christ alone comes to grips with these big problems. Not only comes to grips with them, but gives the answers. Have YOU listened to Him?

LOOKING FOR AN INVESTMENT?

We all covet WEALTH, INFLUENCE, and POWER... well, God has put all three within our reach. To invest with HIM is to be ETERNALLY RICH: to join ourselves to HIS eternal purpose is to be everlastingly INFLUENTIAL. To have unity with the HOLY SPIRIT is to have POWER in the true deepest sense. This POWER and understanding is a FREE gift from God. All we do is provide the vessel, the container, the barrel, if you please. He sends His power, His love, His nature to His own, ACCORDING TO OUR FAITH. The benefits and rewards are priceless.

"Receive ... Knowledge rather than choice gold."
— *Proverbs 8:10*

WALKING AWAY FROM GOD

It is not doing us much good to unravel the nature of the Universe unless we can unravel the nature of man. We live in a day when so many are occupied with the "outer man", while the "inner man" perishes. The tendency today is to ignore man's inner nature and his eternal welfare, as if he did not have a spirit, a mind, or a soul.

As far back as 1874, William Gladstone, perhaps the greatest statesman England ever produced, said, "I am convinced that the welfare of mankind does not now depend on the state; but upon the greatest treasure of mankind: belief in God and the Gospel of Jesus Christ." I wonder what his comment would be today were he still living among us?

That his conclusions were right is conclusively demonstrated by the fact that, since the removal of the Bible from our public schools, an anti-God philosophy of life has taken over that has done exactly what David predicted several thousand years ago: "The nation that forgets God shall be turned into hell." And the hell of the theologians of yesteryear is a pleasant place as compared with the hell we have on hand here and now. With the passing of God has gone conscience, and with the passing of conscience has come lawlessness and crime, lack of restraint and moral decline.

"I do not believe the greatest threat to our future is from bombs or guided missiles. I don't think our civilization will die that way," says Laurence M. Gould, "I THINK IT WILL DIE WHEN WE NO LONGER CARE . . . WHEN THE SPIRITUAL FORCES THAT MAKE US WITHIN TO BE RIGHT AND NOBLE, DIE IN THE HEARTS OF MEN." Arnold Toynbee has pointed out that nineteen of twenty-one notable nations have died from within and not by conquest from without. There were no bands playing and flags waving when these civilizations decayed. It happened slowly, in the quiet and the dark when no one was aware. THIS IS EXACTLY WHAT IS TAKING PLACE NOW!

A WORD OF COMFORT

If these are "times that try men's souls" they are by the same token times that build the strength of men's souls. This is an opportunity to demonstrate the quality of our devotion. Sacrifice takes on added glory when it makes heavy demands. Happy is the man who has found God in his heart, yes, thrice happy is he. For he has found the pearl of great price . . . the Supreme Power.

All the bibles of the entire world teach us of an indwelling presence which enables all of us to receive the guidance and protection of the Infinite Presence and Supreme Power. People of all walks of life and of different creeds have become aware of this God power. Metaphors and figurative language are used in describing its wonder-working power.

David, the Psalmist, put it all together when he said: *"He that dwelleth in the secret place of the most High shall abide under the shadow of the Almighty. I will say of the Lord, He is my refuge and my fortress: my God; in him will I trust. He shall cover thee with his feathers, and under his wings shalt thou trust, his truth shall be thy shield and buckler. Thou shalt not be afraid for the terror by night; nor for the arrow that flieth by day; A thousand shall fall at thy side, and ten thousand at thy right hand; but it shall not come nigh thee. Because thou hast made the Lord, which is my refuge, even the most High, thy habitation; For he shall give his angels charge over thee, to keep thee in all thy ways. Because he hath set his love upon me therefore will I deliver him: I will set him on high, because he hath known my name. He shall call upon me, and I will answer him: I will be with him in trouble; I will deliver him, and honor him. With long life will I satisfy him, and shew him my salvation."*

— Psalm 91

From time immemorial God's problem has been to get men to look from His viewpoint. Man's failure in this particular is the reason for the condition of the world today. Let us all put our faith in this Supreme Power that runs the Universe and is waiting for acceptance and development of every man's soul!

THE WORDS OF JESUS CHRIST

The words of Jesus Christ have proved themselves to be the most dynamic, penetrating and energizing words ever spoken . . .

- They are timeless, ageless words that know no barriers or boundaries.

- They go to the heart of every problem and offer a solution in one syllable words.

- They flood the mind with light and release transforming power in the hearts of men.

- They are a Damascus blade that cuts to the very seat and source of all human ills, and effect a cure by removing first causes.

- They are the light that the stumbling, groping feet of men must have if they are to be saved from the outer darkness where light never penetrates.

- They are the voice that men most need to hear amid the confused questioning of this present hour.

And no marvel . . . for Jesus Christ himself IS THE WORD. To that fact the history of two milleniums attest. If He "spake as never a man spake" it was because He was God. His challenge, "Come unto me" is the challenge that our day must accept or perish with our ears full of the empty words of men as powerless as they are vacuous.

There is more light in Christ's words
than in any other human words.
This is not enough it seems, to be Christian . . .
in addition one must Believe.

— Andre Gide

HUMAN VALUES

The quality of your life is dependent upon your VALUES. ESTABLISH A SOLID SET OF VALUES. Your values will determine the quality of your life and help you make good CHOICES.

INTELLECT is NOT the most important thing in life . . . It is the QUALITIES and VALUES which guide the emotions and the intellect, such as Goodness, Character, Love, Attitude, Heart and the Generous Qualities.

Many people do not know what the HUMAN VALUES are. Some of the true human values of life are:

Loyalty	Culture	Love
Gratitude	Balance	Truth
Achievement	Learning	Character
Moral Fortitude	Action	Happiness
Integrity	Goodness	Attitude
Solid Beliefs	Suffering	Honesty
Self-Esteem	Freedom	Discipline
Mental Health	Patience	Kindness
Confidence	Ethics	Health
Confession	Leisure	Prayer
Contentment	Faith	Creativity
Friendship	Hope	Conduct
Moderation	Courtesy	Peace of Mind
Development	Beauty	A Sense of God
Human Relations	Pride	Responsibility

We must be KIND and LOVING to everyone. We must realize NOW that these may be our best years. Listen to the words of the late Aldous Huxley . . .

"It is a little embarrassing
that after forty-five years of research and study,
the best advice I can give to people is
to be a little kinder to each other."

MIRACLES

You may think that miracles are impossible yet it lies entirely within God's Power to suspend the laws of Nature, since it was HE himself who created them.

In Lourdes, France many people who are dying are cured. That is certainly a miracle. A miracle is a supernatural fact, a suspension of natural law, apparently from the Spiritual World by the power of God.

SCIENCE has a system of its own . . . science deals in tangible facts. CHRISTIANITY has a system of its own . . . CHRISTIANITY deals with the spiritual realm. It is obvious there are two realms. It is not science that nourishes the inner life of man . . . it is the faith of the soul, the spiritual realm.

I was given the words to a song and also the music in the night. It was truly a miracle for I do not write music. This is one of the several miracles that has happened to me during my lifetime.

ONENESS WITH JESUS

IF YOU . . . WANT YOUR ONENESS . . . WITH THE SAVIOUR,
THE LOVE . . . OF THE CRUCIFIED . . . ONE,
YOU MUST . . . SURRENDER YOUR HEART . . . TO JESUS
FOR HE IS . . . THE ALMIGHTY . . . ONE.

THERE IS . . . NO POWER OR LOVE . . . LIKE JESUS
FOR HE . . . IS THE CHOSEN . . . ONE.
HIS LOVE . . . NEVER DIES . . . ONLY HIS LOVE
SATISFIES . . . THE HUNGER . . . OF YOUR HEART.

THERE IS . . . NO ONE . . . LIKE JESUS,
NO ONE ELSE . . . WHO TRULY . . . SATISFIES.
YOU CAN . . . SEARCH THE WORLD . . . AND ITS PLEASURES
BUT YOU'LL . . . BE DISAPPOINTED . . . IF YOU TRY.

THE SOUL . . . WAS MADE . . . FOR JESUS,
HE WILL . . . FILL IT . . . WITH HIS JOY.
JUST OPEN . . . YOUR HEART . . . TO JESUS
AND WITH HIM . . . YOU WILL . . . EVER ABIDE.

LIFE VS EXISTENCE

A distinction that is hard for us to make is the distinction now commonly made by science between existence and life. "A thing is, when it exists, it exists when it is," they assure us. "It lives when in addition to existence it gets correspondence with the full environment for which it was made." And that so fully fulfills the definition of life given by Jesus Christ. The only definition that the world has ever had, does now have, and ever will have . . . in spite of our boasted intellectual progress and scientific research, and experimentation. Here is the only definition of life that the world has ever had. And it makes a sharp distinction between existence and life.

When Jesus announced his commission, his mission in the world, did he say, "*I am come that they might have*" a new theology? NO! A new religious teaching? NO! "*I am come that they might have LIFE.*"

Now he is speaking to those who existed. They had no adjustment to the spiritual environment for which they were built. I am come that they may get that adjustment. He had already said to Dr. Nicodemus as he interviewed him there on the house top that night, "You must be born again." Don't be surprised at that Nicodemus, you are amazed? Well, I am amazed at you. That you should be a teacher and yet you don't know that simple truth.

You MUST be born again. And that MUST is not a theological must. You must be born again because the fundamentalists say you must. You must be born again is not a theological must, it is a biological must. Here is one of the most important MUSTS that any of us will ever face. Makes all the difference between life and mere existence . . . breathing air, and eating food, and taking up room, wearing a few clothes. That's existence in common with the animal creation. Nothing more, nothing less.

The statement of Christ, "*I am come that they might have life,*" throws a different light on the whole concept of Christianity. So it does. Not a religion, not a philosophy, not a theology, what? "*I am come that they might have LIFE.*"

A person or thing may exist without living, and a deeper truth must be stated concerning human beings: they may half exist and half live at one and the same time. To such a group our Lord was speaking when He said, "*I am come that ye might have life.*"

MY PHILOSOPHY

1. Do the BEST you can, EACH DAY.

2. THINK and PLAN first, then DO secondly, then ENJOY the FRUITS of your labor.

3. Do not waste TIME, for time is the RAW MATERIAL of LIFE.

4. Live CONSTRUCTIVELY and live OPTIMISTICALLY.

5. LIVE to ENJOY the money you make.

6. Abide by the GOLDEN RULE . . . Matthew 7:12.

7. Abide by the SERMON ON THE MOUNT . . . Matthew 5,6,7.

8. Nothing in life is STATIC: one must LEARN to make adjustments.

9. Never admit defeat. LIVE CONFIDENTLY.

10. Always look for the GOOD in the other fellow; no one is perfect.

11. Think WELL of yourself, as the world takes you at your own estimate.

12. Beware of THIRST for the wrong kind of pleasures; cut off wrong pleasures and replace with the REAL PLEASURES of life.

13. UNDERSTAND the Law of CAUSE and EFFECT. I will suffer if I violate it. It becomes my greatest friend if I understand it.

14. Every EXCESS has its EFFECT, its AFTERMATH, its HANG-OVER. EVERYTHING that exceeds the BOUNDS OF MODERATION has an UNSTABLE FOUNDATION.

15. HAPPINESS depends not on things around me, but on my ATTITUDE. Everything in my life will depend on my ATTITUDE.

16. YOU serve GOD best by serving your fellow man.

TRUTH

"I am the way . . . the TRUTH . . . and the life."
— John 14:6

THE TRUTH TAUGHT BY JESUS CHRIST IS THE RIGHT WAY TO LIVE. What He taught is not primarily a religion. Christ did not teach a religion. He is God's revelation of how life MUST be lived to be lived at its best. To misunderstand, or fail to grasp this truth, is to miss the whole purpose of God's revelation of Himself in Jesus Christ. To accept and believe it is at once to give us an intelligent conception of the whole scheme of things called life.

The one aim of our life ought to be to purify ourselves from falsehood and to confess the truth. It is within our power to recognize and profess the truth. It all depends, therefore, on the strength of the consciousness of our Christian truth, on the part of each individual person.

"Ye shall know the truth,
and the truth shall make you free."
— John 8:32

Man discovers truth through absurdity . . . through getting what he thought he wanted. In fulfilling his original dream, he comes to realize all the things money can't buy . . . that in the end, all any of us have, is what we are in our relationship to other persons (love) and to ourselves (pride and principles).

— William D. Montapert

The sole means of uniting men . . . is their union in the truth. Therefore, the more sincerely men strive toward the truth, the nearer they get to unity.

I have searched for TRUTH early and late.
TRUTH is all I will have
When I come to the end of my little day.
— Alfred A. Montapert

It doesn't make any difference who says a thing,
or what the position of the man may be.
The great question is:
Is he RIGHT, OR is he WRONG?
— Bernard Baruch

I WOULD

I WOULD have neither joy nor success by incurring a debt to others greater than I can pay. I would give value received for all I draw from the Bank of Life.

I WOULD have a few friends who know me for what I am and who love me in spite of what I am. In return for such friendship, I give my pledge to foster in myself what I ask of others.

I WOULD have some work to do which has such value that without it the day in which I live will be poorer, and richer if I succeed; and I want to do my work without taxing the purse, sympathy, or patience of others beyond the value that I give.

I WOULD cultivate such courage of mind and heart that I shall not be afraid to travel where there is no blazed trail, and I shall not hesitate to sacrifice when, by sacrifice, I can make contribution to others.

I WOULD experience such growth in grace as shall enable me to understand those who rejoice or weep or suffer. I would enter into their joy without covetousness and into their suffering with such sympathy as will give rise to courage and wings to hope.

I WOULD have a deeper appreciation of nature in all her moods and aspects, and a profounder respect for man as he seeks to labor together with God for the highest good of humanity.

I WOULD cultivate a sense of humor, for without it, I have discovered, life is likely to become so serious a business that it will be unlivable. Especially, would I learn to laugh at momentary defeat, smile at gray-cloaked discouragement, and dismiss dejection with the nonchalant carelessness of faith.

I WOULD have a little leisure in which to do . . . nothing. To keep the bow tightly strung all the time is, I have learned, to rob it of its spring and power. Too, I must have time to cultivate the fine art of meditation. God has His best chance at me when I am full of . . . hush.

Finally, I WOULD learn to wait for the best and have the wisdom to know it when it comes.

PRAISE FIRST THEN PRAY

My Grandmother Margaret Burton used to arise from her bed in the morning, go to the open window and with upraised hands . . . "Praise the Lord" for about five minutes. Then she would kneel at her bedside and say her morning prayers. Grandma was "Christ Centered." Her face radiated with goodness, which came from the indwelling presence of God in her heart. She had Peace of Mind and the Joy of the Lord was reflected in her whole being.

SALVATION

About 2000 years ago, Jesus Christ died on the cross
to save everyone from the wages of sin which is death.

SO

Everyone has been Saved.

HOWEVER,

This is not possible until you individually

BELIEVE it with your HEART . . .

This is called FAITH . . . You must say it . . .
confess it with your mouth . . . This is called
CONFESSION . . . Only then are you saved. Only
the indwelling Power of God in your heart
has the power to transform you. Only then
are you born spiritually into the Family of
God. This is called your . . .

NEW SPIRITUAL NATURE.

No one can explain or define this spiritual
power of God. It can only be experienced,
and is better felt than told.

THE TEMPORAL WORLD

The things around us do not enamor us. These things are temporal. We remind ourselves so frequently they are so soon past. We speak of them as ours, but truly they are not. God has loaned them to us for a little moment. It is up to us to use them, so that they will accumulate against that day when all time is bankrupt in eternal wealth. This we seek to do.

The whole of life . . . is our individual task . . . to develop our full potential. HOW ARE WE TO LIVE? We are spirit beings and need more knowledge about the Spiritual Realm, our Spiritual Nature. The answer lies in our spiritual development, for here is the higher power, the guide and strength to the highest and best life ever known to mankind! Apart from God man exists but does not live.

So many are forgetting God utterly, completely. They are going their way thoughtless of what will eventually come to pass. Sooner or later we must go to spiritual sources for real satisfaction and happiness. God in the soul satisfies the inner man. Having a sense of God is man's only real security. Let the supreme purpose of our daily life be to open our life to the higher powers of the mind and spirit, then KNOW AND DO THE WILL OF GOD.

Today people are looking to Astrology, cults, isms, and mystics, instead of going to the true source for all their needs. Living is a continuous adventure. We must learn to simplify our lives. Discuss the presence of God in our lives. God is revealed by his Love and Creation.

When the old timers used to greet one another they used to say, "How is your Faith?" They meant just that: "How positive are you? How much trust do you have in God? 5%, 10%, 70%, 80%, or 90%?" It is knowing the VALUE of this FAITH, then ACTING on it. Without Action and Doing or Using it, Knowledge is sterile.

The thing that makes me so sorry for this whole modern generation is, they have never experienced anything where God manifested himself in that manner. They have been cheated. Cheated as perhaps no generation in the history of mankind has been cheated. Oh, we've given them automobiles, we've given them good homes, we've given them education, we've given them money. In fact, we've given them about everything except God.

CHAPTER TWENTY-TWO

DESTINY

The destiny of man lies in his soul.

— Herodotus

One day Michaelangelo ordered the workmen to pull down the scaffolding, remove the ropes, clear away plaster, litter and rubble, and disclose the finished work of the Sistine Chapel. Men stood in awe as they gazed upon the figures of angels and seraphs wrought into the ceiling by the Artist's Master. So one day death shall pull down the scaffolding and disclose to full view the finished work of Jesus Christ in men who have yielded their lives to Him. The sunlight of eternal years will then shine upon the structure which God shall have reared. The building material we must furnish . . . honesty, integrity, sincerity, truth, honor and devotion. God grant to all of us the foresight to send on good material against that day.

Our little day will soon be done. We will have followed Life's footpath to where sunset shadows lie softly upon autumn hills. Two worlds will blend into one, as twilight blends day and night where the cherry thicket is crimson with the first touch of frost. The fading day will burn with the goldenfire of eternal sunrise. Through the open door of resurrection dawning, we will glimpse the Holy Grail.

Dreams will begin to come true and half seen visions will begin to unfold in reality. On anxious feet, we will hurry out of hemmed in circumstances into immortal freedom. No longer will we turn a puzzled gaze upon the pain and imperfection of life's blurred picture. We will see no longer *"through a glass darkly,"* but face to face. Crystal clear will be the flood of light that, rolling in billowy tides, will wash life's yesterday and make it resplendent with God's unsullied beauty.

Redemption will have struck the major notes of its final triumph. Pain-twisted bodies will be made "like Him." White-faced suffering will blush into eternal health. God will wipe away all tears and smooth every wrinkle. Eternal youth will join its voice in the song of praise that will swell in mighty volume, like the "sound of many waters."

Trails end? No! It is the place where the Footpath widens into the . . . FOREVER.

THE GREAT ADVENTURE

Men have tried in various ways through the centuries to build society on secure foundations, but all of men's schemes have failed. Political, economic, and scientific programs have been tried ... but these have failed to bring peace and prosperity to mankind.

It is the author's conviction that hope and certainty are to be found only in God. Apart from the grace of God and His purpose for the human race all is frustration and confusion. But in the divine relation of the love of God there is a clear, shining light that beckons us on to the perfection that is to be. We have tried everything else but true Christianity.

It is an undeniable fact that young people today face greater distractions and more subtle temptations than in the past. Where is there safe anchorage for our youth? Secular education and scientific dogmas tend to undermine religious faith and moral principles. To what greater inspiration and counsel can we turn than to the imperishable truth to be found in this treasure house ... THE BIBLE. Many methods of success are found in the Bible.

Sad to say, much of the instruction in the schools of today tends to destroy faith in God and the Bible. Science all too often is exalted as man's only saviour.

When you come to the end of your little day and life is fast fading away, will you die spiritually bankrupt? Have you developed your Spiritual Dimension, so that when you enter the Kingdom of God you will feel at Home?

The physical body is bound to the physical universe by its incessant needs of the oxygen of the air and the foods provided by the earth.

The time will come when your physical body will die and returns to the dust. The spirit will leave your body and return to the creator who gave it.

THE ROAD OF LIFE

Each day is a new road. Like the prophet of old, the morning warns us that "We have not passed this way before." It is the love of the unknown that makes life a thrilling adventure.

If our days were all mapped, and scheduled, life would soon become an unbearable monotony. It is the arrangement of a wise providence that the road of life may reveal itself only as it is travelled.

If fortune tellers and seers could reveal the future, I would not visit them. I much prefer to allow each bend in the road to reveal its own joy or sorrow.

Disappointment has met me at more than one bend in the road, but out of the darkness a new sunrise of courage has given strength against another day of battle.

Looking back I can see the road winding thru sunlight and shadows; over hills, and down into the valleys; along an easy level place, and then up a steep and difficult climb. But these vicissitudes have all had their advantages; they have increased my checking account in the bank of experience, and I am drawing on this account for the duties, responsibilities, and opportunities of a present which would be bankrupt in courage were it not for the sunny, shadowy, sorrowful, joyful yesterday.

I turn toward the West. The road is hidden. Yonder I can see the dim outline of the last hill silhouetted against the shadows of the evening sky. With trembling hand . . . not from fear, but from the excitement of breathless, expectant wonder . . . I shall one day part the curtains and pass from sight into the great unknown. WHAT DOES IT HOLD? I do not know; only that the Master with whom I have journeyed is there, and with HIM the unnumbered years can but mean adventurous living.

Toward the last bend in the trail then, I hurry on, buoyed up by the hope that yet more thrilling experiences with life await me.

FOR WHOM THE BELL TOLLS

Jesus rarely ever used the word, DEATH. When He went to visit the little girl who was ill and had finally passed on, He said, "Stop your nonsense; why are you weeping and howling around? She is not dead, she is but asleep. I have come to awaken her." He said, *"I am the resurrection and the life,"* you know.

Now, I want you to read the words of the Apostle Paul, who is speaking to his son, Timothy. He too, has come to the lengthening shadows of the final days. The sun is setting behind the hills. He is writing a last, final note to his son, Timothy, a young fellow who was converted in his early ministry. And he says to Timothy, "If it is all possible, I wish you'd come and see me. But if not, very well. The time of my departure has come." The literal Greek translation says, *"the time of my sailing has arrived."* The figure is of a ship that has been in port, taking on cargo; hulls all full now, flags are run, the band is playing. The Apostle Paul says, "The time of my sailing has arrived. I have taken on my cargo and I am now about to turn my bow into the strong current, out where the deep tides run. Out where I shall experience what I was made to experience."

Why should this be a fearsome thing?

He said, "By the way Timothy, my books are all balanced, everything is in order. No erasures that I want to make, nothing to correct. Oh, I've made my mistakes here and there, but, through it all, I have been God's transformed man. Ambition which now consumes me, is to know the power of His resurrection. I have made it my first job to, at any price, be ready. *'I have fought a good fight, I have kept the faith.'* I passed it on to you; that faith, once and for all, delivered."

And, he said, "By the way, Timothy, at last I feel, at last I am laying hold of that for which Christ laid hold on me. I am about to lose my head but Christ, He is about to hand it back to me, nicely crowned." God doesn't crown us by a mistake of birth, you know. He crowns us, when we prove ourselves worthy to wear a crown.

FOR WHOM THE BELL TOLLS
CONTINUED

You know why I am so insistent on things like these? Because I am exceedingly anxious that your day and my day shall close like that. Nothing to fix up, no books to balance, no erasures to make, no corrections to make. Everything in order. How about that! That's my idea of being a Christian. Is it yours? T'was the Apostle Paul's.

It'll be a great day, when the sun is sinking in splendor and casting long shadows across the final moments. It'll be a great day, to be able to say, with this man, "By the way, Timothy, the time of my departure has arrived . . . "

Time is so short, opportunity is so fleeting. Our little day soon will be done. As says Tennyson, the poet, "It will soon be twilight and evening bell and clear call . . . " for all of us.

CROSSING THE BAR

Sunset and evening star,
    And one clear call for me,
And may there be no moaning of the bar,
    When I put out to sea.

But such a tide as moving seems asleep,
    Too full for sound and foam,
When that which drew from out the boundless deep
    Turns again home.

Twilight and evening bell
    And after that the dark!
And may there be no sadness of farewell,
    When I embark;

For tho' from out our bourne of time and place
    The flood may bear me far,
I hope to see my Pilot face to face,
    When I have cross't the bar.

— *Alfred Lord Tennyson*

DEATH IS A DOOR

For a Christian, death does not exist . . . rather, it is only a change into eternal life . . .

"And this is life eternal, that they might know thee the only true God, and Jesus Christ, whom thou hast sent."

— John 17:3

"Verily, verily, I say unto you, If a man keep my saying, he shall never see death."

— John 8:51

"I am the resurrection and the life."

— John 11:25

"I am the living bread which came down from heaven, and if any man eat of this bread, he shall live for ever."

— John 6:51

"For half a century I have been writing my thoughts in prose and in verse . . . history, philosophy, drama, romance, tradition, satire, ode, and song. I have tried all. But I feel I have not said the thousandth part of what is in me. When I go down to the grave, I can say, like many others, 'I have finished my day's work.' But I cannot say, 'I have finished my life.' My day's work will begin again the next morning. The tomb is not a blind alley; it is a thoroughfare. It closes on the twilight, it opens on the dawn."
                                                                — *Victor Hugo*

Leaving the cemetery, some one remarked: "All is finished." Some one murmured, "Poor soul, that's how we'll all finish." But the truth is, for the Christian it is just the beginning of the eternal life. Yes, the person had finished the last rehearsal, but the play was just beginning. The years of training were over, but the eternal work was about to start. The person had just been born to eternal life. The real life . . . life that's going to last, life eternal. A step from temporal to eternal. As in the death of the caterpillar, emerges the butterfly. From the seed of grain, the full-blown sheath.

"For I am now ready to be offered, and the time of my departure is at hand. I have fought a good fight, I have finished my course, I have kept the faith: Henceforth there is laid up for me a crown of righteousness, which the Lord, the righteous judge, shall give me at that day: and not to me only, but unto all them also that love his appearing."

— II Timothy 4:6-8

SHOULD YOU GO FIRST

Should you go first and I remain
    To walk the road alone,
I'll live in memory's garden, dear,
    With happy days we've known.
In Spring I'll watch for roses red,
    When fades the lilac blue,
In early Fall when brown leaves call
    I'll catch a glimpse of you.

Should you go first and I remain
    For battles to be fought,
Each thing you've touched along the way
    Will be a hallowed spot.
I'll hear your voice, I'll see your smile,
    Though blindly I may grope,
The memory of your helping hand
    Will buoy me on with hope.

Should you go first and I remain
    To finish with the scroll,
No length'ning shadows shall creep in
    To make this life seem droll.
We've known so much of happiness,
    We've had our cup of joy,
And memory is one gift of God
    That death cannot destroy.

Should you go first and I remain,
    One thing I'd have you do:
Walk slowly down that long, lone path,
    For soon I'll follow you.
I'll want to know each step you take
    That I may walk the same,
For some day down that lonely road
    You'll hear me call . . . your name.

                — *Albert Kennedy Rowswell*

MAMA WE LOVE YOU

Both life and death are inexplicable mysteries. To undertake to fathom or explain life is hopelessly impossible. But as far as I am concerned, the mystery of life but argues the necessity for continuation, and continuation God has demonstrated in a thousand ways.

It is unthinkable that the God who so carefully attends a shrunken seed in its wintry grave of death should allow a life as nobly lived as the life of my dear mother to utterly perish in that mystery of death. If pressed for a stated doctrine or creed . . . that would be my doctrine, faith and creed, it was the faith, doctrine and creed of my dear mother. Nor does one need more.

"Who believes," said Jesus Christ, *"shall be saved"* . . . saved FROM the futility of a materialistic philosophy of life that gives no hope beyond the place where the sun dips behind the skyline of death, and saved TO an awareness of God that reassures one as one journeys beyond a shadow-hung horizon of time that we count years.

Be the reasons what they may, it DOES make a difference where, when, and of what stock one is born. Those born in mountain country INHERIT something of the rugged strength of the mountains. The prairies weave their spell of vastness, breadth and solitude into the life and character of those who tramp their star-studded skies of blue, and become a part of their silent muse. All of this was a part of Mama's early life. She was born and reared in the State of Connecticut when the country was young and new. The traditions of our National life became a part of her and to the last she retained her rugged New England idealism. Their spiritual conception and lofty principles clothed her like a garment and she wore them worthily.

Mama had lived so long in intimate fellowship with God that He was ever "nearer to her than breathing, closer than hands or feet." Like Enoch of old, Mama walked with God out into the vast expanse known to us only as the forever . . . the forever which alone explains the vastness of our hopes and dreams and longings. The forever which accounts for the awareness that we are overmade for everything time and the present has to offer.

WHEN I MUST LEAVE YOU

When I must leave you
 for a little while,
Please do not grieve
 and shed wild tears
And hug your sorrow
 to you through the years,
But start out bravely
 with a gallant smile;
And for my sake
 and in my name
Live on and do
 all things the same,
Feed not your loneliness
 on empty days,
But fill each waking hour
 in useful ways,
Reach out your hand
 in comfort and in cheer
And I in turn will comfort you
 and hold you near;
And never, never
 be afraid to die,
For I am waiting
 for you in the sky!

— *Helen Steiner Rice*

PRAYER

The grass withereth, the flower fadeth,
but the word of our God
shall stand for ever.

— *Isaiah 40:8*

THE HOUR GLASS RUNS OUT ON ALL OF US

The passing of a friend has just reminded me again that my little day will soon be done. With the sundown may it be mine and yours to have the assurance of both God and conscience that we have done the best job that is possible for us to do.

WHAT APPEARS AS DEATH
IS ONLY CHANGE

"He that believeth on me hath everlasting life," the Bible admonishes in John 6:47. It is something more than passing strange to me, that our day that boasts its enlightenment, glories in its emotional maturity, and is devoted to objective reality, should more and more refuse to think on the one event that dominates all life, from its very beginning . . . Death.

A survey has been recently taken among the leading universities of the nation. Indeed, it lapped over in the European countries. The students were questioned something after this manner: "If you were seriously ill and the physician had misgivings, would you desire to know the worst?" 98 and a fraction percent of these university students answered "NO". THEY DID NOT WANT TO FACE THE REALITY OF DEATH.

Like the Warden in Dr. F.B. Myers' church, when asked by Dr. Myer one day, "What will happen to you after you die?" Dutifully and with precise accuracy, the church warden quoted the catechism, "I shall immediately part into everlasting felicity and bliss." Then he hurried to add, "But doctor, I wish you would not talk to me about such unpleasant matters."

Perhaps it is not strange that men generally should shrink away from death, but Christians? Voltaire, when told by his physician that he had but a few hours to live turned his face to the wall and he was heard to mutter, "Death, thou art a monster, thou art a thief, now thou art come to snatch away everything that I love, what a mockery is life." Turning back to his physician he said to him, "I will give you half of my fortune for a month to live." Said his doctor, "Life is not mine to give, much less is it mine to sell. I have told you frankly what you may expect."

And it is a fact that money cannot buy it off. It slips into the mansion as surely and as easily as it slips into the cottage of the poor. Education has no solution. No research chemist has found an answer. Medicine must bow before this last relentless enemy.

Sir William Osler, professor of medicine in Oxford University, speaks for all scientists when he says, "Whether across death's threshold we shall step from life to life, the scientist cannot answer."

No, science does not have the answer, it must come from the other side. GOD'S SIDE. That is the reason WHY I have approached the whole matter as I have. Simply to say to us, that our day, as every other day, bows in total abject defeat, before the question of death.

Yet, as I said at the very beginning, it is the one thing which begins the minute we are born. It is the one thing, that cannot be escaped. And I repeat . . . education has no answer.

Our boasted intellectualism has no answer. All of these mental philosphies which we concoct daily, have no answer. All they can do is act the fool, and refuse to recognize the facts. And I am speaking advisedly, and speaking carefully when I say, "act the fool". And deny the reality. How stupid, how utterly brainless, for anybody to stand beside a casket containing a lifeless body and say, "This is all an error of mortal mind."

The answers must come from the other side. The most brilliant scientific researcher cannot solve the problems. Professor Osler, known to his students and known to the city of London as one of the most brilliant minds who ever entered the University of Oxford, dealt with problems far and away beyond the reach of the average intellect. Yet when it comes to the problem of death, he says frankly to his students, "Whether death is the threshold across which we pass from life to life, I do not know."

> WHAT the caterpillar calls the end of the world, the MASTER calls a butterfly.
>
> — *Bach*

And I repeat, whatever answers we have must come from the other side. From GOD'S SIDE. Now I have appealed to God. He affirms three tremendous truths. Nor do I pass from the intransitive verb "speculate" to the transitive verb "affirm" by accident. When Christ uses what to others would be dogmatic affirmation he is but using his own language.

He was in the beginning with God, so we are told, and He is God. He speaks with authority, because HE IS AUTHORITY. I am stating this because so many seem to suppose that Christians, and especially if they are believing Christians, live for the most part in a daze and a fog. But I would remind us once again, Christianity brings us into the most positive realm of certain knowledge to which human beings have access. We Christians affirm what we know. Granted that it is infinitely beyond the reach of an intellectual process, it is nevertheless true knowledge. For I remind us once again that faith takes journeys in the realms where the intellect cannot go. And no apologies for saying that to the smart day in which we live.

Since Jesus Christ is God, I'm interested to know what he says about death. He says, in the first place, that death is not the end of existence. This great medical scientist whom I have quoted, "Whether death is a threshold over which we pass from life to life, I know not." Jesus Christ says positively, "It is not the end." That's the reason why I said nonchristians . . . I can understand why they do not choose to think about death. But Christians? It is an ever increasing mystery to me why Christians should fear this that we call death.

Listen to Him. He did not say, "Who believes on me shall AFTER AWHILE go to a world that is everlasting." He said, *"Who believes on me HATH everlasting life."* It isn't a question, Dr. Osler, of crossing a threshold from life to life, it is simply a question of crossing from life to LARGER LIFE, according to Jesus Christ. Then why should we dread it?

Oh to be sure, there is a physical shrinking from the unknown. That's understandable. Jesus Christ saw life as a part of two worlds. And notice how I am stating it. He did not think of the other world as something apart. He did not think of THIS present and THAT future, as air-tight compartments mutually exclusive, the one to the other. He thought of them as ONE WORLD. That is . . . to Christians.

Life on earth, Jesus said, is but a preparation for that other life. It's the kindergarten. Listen to Him speak, he's visualizing the end of this probation. We look forward to graduation with great joy, do we not . . . In everything but Christianity. Some of you people look back on your graduation day as the greatest day in the memory of yesterday, do you not? When you marched so straight and with that rare smile, and the professor handed you a diploma, and he announced to all, within hearing, that you had graduated Magna Cum Laude. What a proud day that was!

Jesus Christ says, this was but preparation. Do you believe that? Well, why aren't you a little more careful then to get your work caught up? He visualizes that day and he says, "Those who have graduated, well done." I don't know how it is with you, but I think that will be the greatest day within the range of eternal years, if I can hear him say to me, "*Well done, good and faithful servant; thou hast been faithful over a few things, I will make thee ruler over many things.*" This is what authority is saying, about this question of death.

The second thing He says about death, is that physical death is not the most serious thing that can happen to any person. I want to say that again, death is NOT the most serious thing that could happen to any person.

Physical death is NOT the most serious thing that can happen to us. Listen to Jesus speak once again, "*Fear not them which kill the body.*" Now you read that and re-read it until the full impact of it comes home to you. "*Fear not them which kill the body, RATHER, FEAR HIM WHO IS ABLE BOTH TO DESTROY SOUL AND BODY.*"

The physical body is made for just a few years at best. How fleeting those years are. It is difficult for me to think of myself as a man now well on in years. It seems yesterday, or the day before, I was a barefoot lad, on my grandfather's farm, whistling blissfully down by the creek.

This physical is made for a few passing years, at best. But the part of me to which Christ refers is built for eternity. Augustine was exactly right when he said, "We were built for God and homesick will we be until we find our place in Him." And separation from what I was made for will be the worst possible thing that can happen to me. Death is not the worse thing that can happen to us. THE WORST THING THAT CAN HAPPEN TO US IS TO BE SEPARATED FROM GOD.

Have you ever noticed how triumphant the New Testament is from the beginning to its end? It sings about victory over death on almost every page. The Christian is the only person in the world who knows what that means. I say once again, "I do not marvel at men who do not know Jesus Christ, and are loath to think about death."

All I am trying to say to you is, that death for the Christian is not the flickering out of a candle in the dark. A noted atheist said as he lay on his death bed, "I feel like a child going out into the dark and all alone."

Not the Christian. Once again, and the last word, Jesus gives me final assurance that death is but the beginning. Oh, there are so many things He said that I'd like to quote in this connection. Among other things He said, *"No man taketh my life from me."*

Not only did He demonstrate his power over death, but He himself rose from the grave. Now you say, that's exactly what I've heard them preach all my life, but how do I know? Well, I have just to say that there is as good evidence that Jesus Christ rose from the dead the third day after his crucifixion as there is to substantiate any fact whatsoever within the range of history. Christians do not believe on the hearsay. They live in the realm of positive knowledge. He said, *"Because I live you shall live also."* We do not speculate.

1867 saw the death of Michael Faraday, one of the really, truly, outstanding scientists of the century. When he lay on his death bed an attendant said to him, "Sir, what are your speculations now?" Faraday raised himself on one elbow and said with his last remaining strength, "I have NO speculations, I am resting on certainty!"

After the Napoleonic wars in Europe, the whole of Europe was in a state of chaos. A young man came to Talleyrand, the great statesman, and remarked to him, "What Europe needs is a new religion." They get that idea every little while you know. The world is full of John-ny-come-latelys who are telling us the world needs a new religion. Said Talleyrand to this young man, "Well, young man, if you're convinced the world needs a new religion, go out into the highways and byways and preach your idea of this new religion." Then he said, "Lay down your life, for what you say you believe. Then experience a resurrection from the dead and triumphantly ascend back to him who revealed this new religion to you. When you have done all that, I shall be ready to listen to your new religion. When you demonstrate something new to me as powerful as Christianity, I'll exchange what has stood me so well in hand all these years, for your new conception."

An Englishman was in conversation with a United States citizen. He, like the British so frequently are, was a bit sarcastic. "If you say your declaration is an inspired instrument, what proof have you of that?" This man confidently answered him, "The United States of America." What proof have I of the resurrection of Jesus Christ? The Kingdom of God.

A Russian leader was lecturing in Moscow on the absurdities of Christianity. At the conclusion of his lecture it was thrown open for question. There was a young priest standing with others, who asked permission to speak to the people. Said the communist leader, "Five minutes, no more." He said, "I shall not need so long."

He got to the platform and said, "Brethren and sisters, HE is risen." They answered as is their custom over there, "He is risen indeed." With that shout he turned to leave the platform, the communist said, "Have you finished?" He said, "I have finished. There is nothing more to say. Christ is risen. You ask me how I know? He lives within my heart."

"FOR TO ME TO LIVE IS CHRIST"

We thank thee for these words of Thine, Lord. These assurances, and they are so numerous. When we are born again, when we are supernaturally regenerated, and become a Christian, thou dost open to us a whole new vista. Eternal years but glow and glitter as filled with rare promises as the sky is filled with stars. Oh God, grant to me, and grant to all of us that the heart of us shall be so involved with God, we shall have no misgivings. We'll begin at long last to say what we mean and mean what we say and sing. With the Apostle Paul, we shall be enabled to say, *"For to me to live is Christ,"* not money, nor fame, nor getting ahead, nor finding my place in the sun. *"For to me to live is Christ, and to die is gain."* And it isn't such a fearsome thing, to exchange mud pies for a gold mine. Amen.

EVERYTHING WILL PASS

How few indeed are the works of men that survive. When first brought into being they boast, this will abide. But their bones have hardly crumbled into dust until the things of which they boast become obsolete and perish. The past is characterized by nothing quite so much as making useful such words as gone, perished, old-fashioned, antiquated, and the things of which we boast today will soon go the way of all the past.

CHAPTER TWENTY-THREE

ETERNITY

We shall think of these things. These worthwhile things. Most of the things with which we have to do will pass in a day or two, three. They will be no more. The things which engage our thinking at the moment will endure eternally. They combine to lead us to do the will of God and thou hast said that those of us who incorporate the will of God, who make it their first business to do the will of God, shall be like Mount Zion, which never can be moved.

Things which are seen are temporal, but the things which are not seen are eternal. We are in what is called eternity. It is the same Arno river that flows through Florence which was there in the days of Dante; Julius Caesar saw the same Iber river we see now; Joan of Arc looked upon the same Seine. And King Alfred saw the same Thames we note today. Paul walked on the Appian Way which we can walk on today. Jesus of Nazareth walked from one small village to another and was baptized in the Jordan River which we can visit today.

"And this is life eternal, that they might know thee the only true God, and Jesus Christ, whom thou hast sent."

— John 17:3

Each goes to his own . . . earth to earth, ashes to ashes, dust to dust, spirit to spirit . . . *"Then shall the dust return to the earth as it was: and the spirit shall return unto God who gave it."*

— Ecclesiastes 12:7

"And this is the record, that God hath given to us eternal life, and this is in his Son. He that hath the Son hath life; and he that hath not the Son of God hath not life. These things have I written unto you that believe on the name of the Son of God; that ye may know that ye have eternal life, and that ye may believe on the name of the Son of God."

— 1 John 5:11-13

"Everything science has taught me . . . and continues to teach me . . . strengthens my belief in the continuity of our spiritual existence after death."

— Dr. Wernher von Braun
Space Age Scientist

OVERBUILT FOR THIS WORLD

Man is overbuilt for this world. Both life and death are beyond the comprehension of the human intellect. *"This is life and life eternal that you may know God."* The reason that Jesus uses the word eternal is that we are built for eternal years. David was right when he said of God, *"He hath set eternity in our hearts."*

This is the reason why you are TOO BIG for this physical world. You place man on the biggest thing this world has to offer and he'd hang over on four sides. Doesn't fit him. This present world doesn't fit us, nor do we fit it. Every one of us who is honest will own up to that truth. MAN IS OVER-MADE FOR EVERYTHING YOU FIND HERE.

I have yet to find a man who is entirely satisfied, regardless of how much he possesses. Man is the offspring of God. Man has something unshared by the rest of the universe. Man thinks thoughts and sees visions infinitely beyond the mortal. The only creature that does. THE FULLNESS OF GOD IS THE ONLY THING THAT SATISFIES A MAN'S SOUL.

This is not intended to be an attempt to take away from us all laughter, and mingling with people in social contact. It certainly isn't intended to do that at all. It is intended to lift our thinking to God's viewpoint. It is intended to help train us in the use of God's viewpoint, in the use of God's thinking, in the use of God's words. For Christ said, *"Whosoever is ashamed of me and of my words of him shall the Son of man be ashamed before the Father and the holy angels."*

God has set eternity in our hearts. We are built for two worlds, the physical and the spiritual. It is impossible for any of us to live within the narrow confines of this immediate materialistic present. Man's heart is hungry for the Spiritual World. Get what you will, your heart will still seek adjustment for what it was built for. I have seen supreme happiness and joy in lives where the God-Nature has awakened within. This love of God may be experienced in the heart of us, and God help the person who hasn't experienced it.

ETERNITY IS SET IN YOUR HEART

The Bible says when a person dies his spirit returns to God who gave it and his body returns to the earth. We know the body has the same elements as the earth . . . Carbon . . . Oxygen . . . Hydrogen . . . Nitrogen. That takes care of the physical side. But man is more than 170 pounds of meat.

Now if we are going to find out about the Spirit, we must go to God's side, for that is His realm. What information do we find? God is Spirit, man is Spirit. Even while you are alive, you are Spirit, living in a physical body. You know this much as you have seen your own body develop since you were a baby, when all you were then was a bundle of possibilities.

It will be much better for each individual to realize that most of his existence is out of this world. It will be far more important for him to build into the integrity of the Universe, than to satisfy his own ambitions here. If we live right here, we are right forever and it behooves us to start immediately to make any corrections which will enable us to live better, more constructive lives.

Human philosophy . . . be it social, political, educational or economic . . . is, and always has been, busy with the incidentals of life. The best of men have never gone deeper than the animal surface . . . what shall we eat, what shall we drink, what shall we wear. But here is one who goes deep enough to elevate man to his proper place. Life, He said, is more than raiment and food; more than merely breathing air and taking up room. Life, He said, is a Kingdom within you. You, He said, are potential eternity. You are time without beginning and without end. Eternity is "set in your heart."

ETERNITY . . .
a world where there is TIME ENOUGH,
and ROOM ENOUGH, to do all the things
we always wanted to do.

LAW OF ETERNITY

We are built for God. Things here do not, because they cannot, satisfy us. We are contrived on too vast a scale to be content with a handful of things. We must have close contact with the eternal, for this alone we were made.

We thank Thee for the world in which we live. Thou has so contrived it that it speaks to us of the thing for which we were made. It reassures us day by day that we are built for more than 50 years, or 70 years. We are built for the eternal years.

The day utters speech to the heart of those of us who have eyes to see and ears to hear. Having lived in this world for even so short a time, there could be no mistake about our immortality. The stars that glitter overhead like 10,000 diamonds set in blue, speak to us of these eternal things. A flock of geese passing across a moonlight sky talk to us about the heart of us and its yearning for far places beyond. Their lonely call speaks to us pointedly about our crying out for God. With Job we find ourselves saying so often, Oh, that I knew where I might find Him. Some of us have found that secret place where the heart of us tabernacles with God. A thousand violets that pushed themselves up through a mass of decaying leaves talks to us about our hearts and its eternal push Godward.

Notwithstanding we live in a world so confused, so filled with human depravity, so bewilderingly confusing, our hearts still push upward toward God. When we speak of such things we may have the intellect of some opposed, but the heart of everyone is in full sympathy with the truth revealed by Jesus Christ. Help us then, as wise men and women should, to give our undivided attention to these eternal things. Give us the wisdom to keep first things in first place.

God grant that individually and collectively we may fill that purpose, accomplish our God given tasks, and when it comes our time to fall on sleep, may it not be amid shadows dark and dismal. May the sunset on our day burn the brighter because we have experienced God and Eternal things. It seems far to us at the moment across into that other realm, but it is not far. God grant to keep us reminded of these things continually.

PARTING

We live to serve. To God and man we must give our best. And so, dear reader, we come to the end of our little journey through this book together. May we meet again. God has blessed me so abundantly with all His benefits. My books are the seeds I sow for His purpose and Glory. May His Love and Blessings blanket your life.

Looking back over the years . . . and there are more than I care to think about . . . there have been more blessings than I could ever catalogue. For each and every one, seen and unseen, I am eternally grateful. And each and every one has been a spur that I may be worthy of all I have received.

PRAY TO WIN! is written for both people who pray and for those who neglect prayer. Prayer is a natural instinct of man's nature. Why short-change yourself and deprive yourself of one of your most important Divine Dimensions. If even one cylinder in your automobile was not functioning you would have it fixed. Prayer affects your whole life and will help you choose the REAL VALUES in Life.

Man today will protest that he has risen from primitive man to the highly civilized, cultured man that he is today. But, we ask, what have we accomplished for the good of man's life, for the good of his soul? Have we eased his mind? Have we produced harmony, joy, and serenity within?

Many people wake up when they are old and find out that they have merely existed, that they have not lived the way they were created or designed to live, and they will die spiritually bankrupt. THE ONLY THING THAT WILL SATISFY YOUR SOUL PERMANENTLY IS THE JOY YOU GET WHEN YOU FEEL THE INDWELLING PRESENCE OF GOD. If you, my friend, know of any other safe principle of which to live, you know of something I have not been able to find in Science, Logic, or the Christian Scriptures.

Your friend,

Alfred Armand Montapert